Mak
5.24

W9-DJN-206

MARK TWAIN

Mr. Clemens and Mark Twain

Also by Justin Kaplan

Mr. Clemens and Mark Twain

Title: MARK TWAIN,

A PROFILE.

EDITED BY

JUSTIN KAPLAN

AMERICAN PROFILES

General Editor: Aïda DiPace Donald

American Century Series
HILL AND WANG · NEW YORK

Manufactured in the United States of America

Contents

Introduction

On and off, beginning in his middle thirties, Mark Twain had been writing or dictating an autobiography in which he hoped eventually to be able to tell the black heart's-truth and strip himself nakeder than Adam. In 1906, when he was seventy, he made another approach to his life and legend and consented to have Albert Bigelow Paine undertake what was to be the authorized biography published in 1912. With only an occasional caution for Paine ("That is the tale—some of it is true") he proposed to give his continuing autobiographical dictations to his biographer to use as primary material. Paine was an experienced editor and writer, the author of a distinguished biography of Thomas Nast. It took him no more than a week or two of residence at 21 Fifth Avenue to realize that Clemens' spellbinding, wild and wonderful reminiscences "bore only an atmospheric relation to history." Paine had discovered that his subject was able to recount with absolute certainty something that had happened just the day before and in the telling to turn around all the essential circumstances. When Paine tried to hold him to the actuality, Clemens took on a blank look, as if he had just waked up. "When I was younger I could remember anything, whether it happened or not," he explained, "but I am getting older, and soon I shall remember only the latter." But was this, as he tried to suggest, simply an old man's rueful joke about his failing memory?

Paine soon encountered another, related difficulty. With curses and threats of litigation, Clemens had long fought off even the best-intentioned invasions of his privacy. Whether friend or stranger, anyone who published (even in the loosest sense) a private letter of his was immediately classified as skunk, dog, eunuch, and pickpocket. "All private letters of mine," Clemens said, "make my flesh creep when I see them again after a lapse of years." Once, when asked why the past was so hateful, he had answered, "It's so damned humiliating."

Consequently, with an accredited biographer in full pursuit of the past, Clemens had his worries. So did Paine and some of Clemens' closest friends. "I don't like to have those privacies exposed in such a way even to my biographer," Clemens scolded William Dean Howells: "If Paine should apply to you for letters, please don't comply." Paine had been zealous but indiscreet in his research—one of the servants saw him reading Clemens' love letters and reported him. After a series of such crises during which he was very nearly fired as official biographer, an impossible situation was resolved, in a way. Clemens was to decide which letters and papers his biographer should be allowed to consult.

What was at stake in these conflicts was more than a Victorian reticence about privacy and propriety, more even than Mark Twain's occasionally ferocious restatements of that reticence. As much as any of his biographers or readers he knew how hard it was to shape an integral view of his life and personality. He was, first of all, keenly aware of an autobiographical enigma which he was never able to solve: he thought of himself as one of the mysteriously stranger of God's creatures, as a freak of nature or a prodigy on the order of Halley's comet. Therefore, he seemed to be saying, he was not accessible by any of the modes of biography. But at times he saw this inaccessibility as a problem common to all men and biographies. "Every one is a moon," he said, "and has a dark side which he never shows to anybody." And he might have added, not even to himself.

Moreover, to the end of his life, Mark Twain was a storyteller whose materials and inspiration were autobiographical, who was determined to tell his own story himself, in his own way, and who, in the telling, constantly reshaped his past. The question of "whether it happened or not" is as relevant to certain parts of his autobiography as it is to "The Celebrated Jumping Frog of Calaveras County," and Mark Twain, instead of playing the bookish interlocutor in that story (Simon Wheeler's biographer, in a sense), had become, instead, Simon Wheeler himself, wearing an "expression of winning gentleness and simplicity upon his tranquil countenance." In that story, written just before he turned thirty, Mark Twain might have been describing himself as seventy-year-old autobiographer:

He never smiled, he never frowned, he never changed his voice from the gentle-flowing key to which he tuned the initial sentence, he never betrayed the slightest suspicion of enthusiasm; but all through the interminable narrative there ran a vein of impressive earnestness and sincerity, which showed me plainly that, so far from his imagining that there was anything ridiculous or funny about his story, he regarded it as a really important matter. . . . To me, the spectacle of a man drifting serenely along through such a queer yarn without ever smiling, was exquisitely absurd.

The central drama of Clemens' mature literary life was his discovery of a usable past—chiefly his boyhood in Hannibal, where his imagination continued to dwell for the rest of his days. ("He mourned his exile from youth," Winfield Townley Scott writes in an essay in this collection, "out of it he assembled his finest fabrications.") He began to make this discovery in his early and middle thirties—a classic watershed age for self-redefinition—as he explored the literary and psychological options of a newly created comic identity soon known the world over as Mark Twain. The terms and directions of his discovery were dictated not only from within but also by his exuberant response to the three or four decades of post-Civil War life which he named the Gilded Age, successor to the Golden Age of his boyhood. One of the most celebrated and frequently exercised of Mark Twain's options was to mingle lies and truth without any warning at all. At the start of his career his preferred form was the tall story. Toward the end of his career, in 1900, he gave this explanation to an interviewer:

I have found that when I speak the truth, I am not believed, and that I have never told a lie so big but that some one had sublime confidence in my veracity. I have, therefore, been forced by fate to adopt fiction as a medium of truth. Most liars lie for the love of the lie. I lie for the love of the truth. I disseminate my true views by means of a series of apparently humorous and mendacious stories.

The mature Mark Twain was a myth-maker who was frequently caught in his own confusion of lies and truth and thought of himself as an anomaly, a freak and wonder of nature. Like the best of his own literature, he seems to have sprung out of folklore and legend, and he defied categorizing. "Of all the literary men I have known he was the most unliterary in his make and manner," Howells wrote of him, and even after considering Mark Twain's literary antecedents and contemporaries he concluded that *his* Mark Twain was "sole, incomparable," unlike "all the rest of our sages, poets, seers, critics, humorists." Moreover, this most anomalous and richly endowed of American writers drunkenly scattered his energies as publisher, entrepreneur, entertainer, dramatist, host, householder, family man, world celebrity, friend of the rich and powerful.

The contrast between Samuel L. Clemens and the pseudonymous but real Mark Twain is only the roughest framework for enclosing a cluster of biographical identities: S.L.C., "Youth" (to his wife), Sam, Mark, and even such hotel-register incognitos as J. B. Smith and Mr. C. L. Samuel of New York. He was, or they were, a demonstration of the truth of La Rochefoucauld's maxim: "We are so much in the habit of wearing disguises that we end by failing to recognize ourselves." "Duplicitous" is the word Leslie Fiedler uses in his essay to suggest the evasiveness and changeableness of the core personality. Even the famous pseudonym "Mark Twain" has at least a double meaning as well as a suspicious history. Taken in its river leadsman's sense of two fathoms (or twelve feet) of bottom, it can mean, as Clemens often suggested, safe water and clear sailing. But if the steamboat has come out of deep water into two fathoms, and perhaps less, then "Mark Twain" means precisely the opposite. And Paul Fatout's discussion of the possibility that the pseudonym may have originated in the saloon rather than the pilot house shows the extent to which the core personality of Samuel Clemens was compelled to soften or color part of its own history.

When Clemens' psychological accounts became strained and finally overdrawn in his fifties and sixties, he turned inward, hoping to find some explanation for his oppressive sense of self-divisiveness. For a while he had believed that conscience (most often representing the voice and views of society) was the villain, and he was to describe Huck Finn as being torn between the dictates of a sound heart and a deformed conscience. During the 1890's, after bankruptcy, family tragedy, creative exhaustion, and general disillusion destroyed the entire opulent structure of his life and even threatened his sanity, he turned to the idea of a dream self, a demonic, lawless, quite Freudian unconscious which did unmentionable things and went to far-off places.

During this same period Clemens felt the need not only to restore wholeness to a gravely fragmented psyche but also to restore integrity and direction to a rich, sprawling, and, as he saw it, meaningless and pointless life. The biographical impulse worked on a public as well as a private level. Mark Twain, as opposed to Samuel Clemens, had become an official and historical identity, encrusted with legend, stereotype, and romance. Part of this heritage is the celebrated story of how Olivia Langdon of Elmira, New York, a figure of angelic refinement, shaped, scolded, tutored, and censored Sam Clemens from rough diamond into polished obedience. "It was no mere accident," James M. Cox says in his essay on the marriage, "that she came to be seen as the figure representing all the social and artistic values antithetical to Mark Twain's native genius." Clemens deliberately created an image of himself as a repressed writer and represented his wife as his censor. In terms of the values she represented for him and the productive tensions she introduced she was more nearly his muse.

Long before Paine came on the scene Samuel Clemens himself had been at work as Mark Twain's authorized biographer. How he carried out the assignment demonstrates the difficulties and temptations involved in achieving an integral and at the same time "accurate" profile.

While in Vienna in 1899 Clemens wrote a fourteen-page biographical sketch to be published in a forthcoming edition of his
collected works. After exposing the manuscript to his wife, who
softened a few, small asperities, Clemens sent it on to his nephew,
Samuel E. Moffett, a journalist, along with the reminder that what
he hated above all was "gush and vulgarity." Moffett was to
rewrite the sketch in his own words, add to it and elaborate
according to his judgment, and, after showing it to Clemens for
final approval, sign it for publication. The published sketch is
therefore not only authorized biography but something more. It
can be read as a statement about himself, made in the freedom of
anonymity by a man who had already in his lifetime become a
legend and who continued to manipulate and rearrange the symbols of that legend.

Viewing his life as history from the start, the sketch places Mark
Twain's birth in the context of America's new "Western Empire"
and of the frontier, defined in terms similar to Turner's as "the
extreme fringe of settlement" between cultivated land and wilderness. The "sleepy river towns" of the frontier, which Mark Twain
grew up in and later knew as a pilot, are now a "vanished estate"
whose charm and "warm, indolent existence" are preserved in his
books. Later on, the sketch introduces another symbol as powerful
for turn-of-the-century Americans as the frontier: Mark Twain's
humor is "as irrepressible as Lincoln's," and again like Lincoln's,
it has a profound aptness (writing in 1910 Howells was to invoke
this comparison in its broadest sense when he called Mark Twain
"the Lincoln of our literature").

Instead of being swept on to wealth by the great westward tide
of American expansion, Mark Twain's parents, we are told, had an
almost "miraculous" faculty for inhabiting "eddies and back-
currents," and they remained poor. But even so they owned land
and slaves, and the ancient Anglo-Saxon antecedents which the
sketch cites complete a stereotype, familiar in success literature, of
poor but blood-pure and proud gentry. Mark Twain's father was
descended from Gregory Clemens, identified as one of the judges
who sent King Charles I to the block, and through his mother the
boy was descended from the belted "Lamptons of Durham." His

formal education ended at the age of twelve, a reminder that even as late as 1890 the average American did not go beyond the fifth grade. "His high school was a village printing-office," and his "education in real life" had begun. The sketch heavily underscores the self-made man's traditional anti-intellectualism—or, at the very least, mistrust of higher education: "It is a fortunate thing for literature that Mark Twain was never ground into smooth uniformity under the scholastic emery wheel." He "made the world his university." His preparation to be a pilot was "a labor compared with which the efforts needed to acquire the degree of Doctor of Philosophy at a university are as light as a summer course of modern novels" (for which, generally, Mark Twain had only contempt).

At one point, without warning, the sketch turns into tall story. While a journalist in Nevada, Mark Twain had in fact been challenged to a duel by a rival editor; the duel had ended in apologies; but to escape imprisonment under the territory's anti-dueling statute, Mark Twain had left for California. According to the sketch, he and his second went out to a gorge to practice with Colt revolvers. "A small bird lit on a sage-brush thirty yards away, and Mark Twain's second fired and knocked off its head." The opponent believed that this was Mark Twain's marksmanship and, terrified by this deadly display, he offered a formal apology, "thus leaving Mark Twain with the honors of war." The incident is borrowed from a comic story long familiar in the West in countless versions.

After this interlude the sketch goes on with a number of historically oriented or overtly self-vindicating statements. *The Innocents Abroad* established the author as "a literary force of the first order." His acquaintance with Olivia Langdon led "to one of the most ideal marriages in literary history." The gaudy, spacious, and idiosyncratic house which Mark Twain built in Hartford was, we are told, neither a practical joke nor a public demonstration of "the financial success possible in literature," but instead "one of the earliest fruits of the artistic revolt against the mid-century Philistinism of domestic architecture in America." The sketch goes into considerable detail about Mark Twain's career as a business-

JUSTIN KAPLAN

man and emphasizes "the series of unfortunate investments" that followed the "brilliant *coup*" of his publication of General Grant's *Personal Memoirs*. Bankrupt, he "could easily have avoided any legal liability for the debts," but he "felt bound in honor to pay them," and he paid them in full, thus re-enacting, it now seems, a sort of capitalist passion and resurrection. His work as a writer has been "irresistibly laughter-provoking," but its more important purpose has been to make people "think and feel," and in *Joan of Arc* he emerged most distinctly as "a prophet of humanity." The sketch concludes with a discussion of Mark Twain as "characteristically American in every fiber," yet possessing a "universal quality" which has made him "a classic, not only at home, but in all lands where people read and think about the common joys and sorrows of humanity."

In his own lifetime his life had become history and biography, legend and tradition, all expressing the values and aspirations of his country and his century. Mark Twain had become a hero of the American experience, and when he came home from Europe in 1900, after a self-imposed exile of nearly ten years and an unbroken absence of over five, he was given a hero's welcome and led a hero's public life. He was probably the most conspicuous and widely admired American of his time. And he continued to lead a hero's posthumous life until 1920 when Van Wyck Brooks, in *The Ordeal of Mark Twain,* seriously called into question the man, his achievement, and the times that fostered him. Often reasoning from frail data to sweeping conclusions and making somewhat indiscriminate use of Freudian psychology, Brooks still wrote what remains the strongest and most suggestive book about Mark Twain.

Brooks's view of Mark Twain as a failure, the victim from boyhood on of backgrounds and influences fatally hurtful to the writer, was angrily challenged by Bernard DeVoto whose book, *Mark Twain's America,* may, in rebuttal, have made too much of a case for the frontier tradition, which simply was not that rich. By 1942, when he published *Mark Twain at Work* (a section of which is included in this collection), DeVoto had not only sifted and studied Mark Twain's unpublished papers but had also gone through some dialectic by which he arrived at a position remarkably sympathetic if not similar to that of Brooks. And by this time Brooks himself was less disposed to write off Mark Twain as a failure whose life was to be read as a cautionary tale for American writers.

As crudely suggested by the multiplex, often warring identities of Samuel Clemens and Mark Twain, the man never did, in any definitive sense, achieve unity of personality or unity of statement about himself. And his biographers, having been in the past no more successful than he was, have, in a sense, abandoned the attempt. Partly through the interplay of Brooks and DeVoto, partly through the study of letters and papers which Paine either ignored or was not permitted to see, partly through a more subtle and complex viewing of our past as a whole, we no longer try to force Mark Twain into the mold of the genial humorist and rough-hewn philosopher of his official biographies.

Instead, as Dixon Wecter's article shows most comprehensively, he is to be seen as a deeply conflicted, intermittent genius whose life-style and life-work can best be judged as the hard-won, rich products of his many disunities and in the light of a series of central problems and interactions. The external movement of Mark Twain's life was away from Hannibal, poverty, and obscurity; its internal movement was back to Hannibal again. Out of the opposition of these river currents, out of the turbulent dark waters, came one of the great styles and dazzling personalities of our literature, one of its few undisputed masterpieces, and half a dozen of its major books. Mark Twain's laughter and his bitterness (which became as distinctive a manifestation of his late years as his white suits) were twinned. "The secret source of humor itself is not joy but sorrow," he wrote: "There is no humor in heaven."

As writer, lecturer, and entertainer, he worked through popular forms in order to reach a large, popular audience. He had never, he claimed in the 1890's, tried to "cultivate the cultivated classes," but had "always hunted for bigger game—the masses." Yet he dreaded being simply a humorist, because for him and for his public "humorist" implied "mere" and also "buffoon." (Mark Twain's "tragedy," Dwight Macdonald says, may be a "peculiar inability to speak in his own voice.") But he found that the "masses," in their taste for conventional, genteel productions like *The Prince and the Pauper,* were remarkably like "the cultivated classes," thus leaving him, as the author of a vernacular masterpiece, *Huckleberry Finn,* in an uncomfortable relation to his goals as well as to his audience. The painful abrasions of such conflicts between the dominant culture and Mark Twain's only dimly formulated and evolving purposes are examined in Henry Nash Smith's account of the Whittier birthday dinner in 1877. Clemens' extended comic speech about Longfellow, Emerson, and Holmes as tramps and deadbeats was clearly "an act of aggression against the three poets as representatives of the sacerdotal cult of the man of letters," Smith writes. Even so, Clemens was not consciously prepared to acknowledge his true stance. "I am only heedlessly a savage, not premeditatedly," he said in apology.

The representative of a broad spectrum of paradox, as a writer Mark Twain stood outside American society of the Gilded Age, but as a businessman he embraced its business values and its industrial aspirations. As the concluding article in this book suggests, Mark Twain's concurrent preoccupations with *A Connecticut Yankee* and his typesetting machine tested all his values to the breaking point. Torn between a passionate morality and the compulsion to succeed, he believed money corrupted absolutely; but he wanted to be rich, not merely to get along; and the public who worshiped him as the people's writer were only occasionally perturbed by the fact that he was also the pet, protegé, and crony of Andrew Carnegie, of H. H. Rogers of Standard Oil, and of Colonel George Harvey, agent of the Morgan interests.

Some of these apparent contradictions only suggest further mysteries. For something of Walt Whitman's riddle surrounds Mark Twain: How does one account for their sudden flowering? Reborn in their thirties, both took on new names, new identities. Walter Whitman, the foppish hack journalist who strolled languidly up Broadway, became the poet Walt, who wore an open shirt, celebrated the open road, and thought of himself as "one of the roughs." Sam Clemens, who once wore miner's clothes and worked with pick and shovel, became the Mark Twain who said his biceps muscles had the tone of an oyster wrapped up in an old rag and who was something of a dandy in his eccentric, eye-catching way. Tacitly acknowledging this mystery in himself, Mark Twain was all his life fascinated by the archetypal lore of small men (like him) with the power of giants, of failures (like Ulysses Grant) who became heroes, of "mere" humorists whose laughter could rock belief and the state, and of writers who, through their art (and despite the copyright laws he attacked as iniquitous), seem never to have died.

JUSTIN KAPLAN

Cambridge, Massachusetts
May 18, 1967

Samuel L. Clemens, 1835–1910

Samuel Langhorne Clemens was born on November 30, 1835, in Florida, Missouri, a tiny hamlet about forty miles east of Hannibal, where the Clemens family resettled in 1839 and which the boy was to celebrate all his life. His father died in 1847, and Sam was apprenticed to a printer. In 1853 he left home, set out on his travels, and earned a living as an itinerant typesetter. Four years later he became an apprentice pilot and learned the Mississippi; his career as a river pilot was cut short by the outbreak of the Civil War. During the summer of 1861 he served two weeks as a Confederate irregular, deserted along with the rest of his company, and set out west by stagecoach with his brother Orion, who held a federal appointment in the Nevada Territory. For five years, as prospector and journalist, Clemens lived in Nevada and California. In February, 1863, he first signed the pseudonym "Mark Twain" to a humorous travel letter; two years later he had his first taste of national fame when his "Jumping Frog" story was published and widely circulated; and he began his career as a lecturer. Early in 1867, hungry for greater challenges and rewards, he arrived in the East, to stay.

Clemens' trip to Europe and the Holy Land that summer and fall was to be the basis of his first major book, *The Innocents Abroad* (1869), and to inaugurate a period during which it often seemed that nothing could go wrong for him. He married Olivia Langdon, a coal heiress from Elmira, New York, who bore him three adored daughters (and a son, who died in infancy), he settled affluently in Hartford, Connecticut, he made a rapid transition from sagebrush bohemian to man of letters and man of property, and through his books, his lecturing, his speeches and random statements, and his dazzling personality he became one of the few American writers of his time who had both a flourishing income and an international reputation. *Roughing It* (1872), his account of his Western experiences, was followed by his satirical novel, *The Gilded Age* (1873), which he wrote in collaboration with Charles Dudley Warner, and by *Sketches: New and Old* (1875), *Tom Sawyer* (1876), *A Tramp Abroad* (1880), *The Prince and the Pauper* (1882), and *Life on the Mississippi* (1883). In 1885, when he published his masterpiece, *Huckleberry Finn,* he was also the owner of a publishing house which was to make a historic success out of General Grant's *Personal Memoirs,* and among other business interests which promised huge returns was his stake in an automatic typesetting machine.

Clemens published *A Connecticut Yankee* in 1889 and *Pudd'nhead Wilson* in 1894, but with these major exceptions the fifteen years between 1885 and 1900 proved to be his severest ordeal by failure. Overinvested in both the publishing house and the typesetting machine, he was compelled to close his Hartford house in 1891 and move his family abroad; three years later he went into bankruptcy; and in 1896, just as he arrived in England after a round-the-world lecture tour which he undertook to help pay off his debts, his favorite daughter, Susy, died of meningitis, and he was nearly unhinged by grief and despair.

By 1900 his fortunes and his psyche were sufficiently mended for him to return to America and to an ovation that went on for the rest of his life. He became as celebrated for his white suits and his great mane of white hair as he was for his uncompromising stand against injustice and imperialism and for his invariably quotable comments on any subject under the sun. The climax of his public career, he felt, was the honorary doctorate of letters which Oxford awarded him in 1907. His wife had died in 1904, his second daughter in 1909. On April 21, 1910, Samuel Clemens died in Redding, Connecticut, where he had built a splendid house on a hilltop.

J.K.

MARK TWAIN

Mark Twain

"I am persuaded," wrote Bernard Shaw to Mark Twain, "that the future historian of America will find your works as indispensable to him as a French historian finds the political tracts of Voltaire." By his own participation, no artist in our literature save Lincoln spans so broad a segment of typical American experience in the last century. Samuel Langhorne Clemens, known by the most famous pen name that an American ever bore, is a matchless annalist of his times. His life makes those of literary men in Boston and Concord and New York resemble (in Hawthorne's phrase) the flowering of talents that blossomed in too retired a shade. He knew the greatest river of the continent as Melville knew the high seas. He witnessed the epic of America, the westward tide at its full, with perception keener than the shallow appraisals of Bret Harte and Joaquin Miller. When in his *Autobiography* Mark Twain recalls after forty years the tragedy of an emigrant lad stabbed to death by a drunken comrade, and adds, "I saw the red life gush from his breast," we are reminded of Whitman's affirmation, "I was there"—with the difference that Walt's immediacy was imaginative, Mark's actual. In the activities of the external man as well as in character and temperament, Mark Twain was a representative American—from idyllic ante-bellum boyhood in a

Reprinted with permission of The Macmillan Company from *Literary History of the United States*, edited by Robert E. Spiller. Copyright 1946, 1947, 1948 by The Macmillan Company.

1

river town, to maturity enmeshed in the cross-purposes of the Gilded Age which he christened, and thence to the sunset years of mingled hope and disillusion in the Progressive Era. Despite his own avowal, "There is not a single human characteristic which can be safely labeled as 'American,' " Mark Twain is stamped unforgettably with the national brand. If he failed finally to reconcile reality and ideality, he absorbed and gave expression to both. That failure was not his; it belonged to his generation.

In old age his incurably Calvinist mind saw all the events of his life, from birth on November 30, 1835, in the village of Florida, Missouri, as a chain of causation forged by some power outside his will. Like his Connecticut Yankee he was led to reflect upon heredity, "a procession of ancestors that stretches back a billion years to the Adam-clam or grasshopper or monkey from whom our race has been so tediously and ostentatiously and unprofitably developed." His father, an austere restless Virginian, bequeathed the family a vain hope of fortune from "the Tennessee lands," like Squire Hawkins in *The Gilded Age;* he also gave his son an object lesson in failure like the example set by the father of a genius whom Mark the Baconian once rose to challenge, Shakespeare of Stratford. The wife and mother, Jane Lampton Clemens, of Kentucky pioneer stock, sought by her strong Presbyterianism to balance her husband's village-lawyer agnosticism; their famous son inherited the self-tormenting conscience with the latter's will to disbelieve. As for derivations more remote, Twain the romantic relished his maternal tie with the Earls of Durham through "the American claimant," while Twain the democrat reserved his sole ancestral pride for a regicide judge, who "did what he could toward reducing the list of crowned shams of his day."

In 1839 the Clemenses moved to Hannibal, on the west bank of the Mississippi, and set the conditions of boyhood and youth from which flowed the wellspring of Mark Twain's clearest inspiration. Thanks to *Tom Sawyer* and *Huckleberry Finn,* its aspect in the forties has become the property of millions: the wharf giving upon the turbid waters where rafts and broadhorns, fast packets and gay showboats passed endlessly, the plank sidewalks where Tom and Becky trudged to school, the tanyard where Huck's drunken father slept among the hogs, the steep slope of Cardiff (really Holliday's) Hill, the surrounding woods of oak and hickory and sumach, and a few miles downstream the cave where Injun Joe met death. Hannibal lay in its halcyon summer between frontier days and the convulsions of the Civil War, the latter forecast in the mobbing of an occasional abolitionist and the tracking down of runaway slaves. On the whole, happiness outweighed grief; prized in retrospect was the large freedom of a boy's life, with the swimming hole and woods full of game, jolly playmates banded against a world of adult supremacy, and dinner tables groaning with prodigal hospitality. "It was a heavenly place for a boy," Hannibal's first citizen remembered.

Sam Clemens' schooling ended early, when he was about twelve. After his father's death the lad was apprenticed to a printer's shop—"the poor boy's college," Lincoln called it. Lack of formal education doubtless gave the later Mark Twain an eagerness to have his genius certified by convention, and also led him occasionally to discover shopworn ideas with a thrill impossible to sophisticates; but it also delivered him from those cultural stereotypes into which the genius of New England, for example, for generations had been poured. Fatalist that he was, Twain liked to date his career from certain accidents. The first of them came one day on the streets of Hannibal, when the young printer picked up a stray leaf from a book about Joan of Arc, and for the first time saw magic in the printed word. Henceforth the itch of scribbling was strong upon him. His earliest known appearance in print, a crudely humorous sketch called "The Dandy Frightening the Squatter," appeared in the Boston *Carpet Bag* of May 1, 1852. He left Hannibal the next year, wandering on to New York and Philadelphia, and began to send home-town papers the first of those facetious travel pieces which he wrote sporadically for the next half-century. In 1857, after tarrying a while in Cincinnati, he set out for New Orleans with a notion of shipping for the Amazon. But, lacking funds, he became a steamboat pilot under the tutelage of Horace Bixby. That veteran gradually taught him the ever-changing aspects of the Mississippi, by sun and starlight, at low water and in flood.

For two years after that Clemens turned his wheel atop the texas deck, drawing a licensed pilot's high wages, while he gained postgraduate schooling in human nature. Oft quoted is his later assertion: "When I find a well-drawn character in fiction or biography I generally take a warm personal interest in him, for the reason that I have known him before—met him on the river." A born worrier, he felt the responsibility that lay within a pilot's hands as he steered past narrows and snags and sand bars, or for the sake of prestige raced his rivals until the boiler nearly burst under its head of steam. His old master, many years later, stated that Clemens "knew the river like a book, but he lacked confidence." One may speculate whether a very human incertitude, deep in his being, did not chime with a classic type of humor in his constant self-portrayal as the man who gets slapped: the bumptious yet timid cub of *Life on the Mississippi;* the fear-bedeviled soldier of "The Campaign That Failed"; the tenderfoot of *Roughing It,* setting forest fires and just missing wealth through sheer stupidity; or the harassed traveler losing his tickets, browbeaten by porters and shopkeepers, falling foul of the authorities, who appears in a long sequence from the juvenile Snodgrass letters to *A Tramp Abroad.*

II

Clemens' career on the river ended in the spring of 1861 with the outbreak of hostilities. With brief enthusiasm he joined a Confederate militia band, savoring the boyish conspiracy of war in its early stages. In the lack of discipline the band soon broke up; and Sam, with qualms about fighting for slavery, yielded to persuasion from his Unionist brother Orion, lately appointed Secretary of the Territory of Nevada. In July, 1861, the two set out for the West. The outlines of the story told in *Roughing It* are true enough: the nineteen-day trip across the plains and Rockies to Carson City; an attack of mining fever that left Sam none the richer; his acceptance of a job on the Virginia City *Enterprise;* a journalist's view of San Francisco in flush times; and a newspaper-sponsored voyage to the Sandwich Islands. His dream of becoming a millionaire by a stroke of fortune never forsook him; lingering in his blood, the bonanza fever made him a lifelong victim of gold bricks, quick-profit schemes, and dazzling inventions. But his return to journalistic humor—the vein he had worked in his late teens and early twenties, imitative of such professional humorists as Seba Smith, J. J. Hooper, and B. P. Shillaber, in whose productions every newspaper office abounded—proved to be his really lucky strike. In 1863 the Missourian of twenty-eight met Artemus Ward on the latter's Western lecture tour, and watched a master storyteller in action: the adroit timing, change of pace, and deadpan obliviousness to the point of one's own wit. Twain's "How to Tell a Story" (1895) acknowledges these profitable lessons.

It was Ward who encouraged him to seek a wider audience than the red-shirted miners of Washoe and nabobs of the Golden Gate. The first fruit of this encouragement to appear in the East—a piece of jocular sadism against the small fry who made day and night hideous at resort hotels, "Those Blasted Children"—was printed early in 1864 by the New York *Mercury*. Meanwhile in 1863 Clemens had begun to imitate current funny men like Ward, Orpheus C. Kerr, and Josh Billings, by selecting a pen name, the riverboatman's cry for two fathoms, "Mark Twain." Clemens stoutly maintained he appropriated it soon after an eccentric pilot-journalist of New Orleans, Captain Isaiah Sellers, relinquished it by death. No contribution in the New Orleans press, however, has ever been found under that name; also, Sellers' death occurred a year after Clemens adopted this pseudonym. Whether original or borrowed, the name served an important purpose. It created an alter ego, a public character, which Clemens could foster through the years while doffing it in private as he pleased. It set definable limits to his role of being what the age called a "phunny phellow." A speculative critic might guess that his abiding interest in transposed identities, twins, and Siamese prodigies mirrored a dualism which self-observation would have shown running like a paradox through his nature: gullible and skeptical by turns; realistic and sentimental, a satirist who gave hostages to the established order, a frontiersman who bowed his neck obediently to Victorian mores, and an idealist who loved the trappings of pomp and wealth.

Incessantly he contradicted himself on a variety of subjects. His was not a single-track mind, but a whole switchyard. The creation of two more or less separate identities—Clemens the sensitive and perceptive friend, Mark Twain the robust and astringent humorist —springing from the same trunk of personality, helped to make him like those ligatured twins in *Pudd'nhead Wilson,* Luigi and Angelo, "a human philopena."

Under the name of Mark Twain the wild-haired Southwesterner began to contribute to the press yarns swapped about the legislative halls of Carson City, the bars and billiard parlors of San Francisco, and the hot stoves of miners on Jackass Hill. From these last, about February, 1865, he first heard the old folk tale of the Jumping Frog. To the anecdote he added the salt of human values which the genre usually lacked, in garrulous Simon Wheeler and simple Jim Smiley the Frog's owner. Published in the *Saturday Press* of New York, November 18, 1865, it was swiftly broadcast. The author grumbled in a letter home about the irony of riding high on "a villanous backwoods sketch," but already he was tasting that sense of popularity which soon came to be his elixir of life. In October, 1866, back from Honolulu and planted on a San Francisco lecture platform, he first encountered another powerful stimulant, the instant response. Early in 1867, at Cooper Union in New York, he won his Eastern spurs, and began to be hailed as rightful heir to Artemus Ward, lately dead of tuberculosis in England. Soon, as his friend William Dean Howells phrased it, Twain learned "all the stops of that simple instrument, man." The lecturer's effect upon the writer was great. Increasingly Twain came to write by ear, testing his books by reading aloud, while making the expanded anecdote or incident the unit of his literary composition. Sometimes, of course, without benefit of his infectious personal charm, that mane of fiery red hair and hawklike nose, the gestures of an artist's hands, and the inflections of that irresistible drawl, a reader of cold print missed qualities which on the platform redeemed humor of a perishable sort.

"When I began to lecture, and in my earlier writings, my sole idea was to make comic capital out of everything I saw and heard," he told the biographer Archibald Henderson. After his first volume, of chiefly Western sketches, named *The Celebrated Jump-ing Frog* (1867), he reinforced this reputation by distilling a humorous travelogue out of the letters sent back to the *Alta California* from his cruise to the Mediterranean and Holy Land on the *Quaker City* in 1867. Comic capital was readily furnished by the flood of tourists, affluent merchants and their wives, war profiteers, former army officers on holiday, and clergymen for whom Jerusalem justified the junket, which swept over the Old World after Appomattox. Knowing themselves to be innocents, they faced down their provincialism by brag and cockalorum, and haggling over prices. Mark Twain gladly joined them, joking his way among the shrines and taboos of antiquity, comparing Como unfavorably with Tahoe, bathing in the Jordan, finding any foreign tongue incredibly funny, and pitying ignorance, superstition, and lack of modern conveniences. *The Innocents Abroad* (1869) helped to belittle our romantic allegiance to Europe, feeding our emergent nationalism. Instantly a best seller, it delighted those Americans in whom "the sense of Newport" (as Henry James later called it) had never been deeply engrafted. A slender minority like James himself felt that Mark Twain amused only primitive per-sons, was the Philistines' laureate. Years later, in 1889, in a letter to Andrew Lang, Twain would glory in this charge:

Indeed I have been misjudged, from the first. I have never tried in even one single instance, to help cultivate the cultivated classes. I was not equipped for it, either by native gifts or training. And I never had any ambition in that direction, but always hunted for bigger game—the masses. I have seldom deliberately tried to instruct them, but have done my best to entertain them. . . . Yes, you see, I have always catered for the Belly and the Members.

III

Yet this is not the whole story. From an early date, Mark Twain, the playboy of the Western World, had begun to feel the aspirations of an artist, to crave deeper approval than had come to the cracker-box humorist like Sam Slick and Jack Downing. In Honolulu in 1866 the diplomat Anson Burlingame gave him advice by which

the aged Twain avowed he had lived "for forty years": "Seek your
comradeships among your superiors in intellect and character;
always *climb*." On the *Quaker City* voyage the Missourian feil
under the refining spell of "Mother" Fairbanks, wife of a prosperous Ohio publisher, and tore up those travel letters which she
thought crude. Always enjoying petticoat dominion, he eagerly
sought her approval of the revised *Innocents* and was enchanted
when she pronounced it "authentic." "A name I have coveted so
long—and secured at last!" he exclaimed. "*I* don't care anything
about being humorous, or poetical, or eloquent, or anything of that
kind—the end and aim of my ambition is to be authentic—is to be
considered authentic." In a similar thirst for higher recognition he
told Howells, reviewer of *Innocents* in the *Atlantic:* "When I read
that review of yours, I felt like the woman who was so glad her
baby had come white." Nevertheless, as Twain found to his
intermittent chagrin, his reputation throughout life kept returning
to that of a "phunny phellow," turning cartwheels to captivate the
groundlings—until at length he built up the defensive attitude
expressed to Lang. At *Atlantic* dinners, the author of "Old Times
on the Mississippi" and *Tom Sawyer* found himself seated below
the salt, ranked by Longfellow and Lowell and Whittier, as well as
by such adopted sons of Boston as Howells and Aldrich. Despite
the new decorum of his life and the growing richness of his art, the
wild man from the West was expected, some time, somehow, to
disgrace himself. And, by the meridian of Boston, he eventually did
so, when at the celebrated Whittier birthday dinner on December
17, 1877, he made his speech of innocent gaiety about three
drunks in the high Sierras who personated Emerson, Longfellow,
and Holmes. The diners were shocked, refusing their laughter
while he stood solitary (as Howells said) "with his joke dead on
his hands." The next day or so, when Twain's haunting distrust of
himself and his own taste had induced a penitential hangover, he
sent apologies, writing characteristically: "Ah, well, I am a great
and sublime fool. But then I am God's fool, and all his works must
be contemplated with respect." He then begged Howells to exclude
him from the *Atlantic* for a while, in the interest of readers' good
will. The gravity with which both the saints and the sinner

freedom on a raft floating down the Mississippi, now and again he yearned for the lusty old ways of medieval speech, "full of unconscious coarsenesses and innocent indecencies," "good old questionable stories," as the Connecticut Yankee says. But quickly he reminded himself, as he observes in *A Tramp Abroad,* that the license of the printed word had been "sharply curtailed within the past eighty or ninety years." To this curb in the main he gave unstinting consent.

IV

Up to the time of his anchorage in Hartford in 1871, the most important facts about Mark Twain are the things that happened to him, shaping his development as an artist and filling the granaries of memory. After that date the chief milestones are the books he wrote out of that accumulation. His maturity and self-assurance can be gauged, growing from book to book through the next two decades, as he lectured at home and abroad, met the captains of literature and politics and finance, read widely if desultorily, and perfected his early journalistic manner until it became one of the great styles of American letters—easy, incisive, sensitive to nuances of dialect, rich in the resources of comedy, satire, irony, and corrosive anger.

One group, of secondary importance, consists of his travel books. Between *The Innocents Abroad* (1869) and *Roughing It* (1872) he learned, under emancipation from newspaper reporting, to take greater liberties with fact for art's sake. Both books owe such structure as they have to a rough chronology. Upon this thread Mark Twain the raconteur strings one story after another. The latter volume offers us almost all the classic types which Americans in general, frontiersmen in particular, had long since favored: the tall tale, the melodramatic shocker, the yarn of pointless garrulity, malapropian humor, the canard of impossible coincidence, the chain of free association that wanders farther and farther from its announced subject; the comedy of man in his cups, the animal fable, and the delusions of a lunatic. Paradox, surprise, and understatement often heighten his effects. Anecdote continues

regarded this incident reveals the massiveness of the genteel tradition in New England and the probationary status upon which Mark was kept for so many years.

Between the publication of the *Innocents* and this indiscretion, Clemens had taken a wife whose remolding influence has been the subject of much debate. The story of their courtship is familiar: his first sight of her delicate face in a miniature carried by her brother on the *Quaker City* cruise; Twain's meeting with the original, Olivia Langdon, ten years his junior, a semi-invalid who had turned to faith healing; their two years' betrothal while her father, the richest businessman in Elmira, and her kin were slowly won over; and their wedding early in 1870, with Clemens the bridegroom trying unsuccessfully to establish himself as a solid newspaper editor in Buffalo, but moving to Hartford in 1871 to resume a free-lance life. His veneration of women and their purity was almost fanatical. "I wouldn't have a girl that *I* was worthy of," he wrote "Mother" Fairbanks before his engagement. *"She* wouldn't do."

About the sexual make-up of Mark Twain speculation has been indulged since the Freudian era. In that famous sophomoric sketch *1601,* written in mid-career to amuse his clerical friend Joe Twichell, he had Sir Walter Raleigh describe "a people in ye uttermost parts of America, y^t copulate not until they be five-&-thirty yeeres of age." This, it happens, was the age when Clemens married a semi-invalid wife, as if some inadequacy in himself, some low sexual vitality, made such a woman his fitting mate. And yet respecting their physical love for each other and the fruitfulness of their union, with its four children, no doubt can be raised. What illicit experience might have come to a boy growing up in the accessible world of slavery, and passing his green manhood upon riverboats and in bonanza towns, can only be guessed at. In later years, respecting the idealized Hannibal of his boyhood, he went so far as to deny the existence of sexual irregularities; and by confining his two great novels about Hannibal to adolescence he was able in a manner to carry his point. Obviously certain taboos about sex, personal as well as conventional, appear in his writings from beginning to end. Unlike his friend Howells, he attempted no probings of desire, no analysis of the chemical affinity between man and woman beyond the calf love of Tom and Becky and the implausible treatment of Laura the siren of *The Gilded Age*. Only under the protective shield of miscegenation, in the person of the warm-blooded Negress Roxana in *Pudd'nhead Wilson,* does he venture even to approach passion which overleaps the bounds of society. Joan of Arc, a virgin of exquisite purity, plainly is the heroine after his inmost heart. A certain fear of sex, like the shrinking of primitive races and some adolescents from carnality as if it meant degradation of the body, seems to lie at the root of Mark Twain's nature. The exceptions of his occasional bawdry— in *1601* and a few unprinted works like his speech before the Stomach Club in Paris and his manuscript "Letters from the Earth"—but prove the rule, in ridiculing the body and its ways sufficiently to suit the most fanatic Puritan.

Yet Twain was in no sense a misogynist. He loved the company of women, of the refined women whose tastes and restraints fitted his own presuppositions about them. His understanding of the feminine mind has left no more delightful evidence than "Eve's Diary," written in 1905 shortly after Olivia's death, so that Adam's final bereavement becomes the epitaph of his own loss: "Wherever she was, *there* was Eden." In summary, Mark Twain's personal make-up and the conventions of gentility surrounding the kind of success he aspired to, joined to suppress the recognition of sex as a key motive in human actions—leaving woman not an object of desire but of reverential chivalry.

The effect of his wife upon Twain the artist has provoked latter-day discussion. One school of thought holds that Clemens was forced, first by his mother and then by his wife, to "make good," i.e., to make money and be respectable. Moreover, thanks to the censorship of his wife, they say, he became not the New World Rabelais but a frustrated genius incapable of calling his soul or vocabulary his own. It is clear, however, that proof of Livy's "humiliating" dominion rests largely upon Twain's letters to Howells: that pair of devoted husbands married to invalids who made a gallant little joke over being henpecked. The notion that women exercised a gentle tyranny over their menfolk, for the

latter's good, always appealed to Mark Twain, school ern theories that man was coarser clay and woman special being (as among the Washoe miners in *Rough* chipped in $2,500 in gold as a gift at the miraculous si woman). All his life he encouraged women to refor prove his taste and manners. His three little daughters in the family rite known as "dusting off Papa," and fish" of adolescent girls in his Bermudian Indian su among the youngest of the sex whose devoted slave he be. It was a kind of game in the feudal tradition, whic But to assume therefore that Twain the genius was baffled, unmanned by women in general and Livy in to convert a jest into a cry of anguish. About t influence of husband upon wife something deserves to Twain's vitality rescued her from abysses of timorou banter relaxed her serious disposition, and his religiou destroyed her Christian faith.

As for the specific question of censorship, we know liked to read aloud *en famille* the results of his daily usually meeting the approval he craved, sometimes en chill disfavor to which he was equally sensitive. He wa critic and knew it. He plunged into writing without n foresight. Livy's judgment in matters of simple good pruning wordiness and irrelevance was clearly superio in the heat of incubation. A careful examination of his shows that Mrs. Clemens, like that other long-stan William Dean Howells, objected to certain vivid phrases—"wallow," "bowels," "spit," "rotten," and sions to stenches and putrefaction which always te Twain, so that he grumbled about her "steadily we English tongue"—but that in mild profanities (like "comb me all to hell") and in rare inclinations towa (such as the farce of "The Royal Nonesuch") th second thought was his own most attentive censor. above playing an occasional hazard with his critics to he could skate on thin ice; then doubled on his own t safety. Just as he dreamed of the unabashed nakedne

to be the fiber of those later travel books, which show more fluency in repeating the essential pattern, but grow in world-weariness after the early gusto of the Innocents and the Argonauts. They include *A Tramp Abroad* (1880), with more travesty of European languages, guidebooks, and art criticism, and *Following the Equator* (1897), which reports Twain's lecture tour in Australia and India. Inevitable become his burlesques of sentimental poetry, parodies of romantic situations, yarns picked up in new places or recollected from the limbo of years. In this last book, however, flippancy at the expense of peoples and customs vanishes when the traveler reaches the threshold of Asia, as if the ancient disillusioned torpor of that continent had striken the satirist dumb. These travelogues do not show Twain's gifts to greatest advantage. Flashes of notable writing occur, but intrinsically they are the potboilers of a master improviser.

The earliest novel he attempted was *The Gilded Age,* in collaboration with Charles Dudley Warner, published late in 1873, just as the Panic was ringing down the curtain upon the worst excesses of that age. It harks back to their common knowledge of Missouri, where Warner had been a surveyor, and to Twain's passing observation of Washington in the winter of 1867–1868, when after return from the Holy Land he had served briefly and unhappily as private secretary to pompous Senator William Stewart of Nevada and more successfully had begun to write humorous commentaries on the news (anticipative of the late Will Rogers) for the *Tribune* and the *Herald* of New York. This phase left him with an abiding scorn for politicians, their intelligence and honesty. ("Fleas can be taught nearly anything that a Congressman can" is as characteristic as the remark that we have "no distinctly native American criminal class except Congress.") Beside the bungling amateurs of Carson City, these were graduates in graft, scrambling for the spoils of what a later critic termed the Great Barbecue. This same spectacle of post-bellum Washington which sickened fastidious Henry Adams and led even Whitman the optimist to pen the darker pages of *Democratic Vistas,* gave Mark Twain his first shining target for satire.

Warner supplied conventional plot elements of romance, gentility, pluck and luck, harmonized with the theme of material success, which the novel debunks at one level but praises fulsomely at another, when it is sanctioned by what passes among the majority as honesty. Twain himself was always dazzled by the romance of fortune, especially if it followed the ascent from rags to riches, as he shows in a story like "The £1,000,000 Bank Note" (1893). Yet he was aware of the ironies and unhappiness springing from the root of all evil, as revealed in "The $30,000 Bequest" (1904) and most superbly in "The Man That Corrupted Hadleyburg" (1899). In *The Gilded Age* the authors' wavering purpose resembles a mixture of Jonathan Swift and Horatio Alger. Satiric punches are pulled by the constant impulse to strike out in all directions but follow through in none. The vulgarity of a chromo civilization and the urge to keep up with the Joneses mingle with churchly hypocrisy, pork-barrel politics, high tariff, oratorical buncombe, abuse of the franking privilege, bribery, personal immorality in high places, profiteers of "shoddy," and the wider degradation of the democratic dogma.

The Gilded Age is clearly a world of optimistic illusion, proudly putting its best foot forward though the other limp behind in a shabby mud-bespattered boot. In the backwoods, stagecoaches with horns blowing enter and leave town at a furious clip, but once out of sight "drag along stupidly enough"—even as steamboats burn fat pine to make an impressive smoke when they near port. Credit is the basis of society; a typical parvenu boasts: "I wasn't worth a cent a year ago, and now I owe two millions of dollars." Most engaging specimen of this psychology is Colonel Sellers, a New World Micawber, who deals in imaginary millions while he and the family dine off turnips and cold water (man's best diet, he loftily assures them), and warm themselves at a stove through whose isinglass door flickers the illusory glow of a candle. Drawn from Twain's Uncle James Lampton, the Colonel is an epitome of the American dream that remains a mirage—impulsive, generous, hospitable, scheming to enrich not only himself but relatives and friends, and incidentally benefit all humankind, a colossal failure who basks forever in the rushlight of the success cult. Not dishonest by nature, in the heady milieu of Washington he begins to apologize for bribery ("a harsh term"), while hitching his wagon to the baleful star of Senator Dilworthy, drawn from the lineaments of Kansas' notorious Pomeroy. In certain passages Mark Twain's irony is whetted to a cutting edge, but the book's total effect is far from mordant. In many ways both authors were children of the Gilded Age, with hands too unsteady to strike a mortal blow of parricide.

Like everybody else Twain grew fond of Colonel Sellers and tried to resuscitate him. The modest laurels of a dramatic version of *The Gilded Age,* produced in 1874, led Twain and Howells to attempt in 1883 an hilarious sequel which, however, the stage Sellers of the earlier script, John T. Raymond, declined to play because that character had been exaggerated to the brink of lunacy. The plot, as embalmed in Twain's novel, *The American Claimant* (1892), justifies the actor's verdict. It is one of the humorist's most strained and least successful efforts.

V

Three years after *The Gilded Age* Twain published *Tom Sawyer,* the first of three great books about the Mississippi River of his youth. Beyond question, *Huckleberry Finn* (1885), *Life on the Mississippi* (1883), and *Tom Sawyer* (1876) are, in that order, his finest works. The reasons for their superiority are not far to seek. In plotting a book his structural sense was always weak; intoxicated by a hunch, he seldom saw far ahead, and too many of his stories peter out from the author's fatigue or surfeit. His wayward technique, as Howells recognized, came close to free association:

So far as I know, Mr. Clemens is the first writer to use in extended writing the fashion we all use in thinking, and to set down the thing that comes into his mind without fear or favor of the thing that went before or the thing that may be about to follow.

This method served him best after he had conjured up characters from long ago, who on coming to life wrote the narrative for him, passing from incident to incident with a grace their creator could never achieve in manipulating an artificial plot. In travel books and other autobiography written under the heat of recent experience, Mark Twain seemingly put in everything, mixing the trivial, inane, and farcical with his best-grade ore. But in the remembrance of things past, time had dissolved the alloy, leaving only gold. The nostalgia for a youth's paradise "over the hills and far away," for the fast-vanishing freedom of the West, appealed deeply to the age of boyhood sentiment enriched by Longfellow and Whittier. It also led to Mark Twain's strength; namely, the world of the senses and physical action. What he felt was always better expressed than what he had thought or speculated about. A boy's world freed him from those economic and political perplexities, adult dilemmas and introspections, where in rages and knotty casuistries he lost the sureness of touch that came to him through the report of his five senses, or through the championship of justice when the issue was as simple as the conflict between bullies and little folk.

In his heart Mark Twain must have realized that essentially he was a man of feeling, too sensitive to serve merely as a comedian, too undisciplined to be the philosopher he sometimes fancied himself. His forte was to recapture the sheer joy of living, when to be young was very heaven. A great river flowing through the wilderness set the stage for a boy's own dream of self-sufficiency, of being a new Robinson Crusoe on Jackson's Island. In the background moved the pageantry of life, colored by humor, make-believe, and pure melodrama; but the complexity of the machine age and the city lay far, far away.

Mark Twain did not write his first books about this dream world, but let the haze of ideality collect about it, reserving it luckily for the high noon of his powers. Apparently the first hint of this motif comes in one of his New York letters to the *Alta California,* in the spring of 1867, in which he happens to recall the town drunkard of Hannibal, Jimmy Finn (destined to return as Huck's father), and also the Cadets of Temperance which Sam Clemens joined in order to march in funeral processions wearing their red scarf. This latter incident crops up in *Tom Sawyer.* Shortly afterward in *The Innocents,* among the pleasures and palaces of Europe, Twain interpolated other boyhood memories. In February, 1870, on receiving a letter from his "first, and oldest and dearest friend" Will Bowen, one of the flesh-and-blood components of Tom Sawyer, he sat down under the spell of the past and wrote a reply calling up some eight scenes which later appear in *Tom Sawyer* and *Huckleberry Finn*. Around this time he wrote a nameless sketch about a romantic lovesick swain who beyond question is Tom Sawyer. Designated as "Boy's Manuscript" by Twain's first editor, Albert Bigelow Paine, it was not published until 1942 in Bernard DeVoto's *Mark Twain at Work*. Some four years later Twain made a fresh start, scrapping the earlier diary form in favor of third-person narrative. By midsummer, 1875, it was done, and off the press late in the next year (a few months after Clemens with his usual inconsistency had written Will Bowen a stern letter on August 31, 1876, bidding him dwell no more in the sentimental never-never land of boyhood, denying that the past holds anything "worth pickling for present or future use"). In this latter year Twain began *Huckleberry Finn* as a sequel, laid it aside during six fallow years, went back to the story after his visit to Hannibal in 1882, and published it a little over two years later.

The first reader of *Tom Sawyer,* William Dean Howells, disagreed with the author that he had written a book for adults only. He quickly persuaded Twain that it was primarily a story for boys, which grown-ups would enjoy by reading over their shoulder. Twain therefore withdrew a few gibes against Sunday schools and tamed several phrases that smacked of backwoods frankness. Nothing of importance, however, was altered, nor did Tom suffer transformation into the neat, obedient paragon which fiction for the young so long had held up to their resentful gaze. The first chapter announces that Tom "was not the Model Boy of the village. He knew the model boy very well though—and loathed him." The only resemblance Tom bears to the fictional creations of his time is in sensibility: he yields to self-pity, relishes every neighborhood tear shed over his supposed drowning, and almost faints upon hearing that even a villain like Injun Joe has been sealed in the cave. Otherwise, our hero is of very different mettle. He steals from and outwits Aunt Polly, luxuriates in idleness, misbehaves in church, huffs and brags, and like his friend Huck employs lying as protective coloration in a world of adult tyrants. Consequently, in some American homes the new book was read by grown-ups, then tucked away out of a boy's reach; its successor, *Huckleberry Finn,* soon after publication was ejected from the town library of Concord, Massachusetts (where, a generation before, John Brown had been welcomed by Thoreau and Emerson), because Huck elected to "go to Hell" rather than betray his friend, a runaway Negro.

In 1870 Thomas Bailey Aldrich had published his mild *Story of a Bad Boy;* twenty years later Twain's friend Howells would reminisce of adolescents not too bright or good for human nature's daily food in *A Boy's Town;* a little later came Stephen Crane's recollections of Whilomville and William Allen White's of Boyville. They helped maintain the tradition of realism. In extreme recoil from priggishness, a line beginning with *Peck's Bad Boy* in 1883 flaunted incorrigibility above all. It is possible to overstress the picaresque intent of *Tom Sawyer* in turning upside down the world of Peter Parley and the Rollo books, or its analogues with that still greater novel, Cervantes' *Don Quixote,* in which some critics find the model of Tom the dreamer and Huck his commonsense henchman. Mark Twain's verisimilitude should not be overlooked in this search for "purpose." He wrote about boys from having been one in the Gilded Age, in a river town before the war.

To a stranger in 1887 he described this book as "simply a hymn, put into prose form to give it a worldly air." These lads no more resemble Peck's Bad Boy than they do the model children of that improving storyteller, Jacob Abbott. Within a framework of superb dialogue and setting, of sensitive perceptions that turn now and again into poetry, against a background where flicker shadows of adult humanitarianism and irony, Tom and Huck grow visibly as we follow them. The pranks and make-believe of early chapters —whitewashing the fence, releasing a pinchbug in church, playing pirate in *Tom Sawyer,* and in its sequel the rout of a Sunday school picnic under the guise of attacking a desert caravan—are dimmed as the human values deepen and occasional moral issues appear.

The Tom who takes Becky's punishment in school, and testifies for the innocent Muff Potter at risk of the murderer's revenge, parallels the development of Huck from a happy-go-lucky gamin to the epitome of generosity and loyalty. Mark Twain makes no account of rigid consistencies in time. His boys vary between the attitudes of nine-year-olds and those of thirteen or fourteen, despite the fact that *Tom Sawyer's* time span is one Missouri summer, and that of *Huckleberry Finn* a few more unbroken months. Like the creator of perennial comic-strip characters, Twain arrests or syncopates the march of time as he pleases. In the latter novel he also ignores the fact that Nigger Jim could have escaped by swimming across to the free soil of Illinois early in the book, and commits other sins against literalism which he would have ridiculed unmercifully in the pages of his *bête noire* James Fenimore Cooper.

Huckleberry Finn is clearly the finer book, showing a more mature point of view and exploring richer strata of human experience. A joy forever, it is unquestionably one of the masterpieces of American and of world literature. Here Twain returned to his first idea of having the chief actor tell the story, with better results. Huck's speech is saltier than Tom's, his mind freer from the claptrap of romance and sophistication. Huck is poised midway between the town-bred Tom and that scion of woodlore and primitive superstition Nigger Jim, toward whom Huck with his margin of superior worldliness stands in somewhat the same relation that Tom stands toward Huck. When Tom and Huck are together, our sympathy turns invariably toward the latter. A homeless river rat, cheerful in his rags, suspicious of every attempt to civilize him, Huck has none of the unimportant virtues and all the essential ones. The school of hard knocks has taught him skepticism, horse sense, and a tenacious grasp on reality. But it has not toughened him into cynicism or crime. Nature gave him a stanch and faithful heart, friendly to all underdogs and instantly hostile toward bullies and all shapes of overmastering power. One critic has called him the type of the common folk, sample of the run-of-the-mill democracy in America. Twain himself might have objected to the label, for he once declared "there are no common people, except in the highest spheres of society." Huck always

displays a frontier neighborliness, even trying to provide a rescue
for three murderers dying marooned on a wrecked boat, because
"there ain't no telling but I might come to be a murderer myself,
yet, and then how would I like it?" Money does not tempt him to
betray his friend Nigger Jim, though at times his conscience is
troubled by the voice of convention, preaching the sacredness of
property—even in the guise of flesh and blood—and he trembles
on the brink of surrender. Nor can he resist sometimes the
provocation offered by Jim's innocent credulity, only to be cut to
the quick when his friend bears with dignity the discovery that his
trustfulness has been made game of. Even as Huck surpasses Tom
in qualities of courage and heart, so Nigger Jim excels even Huck
in fidelity and innate manliness, to emerge as the book's noblest
character.

Sam Clemens himself (who in the first known letter he wrote his
mother, on the day he reached New York in August, 1853, had
indulged the easy sarcasm, "I reckon I had better black my face,
for in these Eastern States niggers are considerably better than
white people") learned in time, much as Huck learns, to face
down his condescension. In later years he became a warm friend of
the Negro and his rights. He paid the way of a Negro student
through Yale as "his part of the reparation due from every white
to every black man," and savagely attacked King Leopold of
Belgium for the barbarities of his agents in the Congo. Mrs.
Clemens once suggested as a mollifying rule to her husband,
"Consider everybody colored till he is proved white." Howells
thought that as time went on Clemens the Southwesterner was
prone to lose his Southern but cleave to his Western heritage,
finding his real affinities with the broader democracy of the
frontier. On other issues of race prejudice, Twain looked upon the
Jew with unqualified admiration, defended the Chinese whom he
had seen pelted through the streets of San Francisco, and confessed to only one invincible antipathy, namely, against the French
—although his most rhapsodic book was written in praise of their
national heroine.

The final draft of *Huckleberry Finn* was intimately bound up
with the writing of Twain's third great volume about his river

days, *Life on the Mississippi.* Fourteen chapters of these recollections had been published in the *Atlantic* in 1875; before expanding them into a book Twain made a memorable trip in 1882 back to the scenes of his youth. In working more or less simultaneously on both long-unfinished books, he lifted a scene intended for *Huckleberry Finn*—about Huck and the raftsmen—to flavor the other book, but the great gainer from his trip was not the memoir but the novel. The relative pallor of *Life on the Mississippi,* Part II, is due in a measure to the fact that so much lifeblood of reminiscence is drained off into the veins of *Huckleberry Finn.* The travel notes of 1882, written up soon after Twain's return home, are suffused with some of the finest situations in his novel: the Grangerford-Shepherdson feud, Colonel Sherburn and the mob, and the two seedy vagabonds who come on-stage as the Duke and the King, with a posse in their wake, who "said they hadn't been doing nothing, and was being chased for it."

Mark Twain's renewed contact with life among the river towns quickened his sense of realism. For *Huckleberry Finn,* save in its passages about the peace and freedom of Jackson's Island, is no longer "simply a hymn," and so dim has grown the dream of adolescent romancing that Becky Thatcher reappears but perfunctorily under the careless label of "Bessie" Thatcher. The odyssey of Huck's voyage through the South reveals aspects of life darker than the occasional melodrama of *Tom Sawyer.* We are shown the sloth and sadism of poor whites, backwoods loafers with their plug tobacco and Barlow knives, who sic dogs on stray sows and "laugh at the fun and look grateful for the noise," or drench a stray cur with turpentine and set him afire. We remark the cowardice of lynching parties; the chicanery of patent medicine fakers, revivalists, and exploiters of rustic ribaldry; the senseless feudings of the gentry. In the background broods fear: not only a boy's apprehension of ghosts, African superstitions, and the terrors of the night, nor the adults' dread of black insurrection, but the endless implicated strands of robbery, floggings, drowning, and murder. Death by violence lurks at every bend of road or river. Self-preservation becomes the ruling motive, squaring perfectly with the role of the principal characters, Huck the foot-loose orphan and his friend Jim the fugitive—puny in all strengths save loyalty, as they wander among the Brobdingnagian boots of white adult supremacy. The pair belong to the immortals of fiction.

Never keen at self-criticism, Mark Twain passed without soundings from these depths to the adjacent shallows of burlesque and extravaganza. The last fifth of this superb novel, *Huckleberry Finn,* brings back the romantic Tom Sawyer, with a hilarious, intricate, and needless plot for rescuing Jim from captivity. The story thus closes upon the farcical note with which the Hannibal cycle has begun, in the whitewashing episode. On the same note many years later Mark Twain tried to revive his most famous characters, in *Tom Sawyer Abroad* (1894), with Tom, Huck, and Jim as passengers of a mad balloonist and their subsequent adventures in Egypt. Though inferior to its great predecessors, this book does not lack humor, gusto, and rich characterization. *Tom Sawyer, Detective* (1896) dishes up a melodrama of stolen diamonds, double-crossing thieves, and that immortal device of Plautus and Shakespeare, identical twins, whose charm custom could not stale for Mark Twain. Here haste, artifice, and creative fatigue grow painfully apparent.

Uneven quality appears in *Life on the Mississippi,* even though it came at the high tide of his powers. Chapters IV–XVII were written for the *Atlantic* after Twain's chance reminiscences led his friend Twichell to exclaim, "What a virgin subject to hurl into a magazine!" Fresh, vivid, humorous, they recall the great days of river traffic: the problems of navigation, the races, the pilots' association, the resourcefulness and glory of the old-time pilot. The addenda, which came after Twain's return to the river for "copy," sometimes attain the former standard—the description of Pilot Brown the scold, or the account of the *Pennsylvania* disaster and Henry Clemens' death—but more often prove disappointing after the white heat of the book's inception. The first two chapters on the history of the river are merely an afterthought; the later ones too often wander among irrelevant yarns, like the revenge of Ritter the Austrian, or vignettes of picturesque New Orleans. Sam Clemens' year and a half as cub pilot are followed by almost no mention of his two years as a licensed skipper. Instead we are treated to such vagaries as Twain's famous theory about Sir Walter Scott, whose "Middle-Age sham civilization," he claimed, inspired the chivalry of the Old South, which in turn provoked the Civil War.

Yet with all its flaws of disunity and untidyness, *Life on the Mississippi* remains a masterpiece. Its communicable delight in experience, its rich picture of the human comedy and tragedy on the river (which Melville alone among great artists had tried to bring into focus in *The Confidence Man* in 1857), lend it real durability. Howells believed that the author long regarded it his greatest book—pleased with assurance to that effect from the German Kaiser and also from a hotel porter, whose praise he accepted with equal satisfaction. In other moods, toward the end of his life, Twain favored *Joan of Arc,* in part because it cost him "twelve years of preparation and two years of writing. The others needed no preparation, & got none." Thus again he displayed the blindness of self-appraisal. The book that required probably least effort of all, drawn from a brimming native reservoir, *Huckleberry Finn,* unquestionably is his finest, with *Tom Sawyer* and *Life on the Mississippi* as runners-up.

VI

Mark Twain's later years show a drift toward the remote in time and place, in a fitful quest for new themes, new magic—a search that proceeded apace with a growing sense of personal dissatisfaction, frustration, and heartbreak. While the aging artist began to lose much of his creative fire, Clemens the generous, erratic, moody, and vulnerable human being remained, standing at bay against the disillusions and disasters that gathered to ring him around and mock his fame as the world humorist of the century. The development of this last phase is worth tracing.

From recollections of his Hannibal boyhood he gravitated toward a new but distinctly artificial romanticism, "the pageant and fairy-tale" of life in medieval Europe. His earliest treatment of the theme is *The Prince and the Pauper* (1881), a story mainly for children, built upon the old plot of transposed identities. Here to a degree, and still more in *A Connecticut Yankee in King Arthur's Court* (1889) and *Personal Recollections of Joan of Arc* (1896), the romantic's fascination with knights and castles is counterbalanced by the iconoclast's itch to shatter that world of sham and injustice, where crown and miter lorded it over the commons. The savage indignation which Twain so loved to unleash found hunting that gratified him: the prey bore some resemblance to the contemporary, without committing him to the consequences of a frontal attack upon modern authoritarianism, convention, and orthodoxy. *A Connecticut Yankee,* best of the cycle, shows just such an ingenious mechanic as Clemens must often have met on visits to the Hartford shops of Pratt and Whitney, a Yankee who is swept back in time to Camelot. With one hand he transforms Arthurian England into a going concern of steam and electricity; with the other, seeks to plant the seeds of equalitarianism. He remarks that in feudal society six men out of a thousand crack the whip over their fellows' backs: "It seemed to me that what the nine hundred and ninety-four dupes needed was a new deal." This passage, as the late President Roosevelt testified, furnished the most memorable phrase in modern American government. The Connecticut Yankee asserts that the mass of a nation can always produce "the material in abundance whereby to govern itself." Yet the medieval mob is shown collectively to be gullible, vicious, invincibly ignorant, like the populace of Hannibal or Hartford, so that the Yankee sets up not a true democracy but a benign dictatorship centering in himself and his mechanical skills—a kind of technocrat's utopia. Dazzled by the wonders of applied science, Mark Twain always hoped for social as well as technological miracles from the dynamo.

Twain's apotheosis of the Virgin—in terms of Henry Adams' dilemma—of spiritual forces in conflict with materialism and the stupid cruelty of organized society, appears in *Joan of Arc.* The Maid was his favorite character in history. But as Twain's imagination is better than his knowledge of medieval life, the result at best is a *tour de force.*

Joan was published anonymously, in hope of giving this book a head start free from a reputation which the world had come long since to regard as synonymous with comedy. Indeed, most people continued to hail with uproarious mirth Mark Twain's explosive attacks upon power politics, imperialism, malefactors of great wealth, hypocrisy in morals and religion, and other manifestations of what he increasingly came to call "the damned human race." They refused to forget "The Celebrated Jumping Frog," or his reputation for convulsing any crowd whenever his mouth was opened. Meanwhile, as the satirist gained upper hand over the humorist in his nature, and age diminished his ebullience, Mark Twain not only yearned vainly for a serious hearing but also came to flinch from the role of platform zany.

Lecturing, however, became a need more urgent than ever. For, beginning with the Panic of 1893, the tide of Mark Twain's luck suddenly changed. The famous writer, with ample cash in hand and enviable royalties rolling in, still vigorous in health and self-confidence, the adoring husband and beloved father of three charming daughters—this self-made "jour" printer and riverboatman whom the world delighted to honor—upon him fortune suddenly began to rain blow after blow. The first losses were financial. The Paige typesetting machine, brainchild of an erratic inventor who came close to anticipating the fabulous success of Mergenthaler's Linotype, failed after years of costly maintenance from Clemens' pocket; instead of making millions, he lost hundreds of thousands. Then the publishing firm of Charles L. Webster (named for the son-in-law of Mark's sister, but backed by the author himself through suspicion of the big commercial publishers) crashed into bankruptcy. Twain's new friend Henry H. Rogers, Standard Oil magnate and by the lights of the muckraking age a robber baron, advised him that the ethics of literature were higher than those of business, and "you must earn the cent per cent." Mark's own conscience fully acquiesced. Even though his old exuberant energy was flagging, he set out in 1895 on a world lecture tour, after giving a statement to the press:

The law recognizes no mortgage on a man's brain, and a merchant who has given up all he has may take advantage of the laws of insolvency and start free again for himself. But I am not a business man, and honor is a harder master than the law. It cannot compromise for less than 100 cents on the dollar and its debts never outlaw.

The profits, together with royalties and the astute management of Mr. Rogers, eventually enabled him to pay the last dollar to these creditors and add an American parallel to the case of Sir Walter Scott.

Twain's last notable book about American life, *Pudd'nhead Wilson* (1894), written on the brink of financial disaster but before the onset of deeper tragedies, is about a nonconformist who is too witty and wise for the backwoods community where his days are spent; miscalled "Pudd'nhead," he at last wins recognition by solving a murder mystery through his hobby of fingerprints. In so doing he also unravels a case of transposed identities for which the Negress Roxy—a character of magnificent vigor and realism—had been responsible. The novel is a daring, though inconclusive, study of miscegenation. Significant of Mark Twain's growing pessimism are the cynical chapter mottoes ascribed to Pudd'nhead's "Calendar," such as: "If you pick up a starving dog and make him prosperous, he will not bite you. This is the principal difference between a dog and a man." Or, still more typical of the aging Twain: "Whoever has lived long enough to find out what life is, knows how deep a debt of gratitude we owe to Adam, the first great benefactor of our race. He brought death into the world."

These notes—the ingratitude and folly of man, the vanity of human wishes, the praise of death as the nepenthe for life's tragedy—echo increasingly through the later writings of Mark Twain. This drift was no new departure, but the accentuation of a lifelong trend. In youth he had been subject to fits of melancholy and disillusion. In Cincinnati at the age of twenty he had listened avidly to a homespun philosopher expound the gospel of scientific determinism; as a cub pilot he read Tom Paine "with fear and hesitation." Later, in San Francisco, Mark said he had come within a trigger's breadth of suicide, and in 1876 for obscure causes yielded to a bad season of the blues. Still later he discovered Jonathan Edwards, brooding for days over the "dominion of Motive and Necessity," and was powerfully drawn to the agnosticism of Huxley, Haeckel, and Ingersoll. As a boy he had been terrorized by the fickle and vindictive Jehovah of Sunday schools; as a youth he graduated to the God of scientific law, impersonal but just; as an old man he returned to the cruel God, now stripped of anthropomorphic whims, but no less terrible as causation and fate. As early as 1882, in an unpublished dialogue between Negroes written on his river trip, Mark Twain sketched out the logic elaborated sixteen years later in his "wicked book" *What Is Man?*—not printed until 1906, then privately and anonymously because he thought it so blastingly incontrovertible. Its argument, developed between an earnest Young Man and a cynical Old Man, is that self-interest and self-approval are the mainsprings of human conduct, however cleverly they mask themselves as honor, charity, altruism, or love. Hunger for self-esteem is the master passion; under this demon of the ego, free will is nothing but illusion.

While Mark was lecturing around the world for "honor," news reached him that back home his favorite daughter Susy had suddenly succumbed to meningitis. Would the girl have died if her parents had not deserted her? It was perhaps a foolish question, but natural to a self-accusing heart like Clemens'. Unpublished papers bear witness to his bitterness in those days, savage reflections about how God gives us breath and bodies only to undermine us with the million plagues of disease and heartbreak, to show what Twain calls His "fatherly infatuation" toward us. Meanwhile Mrs. Clemens sank deeper and deeper into a hopeless invalidism that ended only with the mercy of her death in 1904; and their daughter Jean, whose moods had long puzzled them, was discovered to be an incurable epileptic. Mark Twain's own robust health was beginning to crumble, and—as a still more tragic circumstance to the artist who had begun to use hard work as an anodyne for grief—his magnificent creative powers were now sadly on the wane. His unpublished papers are full of fragmentary stories and novels that simply would not come out right, and were endlessly reworked, rewritten, finally abandoned. Many are reminiscent, in plot and character, of his golden period; the magician fell back upon his old repertory, made the same passes, but somehow failed to pull off the trick. They are also eloquent with personal revelation. Twain in old age kept tormenting himself, in a dozen allegorical disguises, with the problem of "guilt" which (as his Calvinist conscience whispered) must somehow be antecedent to punishment, the cause of all the failures and bereavements fate had inflicted upon him. The artist keeps asking himself: Was I to blame, for something I did or left undone? The motif of a doting father with a dead or missing child is frequent, and of course transparent.

One such story concerns the dream of a man who has fallen asleep after gazing at a drop of water, swimming with animalculae, beneath the microscope. He dreams that he is on shipboard in the Antarctic seas pursuing his lost child who has been carried off by another ship, in a chase that continues like some nightmare in a fever, while terrible creatures arise to roam the deep and snatch passengers off the deck. The captain of the ship is called the Superintendent of Dreams, and it is his cunning to destroy the seafarers' sense of reality, while they circle toward the ultimate horror of the Great White Glare—actually the beam cast through the microscope's field by the reflector—a vortex of death into which all things, including the craft with the missing child, are being drawn. Seldom has determinism found a grimmer symbol.

The greatest story of Mark Twain's later period, too often neglected in the appraisal of his work, wins at last the personal answer for which he sought so desperately. In the light of those unfinished manuscripts among the Mark Twain Papers, it attains true perspective. This is *The Mysterious Stranger,* begun in the gloom of 1898 after Susy's death and Jean's hopeless prognosis, but not finished until several years later and published post-humously in 1916. Like the last act of a Greek tragedy, or *Samson Agonistes* with "all passion spent," it achieves a wintry serenity beyond despair. The story is that of some boys who are really Tom Sawyer's gang in medieval dress, in the Austrian village of Eseldorf, who strike up acquaintance with a supernatural visitor able to work miracles and juggle with lives. Calling himself "Satan," he claims relationship with the prince of fallen angels, but appears to live in a sphere beyond both good and evil. Laughter and tears, joy and torment, saintliness and sin, to him are but as the sound of lyres and flutes, and at last he grows bored with his own wonder-working caprices. He then tells the wide-eyed Theodor:

It is true, that which I have revealed to you; there is no God, no universe, no human race, no earthly life, no heaven, no hell. It is all a dream—a grotesque and foolish dream. Nothing exists but you. And you are but a *thought*—a vagrant thought, a useless thought, a homeless thought, wandering forlorn among the empty eternities!

And in his heart of hearts the boy knows this is true. Here, in the closing pages of *The Mysterious Stranger,* Mark Twain solved his riddle of grief and self-reproach, and clothed his soul in the only invulnerable armor of desperation. Good and evil, like reality itself, are only illusions, such stuff as dreams are made on, and our little life is rounded with the best gift of the Artist who saves it to the last—extinction.

Like Halley's comet in 1835 and 1910, whose appearance Mark Twain saw as setting the beginning and the end of his life, the luster of his genius flashed forth now and again against this darkened sky of fatalism. He wrote and spoke with sparkles of his old wit, and few were aware of the encircling gloom. Oxford gave him her degree of Doctor of Letters in 1907, and his birthdays became national events. In his famous white clothes he seemed a kind of ghost from America's buried life, recalling the nostalgia of her youth, revisiting these glimpses of the modern city and its vast industrialism. But his great creative genius had almost gone—that energy which he spent and squandered so freely, when he had it, with the recklessness of the Old West. For Mark Twain the artist had always been a kind of pocket miner, stumbling like fortune's darling upon native ore of incredible richness and exploiting it with effortless skill—but often gleefully mistaking fool's gold for the genuine article, or lavishing his strength upon historical diggings long since played out. If latterly he seemed to deny his role as America's great comic spirit, perhaps the key can be found in his last travel book: "Everything human is pathetic. The secret source of humor itself is not joy but sorrow. There is no humor in heaven."

My Mark Twain

It was in the little office of James T. Fields, over the bookstore of
Ticknor & Fields, at 124 Tremont Street, Boston, that I first met
my friend of now forty-four years, Samuel L. Clemens. Mr. Fields
was then the editor of the *Atlantic Monthly,* and I was his proud
and glad assistant, with a pretty free hand as to manuscripts, and
an unmanacled command of the book notices at the end of the
magazine. I wrote nearly all of them myself, and in 1869 I had
written rather a long notice of a book just winning its way to
universal favor. In this review I had intimated my reservations
concerning the *Innocents Abroad,* but I had the luck, if not the
sense, to recognize that it was such fun as we had not had before. I
forget just what I said in praise of it, and it does not matter; it is
enough that I praised it enough to satisfy the author. He now
signified as much, and he stamped his gratitude into my memory
with a story wonderfully allegorizing the situation, which the mock
modesty of print forbids my repeating here. Throughout my long
acquaintance with him his graphic touch was always allowing itself
a freedom which I cannot bring my fainter pencil to illustrate. He
had the Southwestern, the Lincolnian, the Elizabethan breadth of
parlance, which I suppose one ought not to call coarse without
calling one's self prudish; and I was often hiding away in discreet

holes and corners the letters in which he had loosed his bold fancy to stoop on rank suggestion; I could not bear to burn them, and I could not, after the first reading, quite bear to look at them. I shall best give my feeling on this point by saying that in it he was Shakespearian, or if his ghost will not suffer me the word, then he was Baconian.

At the time of our first meeting, which must have been well toward the winter, Clemens (as I must call him instead of Mark Twain, which seemed always somehow to mask him from my personal sense) was wearing a sealskin coat, with the fur out, in the satisfaction of a caprice, or the love of strong effect which he was apt to indulge through life. I do not know what droll comment was in Fields's mind with respect to this garment, but probably he felt that here was an original who was not to be brought to any Bostonian book in the judgment of his vivid qualities. With his crest of dense red hair, and the wide sweep of his flaming mustache, Clemens was not discordantly clothed in that sealskin coat, which afterward, in spite of his own warmth in it, sent the cold chills through me when I once accompanied it down Broadway, and shared the immense publicity it won him. He had always a relish for personal effect, which expressed itself in the white suit of complete serge which he wore in his last years, and in the Oxford gown which he put on for every possible occasion, and said he would like to wear all the time. That was not vanity in him, but a keen feeling for costume which the severity of our modern tailoring forbids men, though it flatters women to every excess in it; yet he also enjoyed the shock, the offense, the pang which it gave the sensibilities of others. Then there were times he played these pranks for pure fun, and for the pleasure of the witness. Once I remember seeing him come into his drawing room at Hartford in a pair of white cowskin slippers, with the hair out, and do a crippled colored uncle to the joy of all beholders. Or, I must not say all, for I remember also the dismay of Mrs. Clemens, and her low, despairing cry of, "Oh, Youth!" That was her name for him among their friends, and it fitted him as no other would, though I fancied with her it was a shrinking from his baptismal Samuel, or the vernacular Sam of his earlier companionships. He was a youth to the end of his days, the heart of a boy with the head of a sage; the heart of a good boy, or a bad boy, but always a willful boy, and willfulest to show himself out at every time for just the boy he was.

There is a gap in my recollections of Clemens, which I think is of a year or two, for the next thing I remember of him is meeting him at a lunch in Boston given us by that genius of hospitality, the tragically destined Ralph Keeler, author of one of the most unjustly forgotten books, *Vagabond Adventures,* a true bit of picaresque autobiography. Keeler never had any money, to the general knowledge, and he never borrowed, and he could not have had credit at the restaurant where he invited us to feast at his expense. There was T. B. Aldrich, there was J. T. Fields, much the oldest of our company, who had just freed himself from the trammels of the publishing business, and was feeling his freedom in every word; there was Bret Harte, who had lately come East in his princely progress from California; and there was Clemens. Nothing remains to me of the happy time but a sense of idle and aimless and joyful talk-play, beginning and ending nowhere, of eager laughter, of countless good stories from Fields, of a heat-lightning shimmer of wit from Aldrich, of an occasional concentration of our joint mockeries upon our host, who took it gladly; and amid the discourse, so little improving, but so full of good fellowship, Bret Harte's fleering dramatization of Clemens' mental attitude toward a symposium of Boston illuminates. "Why, fellows," he spluttered, "this is the dream of Mark's life," and I remember the glance from under Clemens' feathery eyebrows which betrayed his enjoyment of the fun. We had beefsteak with mushrooms, which in recognition of their shape Aldrich hailed as shoe pegs, and to crown the feast we had an omelette soufflé, which the waiter brought in as flat as a pancake, amid our shouts of congratulations to poor Keeler, who took them with appreciative submission. It was in every way what a Boston literary lunch ought not to have been in the popular ideal which Harte attributed to Clemens.

Our next meeting was at Hartford, or, rather, at Springfield, where Clemens greeted us on the way to Hartford. Aldrich was going on to be his guest, and I was going to be Charles Dudley

Warner's, but Clemens had come part way to welcome us both. In the good fellowship of that cordial neighborhood we had two such days as the aging sun no longer shines on in his round. There was constant running in and out of friendly houses where the lively hosts and guests called one another by their Christian names or nicknames, and no such vain ceremony as knocking or ringing at doors. Clemens was then building the stately mansion in which he satisfied his love of magnificence as if it had been another sealskin coat, and he was at the crest of the prosperity which enabled him to humor every whim or extravagance. The house was the design of that most original artist, Edward Potter, who once, when hard pressed by incompetent curiosity for the name of his style in a certain church, proposed that it should be called the English violet order of architecture; and this house was so absolutely suited to the owner's humor that I suppose there never was another house like it; but its character must be for recognition farther along in these reminiscenses. The vividest impression which Clemens gave us two ravenous young Boston authors was of the satisfying, the surfeiting nature of subscription publication. An army of agents was overrunning the country with the prospectuses of his books, and delivering them by the scores of thousands in completed sale. Of the *Innocents Abroad* he said, "It sells right along just like the Bible," and *Roughing It* was swiftly following, without perhaps ever quite overtaking it in popularity. But he lectured Aldrich and me on the folly of that mode of publication in the trade which we had thought it the highest success to achieve a chance in. "Anything but subscription publication is printing for private circulation," he maintained, and he so won upon our greed and hope that on the way back to Boston we planned the joint authorship of a volume adapted to subscription publication. We got a very good name for it, as we believed, in *Memorable Murders,* and we never got farther with it, but by the time we reached Boston we were rolling in wealth so deep that we could hardly walk home in the frugal fashion by which we still thought it best to spare carfare; carriage fare we did not dream of even in that opulence.

The visits to Hartford which had begun with this affluence continued without actual increase of riches for me, but now I went

alone, and in Warner's European and Egyptian absences I formed
the habit of going to Clemens. By this time he was in his new
house, where he used to give me a royal chamber on the ground
floor, and come in at night after I had gone to bed to take off the
burglar alarm so that the family should not be roused if anybody
tried to get in at my window. This would be after we had sat up
late, he smoking the last of his innumerable cigars, and soothing
his tense nerves with a mild hot Scotch, while we both talked and
talked and talked, of everything in the heavens and on the earth,
and the waters under the earth. After two days of this talk I would
come away hollow, realizing myself best in the image of one of
those locust shells which you find sticking to the bark of trees at
the end of summer. Once, after some such bout of brains, we went
down to New York together, and sat facing each other in the
Pullman smoker without passing a syllable till we had occasion to
say, "Well, we're there." Then, with our installation in a now
vanished hotel (the old Brunswick, to be specific), the talk began
again with the inspiration of the novel environment, and went on
and on. We wished to be asleep, but we could not stop, and he
lounged through the rooms in the long nightgown which he always
wore in preference to the pajamas which he despised, and told the
story of his life, the inexhaustible, the fairy, the Arabian Nights
story, which I could never tire of even when it began to be told
over again. Or at times he would reason high—

> Of Providence, foreknowledge, will and fate,
> Fixed fate, free will, foreknowledge absolute,

walking up and down, and halting now and then, with a fine toss
and slant of his shaggy head, as some bold thought or splendid
joke struck him.

He was in those days a constant attendant at the church of his
great friend, the Rev. Joseph H. Twichell, and at least tacitly far
from the entire negation he came to at last. I should say he had
hardly yet examined the grounds of his passive acceptance of his
wife's belief, for it was hers and not his, and he held it unscanned
in the beautiful and tender loyalty to her which was the most
moving quality of his most faithful soul. I make bold to speak of

the love between them, because without it I could not make him known to others as he was known to me. It was a greater part of him than the love of most men for their wives, and she merited all the worship he could give her, all the devotion, all the implicit obedience, by her surpassing force and beauty of character. She was in a way the loveliest person I have ever seen, the gentlest, the kindest, without a touch of weakness; she united wonderful tact with wonderful truth; and Clemens not only accepted her rule implicitly, but he rejoiced, he gloried in it. I am not sure that he noticed all her goodness in the actions that made it a heavenly vision to others, he so had the habit of her goodness; but if there was any forlorn and helpless creature in the room Mrs. Clemens was somehow promptly at his side or hers; she was always seeking occasion of kindness to those in her household or out of it; she loved to let her heart go beyond the reach of her hand, and imagined the whole hard and suffering world with compassion for its structural as well as incidental wrongs. I suppose she had her ladyhood limitations, her female fears of etiquette and convention, but she did not let them hamper the wild and splendid generosity with which Clemens rebelled against the social stupidities and cruelties. She had been a lifelong invalid when he met her, and he liked to tell the beautiful story of their courtship to each new friend whom he found capable of feeling its beauty or worthy of hearing it. Naturally, her father had hesitated to give her into the keeping of the young strange Westerner, who had risen up out of the unknown with his giant reputation of burlesque humorist, and demanded guaranties, demanded proofs. "He asked me," Clemens would say, "if I couldn't give him the names of people who knew me in California, and when it was time to hear from them I heard from him. 'Well, Mr. Clemens,' he said, 'nobody seems to have a very good word for you.' I hadn't referred him to people that I thought were going to whitewash me. I thought it was all up with me, but I was disappointed. 'So I guess I shall have to back you myself.' "

Whether this made him faithfuler to the trust put in him I cannot say, but probably not; it was always in him to be faithful to any trust, and in proportion as a trust of his own was betrayed he was ruthlessly and implacably resentful. But I wish now to speak of the happiness of that household in Hartford which responded so perfectly to the ideals of the mother when the three daughters, so lovely and so gifted, were yet little children. There had been a boy, and "Yes, *I* killed him," Clemens once said, with the unsparing self-blame in which he would wreak an unavailing regret. He meant that he had taken the child out imprudently, and the child had taken the cold which he died of, but it was by no means certain this was through its father's imprudence. I never heard him speak of his son except that once, but no doubt in his deep heart his loss was irreparably present. He was a very tender father and delighted in the minds of his children, but he was wise enough to leave their training altogether to the wisdom of their mother. He left them to that in everything, keeping for himself the pleasure of teaching them little scenes of drama, learning languages with them, and leading them in singing. They came to the table with their parents, and could have set him an example in behavior when, in moments of intense excitement, he used to leave his place and walk up and down the room, flying his napkin and talking and talking.

It was after his first English sojourn that I used to visit him, and he was then full of praise of everything English: the English personal independence and public spirit, and hospitality, and truth. He liked to tell stories in proof of their virtues, but he was not blind to the defects of their virtues: their submissive acceptance of caste, their callousness with strangers, their bluntness with one another. Mrs. Clemens had been in a way to suffer socially more than he, and she praised the English less. She had sat after dinner with ladies who snubbed and ignored one another, and left her to find her own amusement in the absence of the attention with which Americans perhaps cloy their guests, but which she could not help preferring. In their successive sojourns among them I believe he came to like the English less and she more; the fine delight of his first acceptance among them did not renew itself till his Oxford degree was given him; then it made his cup run over, and he was glad the whole world should see it.

His wife would not chill the ardor of his early Anglomania, and in this, as in everything, she wished to humor him to the utmost. No one could have realized more than she his essential fineness, his innate nobleness. Marriages are what the parties to them alone really know them to be, but from the outside I should say that this marriage was one of the most perfect. It lasted in his absolute devotion to the day of her death, that delayed long in cruel suffering, and that left one side of him in lasting night. From Florence there came to me heartbreaking letters from him about the torture she was undergoing, and at last a letter saying she was dead, with the simple-hearted cry, "I wish I was with Livy." I do not know why I have left saying till now that she was a very beautiful woman, classically regular in features, with black hair smooth over her forehead, and with tenderly peering, myopic eyes, always behind glasses, and a smile of angelic kindness. But this kindness went with a sense of humor which qualified her to appreciate the self-lawed genius of a man who will be remembered with the great humorists of all time, with Cervantes, with Swift, or with any others worthy his company; none of them was his equal in humanity. . . .

There is an incident of this time so characteristic of both men that I will yield to the temptation of giving it here. . . . Matthew Arnold arrived in Boston, and one of my family called on him, to explain why I was not at home to receive his introduction: I had gone to see Mark Twain. "Oh, but he doesn't like *that* sort of thing, does he?" "He likes Mr. Clemens very much," my representative answered, "and he thinks him one of the greatest men he ever knew." I was still Clemens' guest at Hartford when Arnold came there to lecture, and one night we went to meet him at a reception. While his hand laxly held mine in greeting, I saw his eyes fixed intensely on the other side of the room. "Who—who in the world is that?" I looked and said, "Oh, that is Mark Twain." I do not remember just how their instant encounter was contrived by Arnold's wish, but I have the impression that they were not parted for long during the evening, and the next night Arnold, as if still under the glamour of that potent presence, was at Clemens' house. I cannot say how they got on, or what they made of each other; if Clemens

ever spoke of Arnold, I do not recall what he said, but Arnold had
shown a sense of him from which the incredulous sniff of the polite
world, now so universally exploded, had already perished. It might
well have done so with his first dramatic vision of that prodigious
head. Clemens was then hard upon fifty, and he had kept, as he did
to the end, the slender figure of his youth, but the ashes of the
burnt-out years were beginning to gray the fires of that splendid
shock of red hair which he held to the height of a stature apparently
greater than it was, and tilted from side to side in his undulating
walk. He glimmered at you from the narrow slits of fine blue-
greenish eyes, under branching brows, which with age grew more
and more like a sort of plumage, and he was apt to smile into your
face with a subtle but amiable perception, and yet with a sort of
remote absence; you were all there for him, but he was not all
there for you. . . .

He satisfied the impassioned demand of his nature for incessant
activities of every kind by taking a personal as well as a pecuniary
interest in the inventions of others. At one moment "the damned
human race" was almost to be redeemed by a process of founding
brass without air bubbles in it; if this could once be accomplished,
as I understood, or misunderstood, brass could be used in art
printing to a degree hitherto impossible. I dare say I have got it
wrong, but I am not mistaken as to Clemens' enthusiasm for the
process, and his heavy losses in paying its way to ultimate failure.
He was simultaneously absorbed in the perfection of a typesetting
machine, which he was paying the inventor a salary to bring to a
perfection so expensive that it was practically impracticable. We
were both printers by trade, and I could take the same interest in
this wonderful piece of mechanism that he could; and it was so
truly wonderful that it did everything but walk and talk. Its
ingenious creator was so bent upon realizing the highest ideal in it
that he produced a machine of quite unimpeachable efficiency. But
it was so costly, when finished, that it could not be made for less
than twenty thousand dollars, if the parts were made by hand. This
sum was prohibitive of its introduction, unless the requisite capital
could be found for making the parts by machinery, and Clemens

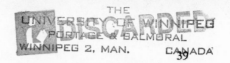

spent many months in vainly trying to get this money together. In the meantime simpler machines had been invented and the market filled, and his investment of three hundred thousand dollars in the beautiful miracle remained permanent but not profitable. I once went with him to witness its performance, and it did seem to me the last word in its way, but it had been spoken too exquisitely, too fastidiously. I never heard him devote the inventor to the infernal gods, as he was apt to do with the geniuses he lost money by, and so I think he did not regard him as a traitor.

In these things, and in his other schemes for the *subiti guadagni* of the speculator and the "sudden making of splendid names" for the benefactors of our species, Clemens satisfied the Colonel Sellers nature in himself (from which he drew the picture of that wild and lovable figure), and perhaps made as good use of his money as he could. He did not care much for money in itself, but he luxuriated in the lavish use of it, and he was as generous with it as ever a man was. He liked giving it, but he commonly wearied of giving it himself, and wherever he lived he established an almoner, whom he fully trusted to keep his left hand ignorant of what his right hand was doing. I believe he felt no finality in charity, but did it because in its provisional way it was the only thing a man could do. I never heard him go really into any sociological inquiry, and I have a feeling that that sort of thing baffled and dispirited him. No one can read the *Connecticut Yankee* and not be aware of the length and breadth of his sympathies with poverty, but apparently he had not thought out any scheme for righting the economic wrongs we abound in. I cannot remember our ever getting quite down to a discussion of the matter; we came very near it once in the day of the vast wave of emotion sent over the world by *Looking Backward,* and again when we were all so troubled by the great coal strike in Pennsylvania; in considering that he seemed to be for the time doubtful of the justice of the workingman's cause. At all other times he seemed to know that whatever wrongs the workingman committed work was always in the right.

When Clemens returned to America with his family, after lecturing round the world, I again saw him in New York, where I so often saw him while he was shaping himself for that heroic enterprise. He would come to me, and talk sorrowfully over his financial ruin, and picture it to himself as the stuff of some unhappy dream, which, after long prosperity, had culminated the wrong way. It was very melancholy, very touching, but the sorrow to which he had come home from his long journey had not that forlorn bewilderment in it. He was looking wonderfully well, and when I wanted the name of his elixir, he said it was plasmon. He was apt, for a man who had put faith so decidedly away from him, to take it back and pin it to some superstition, usually of a hygienic sort. Once, when he was well on in years, he came to New York without glasses, and announced that he and all his family, so astigmatic and myopic and old-sighted, had, so to speak, burned their spectacles behind them upon the instruction of some sage who had found out that they were a delusion. The next time he came he wore spectacles freely, almost ostentatiously, and I heard from others that the whole Clemens family had been near losing their eyesight by the miracle worked in their behalf. Now, I was not surprised to learn that "the damned human race" was to be saved by plasmon, if anything, and that my first duty was to visit the plasmon agency with him, and procure enough plasmon to secure my family against the ills it was heir to forevermore. I did not immediately understand that plasmon was one of the investments which he had made from "the substance of things hoped for," and in the destiny of a disastrous disappointment. But after paying off the creditors of his late publishing firm, he had to do something with his money, and it was not his fault if he did not make a fortune out of plasmon. . . .

My perspectives are not very clear, and in the foreshortening of events which always takes place in our review of the past I may not always time things aright. But I believe it was not until he had taken his house at 21 Fifth Avenue that he began to talk to me of writing his autobiography. He meant that it should be a perfectly veracious record of his life and period; for the first time in literature there should be a true history of a man and a true presentation of the men the man had known. As we talked it over the scheme enlarged itself in our riotous fancy. We said it should be not only a book, it should be a library, not only a library, but a literature. It should make good the world's loss through Omar's barbarity at Alexandria; there was no image so grotesque, so extravagant that we did not play with it; and the work so far as he carried it was really done on a colossal scale. But one day he said that as to veracity it was a failure; he had begun to lie, and that if no man ever yet told the truth about himself it was because no man ever could. How far he had carried his autobiography I cannot say; he dictated the matter several hours each day; and the public has already seen long passages from it, and can judge, probably, of the make and matter of the whole from these. It is immensely inclusive, and it observes no order or sequence. Whether now, after his death, it will be published soon or late I have no means of knowing. Once or twice he said in a vague way that it was not to be published for twenty years, so that the discomfort of publicity might be minimized for all the survivors. Suddenly he told me he was not working at it; but I did not understand whether he had finished it or merely dropped it; I never asked.

We lived in the same city, but for old men rather far apart, he at Tenth Street and I at Seventieth, and with our colds and other disabilities we did not see each other often. He expected me to come to him, and I would not without some return of my visits, but we never ceased to be friends, and good friends, so far as I know. I joked him once as to how I was going to come out in his auto-biography, and he gave me some sort of joking reassurance. There was one incident, however, that brought us very frequently and actively together. He came one Sunday afternoon to have me call with him on Maxim Gorky, who was staying at a hotel a few streets above mine. We were both interested in Gorky, Clemens rather more as a revolutionist and I as a realist, though I too wished the Russian Czar ill, and the novelist well in his mission to the Russian sympathizers in this republic. But I had lived through the episode of Kossuth's visit to us and his vain endeavor to raise funds for the Hungarian cause in 1851, when we were a younger and nobler nation than now, with hearts if not hands opener to the "oppressed of Europe"; the oppressed of America, the four or five millions of slaves, we did not count. I did not believe that Gorky could get the money for the cause of freedom in Russia which he had come to get; as I told a valued friend of his and mine, I did not believe he could get twenty-five hundred dollars, and I think now I set the figure too high. I had already refused to sign the sort of general appeal his friends were making to our principles and pockets because I felt it so wholly idle, and when the paper was produced in Gorky's presence and Clemens put his name to it I still refused. The next day Gorky was expelled from his hotel with the woman who was not his wife, but who, I am bound to say, did not look as if she were not, at least to me, who am, however, not versed in those aspects of human nature.

I might have escaped unnoted, but Clemens' familiar head gave us away to the reporters waiting at the elevator's mouth for all who went to see Gorky. As it was, a hunt of interviewers ensued for us severally and jointly. I could remain aloof in my hotel apartment, returning answer to such guardians of the public right to know everything that I had nothing to say of Gorky's domestic affairs; for the public interest had now strayed far from the revolution, and centered entirely upon these. But with Clemens it was different; he lived in a house with a street door kept by a single butler, and he was constantly rung for. I forget how long the siege lasted, but long enough for us to have fun with it. That was the moment of the great Vesuvian eruption, and we figured ourselves in easy reach of a volcano which was every now and then "blowing a cone off," as the telegraphic phrase was. The roof of the great market in Naples had just broken in under its load of ashes and cinders, and crushed hundreds of people; and we asked each other if we were not sorry we had not been there, where the pressure would have been far less terrific than it was with us in Fifth Avenue. The forbidden butler came up with a message that there were some gentlemen below who wanted to see Clemens.

"How many?" he demanded.

"Five," the butler faltered.

"Reporters?"

The butler feigned uncertainty.

"What would you do?" he asked me.

"I wouldn't see them," I said, and then Clemens went directly down to them. How or by what means he appeased their voracity I cannot say, but I fancy it was by the confession of the exact truth, which was harmless enough. They went away joyfully, and he came back in radiant satisfaction with having seen them. Of course he was right and I wrong, and he was right as to the point at issue between Gorky and those who had helplessly treated him with such cruel ignominy. In America it is not the convention for men to live openly in hotels with women who are not their wives. Gorky had violated this convention and he had to pay the penalty; and concerning the destruction of his efficiency as an emissary of the revolution, his blunder was worse than a crime.

To the period of Clemens' residence in Fifth Avenue belongs his efflorescence in white serge. He was always rather aggressively indifferent about dress, and at a very early date in our acquaintance Aldrich and I attempted his reform by clubbing to buy him a cravat. But he would not put away his stiff little black bow, and until he imagined the suit of white serge, he wore always a suit of black serge, truly deplorable in the cut of the sagging frock. After his measure had once been taken he refused to make his clothes the occasion of personal interviews with his tailor; he sent the stuff by the kind elderly woman who had been in the service of the family from the earliest days of his marriage, and accepted the result without criticism. But the white serge was an inspiration which few men would have had the courage to act upon. The first time I saw him wear it was at the authors' hearing before the Congressional Committee on Copyright in Washington. Nothing could have been more dramatic than the gesture with which he flung off his long loose overcoat, and stood forth in white from his feet to the crown of his silvery head. It was a magnificent *coup,* and he dearly loved a *coup;* but the magnificent speech which he made, tearing to shreds the venerable farrago of nonsense about nonproperty in ideas which had formed the basis of all copyright legislation, made you forget even his spectacularity.

It is well known how proud he was of his Oxford gown, not merely because it symbolized the honor in which he was held by

the highest literary body in the world, but because it was so rich
and so beautiful. The red and the lavender of the cloth flattered his
eyes as the silken black of the same degree of Doctor of Letters,
given him years before at Yale, could not do. His frank, defiant
happiness in it, mixed with a due sense of burlesque, was something that those lacking his poet soul could never imagine; they
accounted it vain, weak; but that would not have mattered to him
if he had known it. In his London sojourn he had formed the top-
hat habit, and for a while he lounged splendidly up and down Fifth
Avenue in that society emblem; but he seemed to tire of it, and to
return kindly to the soft hat of his Southwestern tradition.

He disliked clubs; I don't know whether he belonged to any in
New York, but I never met him in one. As I have told, he himself
had formed the Human Race Club, but as he never could get it
together it hardly counted. There was to have been a meeting of it
the time of my only visit to Stormfield in April of last year; but of
three who were to have come I alone came. We got on very well
without the absentees, after finding them in the wrong, as usual,
and the visit was like those I used to have with him so many years
before in Hartford, but there was not the old ferment of subjects.
Many things had been discussed and put away for good, but we
had our old fondness for nature and for each other, who were so
differently parts of it. He showed his absolute content with his
house, and that was the greater pleasure for me because it was my
son who designed it. The architect had been so fortunate as to be
able to plan it where a natural avenue of savins, the close-knit,
slender, cypresslike cedars of New England, led away from the rear
of the villa to the little level of a pergola, meant someday to be
wreathed and roofed with vines. But in the early spring days all the
landscape was in the beautiful nakedness of the Northern winter. It
opened in the surpassing loveliness of wooded and meadowed
uplands, under skies that were the first days blue, and the last gray
over a rainy and then a snowy floor. We walked up and down, up
and down, between the villa terrace and the pergola, and talked
with the melancholy amusement, the sad tolerance of age for the
sort of men and things that used to excite us or enrage us; now we
were far past turbulence or anger. Once we took a walk together

across the yellow pastures to a chasmal creek on his grounds, where the ice still knit the clayey banks together like crystal mosses; and the stream far down clashed through and over the stones and the shards of ice. Clemens pointed out the scenery he had bought to give himself elbowroom, and showed me the lot he was going to have me build on. The next day we came again with the geologist he had asked up to Stormfield to analyze its rocks. Truly he loved the place, though he had been so weary of change and so indifferent to it that he never saw it till he came to live in it. He left it all to the architect whom he had known from a child in the intimacy which bound our families together, though we bodily lived far enough apart. I loved his little ones and he was sweet to mine and was their delighted-in and wondered-at friend. Once and once again, and yet again and again, the black shadow that shall never be lifted where it falls, fell in his house and in mine, during the forty years and more that we were friends, and endeared us the more to each other.

My visit at Stormfield came to an end with tender relucting on his part and on mine. Every morning before I dressed I heard him sounding my name through the house for the fun of it and I know for the fondness; and if I looked out of my door, there he was in his long nightgown swaying up and down the corridor, and wagging his great white head like a boy that leaves his bed and comes out in the hope of frolic with someone. The last morning a soft sugar snow had fallen and was falling, and I drove through it down to the station in the carriage which had been given him by his wife's father when they were first married, and been kept all those intervening years in honorable retirement for this final use. Its springs had not grown yielding with time; it had rather the stiffness and severity of age; but for him it must have swung low like the sweet chariot of the Negro "spiritual" which I heard him sing with such fervor, when those wonderful hymns of the slaves began to make their way northward. *Go Down, Daniel* was one in which I can hear his quavering tenor now. He was a lover of the things he liked, and full of a passion for them which satisfied itself in reading them matchlessly aloud. No one could read *Uncle Remus* like him;

his voice echoed the voices of the Negro nurses who told his childhood the wonderful tales. I remember especially his rapture with Mr. Cable's *Old Creole Days,* and the thrilling force with which he gave the forbidding of the leper's brother when the city's survey ran the course of an avenue through the cottage where the leper lived in hiding: "Strit must not pass!"

Out of a nature rich and fertile beyond any I have known, the material given him by the Mystery that makes a man and then leaves him to make himself over, he wrought a character of high nobility upon a foundation of clear and solid truth. At the last day he will not have to confess anything, for all his life was the free knowledge of anyone who would ask him of it. The Searcher of hearts will not bring him to shame at that day, for he did not try to hide any of the things for which he was often so bitterly sorry. He knew where the Responsibility lay, and he took a man's share of it bravely; but not the less fearlessly he left the rest of the answer to the God who had imagined men.

It is in vain that I try to give a notion of the intensity with which he pierced to the heart of life, and the breadth of vision with which he compassed the whole world, and tried for the reason of things, and then left trying. We had other meetings, insignificantly sad and brief; but the last time I saw him alive was made memorable to me by the kind, clear judicial sense with which he explained and justified the labor unions as the sole present help of the weak against the strong.

Next I saw him dead, lying in his coffin amid those flowers with which we garland our despair in that pitiless hour. After the voice of his old friend Twichell had been lifted in the prayer which it wailed through in broken-hearted supplication, I looked a moment at the face I knew so well; and it was patient with the patience I had so often seen in it: something of puzzle, a great silent dignity, an assent to what must be, from the depths of a nature whose tragical seriousness broke in the laughter which the unwise took for the whole of him. Emerson, Longfellow, Lowell, Holmes—I knew them all and all the rest of our sages, poets, seers, critics, humorists; they were like one another and like other literary men; but Clemens was sole, incomparable, the Lincoln of our literature.

✪

Mark Twain's Despair

> What a man sees in the human race is merely himself in the
> deep and honest privacy of his own heart. Byron despised the
> race because he despised himself. I feel as Byron did, and for
> the same reason.
>
> —MARGINAL NOTE IN ONE OF MARK TWAIN'S BOOKS

To those who are interested in American life and letters there has
been no question of greater significance, during the last few years,
than the pessimism of Mark Twain. During the last few years, I
say, for his own friends and contemporaries were rather inclined to
make light of his oft-expressed belief that man is the meanest of
the animals and life a tragic mistake.

For some time before his death Mark Twain had appeared
before the public in the role less of a laughing philosopher than of
a somewhat gloomy prophet of modern civilization. But he was old
and he had suffered many misfortunes and the progress of society
is not a matter for anyone to be very jubilant about: to be gloomy
about the world is a sort of prerogative of those who have lived
long and thought much. The public that had grown old with him
could hardly, therefore, accept at its face value a point of view that
seemed to be contradicted by so many of the facts of Mark
Twain's life and character. Howells, who knew him intimately for
forty years, spoke only with an affectionate derision of his "pose"

regarding "the damned human race," and we know the opinion of
his loyal biographer, Mr. Paine, that he was "not a pessimist in his
heart, but only by premeditation." These views were apparently
borne out by his own testimony. "My temperament," he wrote,
shortly after the death of his daughter Jean, "has never allowed my
spirits to remain depressed long at a time." That he continued to
be active and buoyant to the end was, in fact, for his associates,
sufficient evidence that his philosophical despair was only an
anomaly, which had no organic part in the structure of his life.

Was it not natural that they should feel thus about him, those
contemporaries of his, so few of whom had seen his later writings
and all the telltale private memoranda which Mr. Paine has lately
given to the world? What a charmed life was Mark Twain's, after
all! To be able to hold an immense nation in the hollow of one's
hand, to be able to pour out into millions of sympathetic ears, with
calm confidence, as into the ears of a faithful friend, all the private
griefs and intimate humors of a lifetime, to be called "the King" by
those one loves, to be so much more than a king in reality that
every attack of gout one has is "good for a column" in the
newspapers and every phrase one utters girdles the world in twenty
minutes, to be addressed as "the Messiah of a genuine gladness
and joy to the millions of three continents"—what more could
Tom Sawyer, at least, have wished than that? And Mark Twain's
fame was not merely one of sentiment. If the public heart was
moved by everything that concerned him,—an illness in his household, a new campaign against political corruption, a change of
residence, and he was deluged with letters extolling him, whatever
he did or said, if he won the world's pity when he got into debt and
the world's praise when he got out of it, he was no sort of nine-
days' wonder; his country had made him its "general spokesman"
and he was quite within his rights in appointing himself, as he said,
"ambassador-at-large of the United States of America." Since the
day, half a century back, when all official Washington, from the
Cabinet down, had laughed over *The Innocents Abroad* and
offered him his choice of a dozen public offices to the day when the
newspapers were freely proposing that he ought to have the thanks
of the nation and even suggested his name for the Presidency,

when, in his person, the Speaker of the House, for the first time in American history, gave up his private chamber to a lobbyist, and private cars were placed at his disposal whenever he took a journey, and his baggage went round the world with consular dispensations, and his opinion was asked on every subject by everybody, he had been, indeed, a sort of incarnation of the character and quality of modern America. "Everywhere he moved," says Mr. Paine, "a world revolved about him." In London, in Vienna, his apartments were a court, and traffic rules were modified to let him pass in the street. A charmed life, surely, when we consider, in addition to this public acclaim, the tidal waves of wealth that flowed in upon him again and again, the intense happiness of his family relations, and the splendid recognition of those fellow-members of his craft whose word to him was final—Kipling, who "loved to think of the great and godlike Clemens," and Brander Matthews, who freely compared him with the greatest writers of history, and Bernard Shaw, who announced that America had produced just two geniuses, Edgar Allan Poe and Mark Twain. Finally, there was Howells, "the recognized critical Court of Last Resort in this country," as he called him. Did not Howells, like posterity itself, whisper in his ear: "Your foundations are struck so deep that you will catch the sunshine of immortal years, and bask in the same light as Cervantes and Shakespeare"?

The spectators of this drama could hardly have been expected to take the pessimism of Mark Twain seriously, and all the more because he totally refuted the old and popular notion that humorists are always melancholy. I have already quoted the remark he made about his temperament in one of the darkest moments of his life, four months before his own death. It is borne out by all the evidence of all his years. He was certainly not one of those radiant, sunny, sky-blue natures, those June-like natures that sing out their full joy, the day long, under a cloudless heaven. Far from that! He was an August nature, given to sudden storms and thunder; his atmosphere was charged with electricity. But the storm clouds passed as swiftly as they gathered, and the warm, bright, mellow mood invariably returned. "What a child he was," says Mr. Paine,

"always, to the very end!" He was indeed a child in the buoyancy
of his spirits. "People who always feel jolly, no matter where they
are or what happens to them, who have the organ of Hope
preposterously developed, who are endowed with an uncongealable
sanguine temperament!" he writes, referring to himself, in 1861.
"If there is," he adds, thirteen years later, "one individual creature
on all this footstool who is more thoroughly and uniformly and
unceasingly *happy* than I am I defy the world to produce him and
prove him." And it seems always to have been so. Whether he is
"reveling" in his triumphs on the platform or indulging his "rain-
bow-hued impulses" on paper, we see him again and again, as Mr.
Paine saw him in Washington in 1906 when he was expounding
the gospel of copyright to the members of Congress assembled,
"happy and wonderfully excited." Can it surprise us then to find
him, in his seventy-fifth year, adding to the note about his daughter's death: "Shall I ever be cheerful again, happy again? Yes. And
soon. For I know my temperament"?

And his physical health was just what one might expect from
this, from his immense vitality. He was subject to bronchial colds
and he had intermittent attacks of rheumatism in later years:
otherwise, his health appears to have been as perfect as his energy
was inexhaustible. "I have been sick a-bed several days, for the
first time in 21 years," he writes in 1875; from all one gathers he
might have made the same statement twenty-one, thirty-one years
later. Read his letters, at fifty, at sixty, at seventy—during that
extraordinary period, well within the memory of persons who are
still young, when he went about, as Mr. Paine says, "like a
débutante in her first season"—the days when people called him
"the Belle of New York": "By half past 4," he writes to his wife,
"I had danced all those people down—and yet was not tired, merely
breathless. I was in bed at 5 and asleep in ten minutes. Up at 9 and
presently at work on this letter to you." And again, the next year,
his sixtieth year, when he had been playing billiards with H. H.
Rogers, until Rogers looked at him helplessly and asked, "Don't
you ever get tired?": "I was able to say that I had forgotten what
that feeling was like. Don't you remember how almost impossible
it was for me to tire myself at the villa? Well, it is just so in New

York. I go to bed unfatigued at 3, I get up fresh and fine six hours later. I believe I have taken only one daylight nap since I have been here." Finally, let us take the testimony of Mr. Paine, who was with him day in, day out, during the last five years of his life when, even at seventy-four, he was still playing billiards "9 hours a day and 10 or 12 on Sunday": "In no other human being have I ever seen such physical endurance. I was comparatively a young man, and by no means an invalid; but many a time, far in the night, when I was ready to drop with exhaustion, he was still as fresh and buoyant and eager for the game as at the moment of beginning. He smoked and smoked continually, and followed the endless track around the billiard-table with the light step of youth. At 3 or 4 o'clock in the morning he would urge just one more game, and would taunt me for my weariness. I can truthfully testify that never until the last year of his life did he willingly lay down the billiard-cue, or show the least suggestion of fatigue."

Now this was the Mark Twain his contemporaries, his intimates, had ever in their eyes,—this darling of all the gods. No wonder they were inclined to take his view of "the damned human race" as rather a whimsical pose; they would undoubtedly have continued to take it so even if they had known, generally known, that he had a way of referring in private to "God's most elegant invention" as not only "damned" but also "mangy." He was irritable, but literary men are always supposed to be that; he was old, and old people are often afflicted with doubts about the progress and welfare of mankind; he had a warm and tender heart, an abounding scorn of humbug: one did not have to go beyond these facts to explain his contempt for "the Blessings-of-Civilization Trust," with its stock-in-trade, "Glass Beads and Theology," and "Maxim Guns and Hymn-Books," and "Trade Gin and Torches of Progress and Enlightenment." All his closest friends were accustomed to little notes like this: "I have been reading the morning paper. I do it every morning, well knowing that I shall find in it the usual depravities and basenesses and hypocrisies and cruelties that make up civilization and cause me to put in the rest of the day pleading for the damnation of the human race." Might not any sensitive man, young or old, have written that?

Even now, with all the perspective of Mark Twain's writings which only a succeeding generation can really have, it might be possible to explain in this objective way the steady progress toward a pessimistic cynicism which Mr. Paine, at least, has noted in his work. The change in tone between the poetry of the first half of *Life on the Mississippi* and the dull notation of the latter half, between the exuberance of *A Tramp Abroad* and the drab and weary journalism of *Following the Equator,* with those corroding aphorisms of Pudd'nhead Wilson's "New Calendar," that constant running refrain of weariness, exasperation and misery, along the tops of the chapters, as if he wished to get even with the reader for taking his text at its face value—all this might be attributed, as Mr. Paine attributes it, to the burdens of debt and family sorrow. If he was always manifesting, in word and deed, his deep belief that life is inevitably a process of deterioration,—well, did not James Whitcomb Riley do the same thing? Was it not, is it not, a popular American dogma that "the baddest children are better than the goodest men"? A race of people who feel this way could not have thought there was anything amiss with a humorist who wrote maxims like these:

If you pick up a starving dog and make him prosperous, he will not bite you. This is the principal difference between a dog and a man.

It takes your enemy and your friend, working together, to hurt you to the heart: the one to slander you and the other to get the news to you.

They could hardly have been surprised at the bitter, yes, even the vindictive, mockery of "The Man That Corrupted Hadleyburg," at Mark Twain's definition of man as a "mere coffee-mill" which is permitted neither "to supply the coffee nor turn the crank," at his recurring "plan" to exterminate the human race by withdrawing the oxygen from the air for a period of two minutes. Has not the American public, with its invincible habit of "turning hell's back-yard into a playground," gone so far even as to discount *The Mysterious Stranger,* that fearful picture of life as a rigmarole of cruel nonsense, a nightmare of Satanic unrealities, with its frank assertion that slavery, hypocrisy and cowardice are the eternal destiny of man? Stuart P. Sherman, who liked to defend the views of the old-fashioned democratic public and sometimes seemed to forget that all traditions are not of equal validity, said of this book that it "lets one into a temperament and character of more gravity, complexity and interest than the surfaces indicated." But, having made this discovery, for he was openly surprised, Sherman merely revealed, in his new and unexpected Mark Twain, the Mark Twain most people had known before: "What Mark Twain hated was the brutal power resident in monarchies, aristocracies, tribal religions and—minorities bent on mischief, and making a bludgeon of the malleable many." And, after all, he said, "the wicked world visited by the mysterious stranger is sixteenth-century Austria—not these States." But is it? Is not the village of Eseldorf in reality Hannibal, Missouri, all over again, and are not the boys through whose eyes the story is told simply reincarnations of Huck Finn and Tom Sawyer, those characters which, as we know from a hundred evidences, haunted Mark Twain's mind all his life long? They are, at any rate, Mark Twain's boys, and whoever compares their moral attitude with that of the boys of Mark Twain's prime will see how deeply the iron had entered into his soul. "We boys wanted to warn them"—Marget and Ursula, against the danger that was gathering about them—"but we backed down when it came to the pinch, being afraid. We found that we were not manly enough nor brave enough to do a generous action when there was a chance that it could get us into trouble." What, is this Mark Twain speaking, the creator of Huck and Tom, who gladly broke every law of the tribe to protect and rescue Nigger Jim? Mark Twain's boys "not manly enough nor brave enough" to do a generous action when there was a chance that it could get them into trouble? Can we, in the light of this, continue to say that Mark Twain's pessimism was due to anything so external as the hatred of tyranny, and a sixteenth-century Austrian tyranny at that? Is it not perfectly plain that that deep contempt for man, the "coffee-mill," a contempt that has spread now even to the boy-nature of which Mark Twain had been the lifelong hierophant, must have had some far more personal root, must have sprung from some far more intimate chagrin? One goes back to the long series of "Pudd'nhead" maxims, not the bitter ones now, but those

desperate notes that seem to bear no relation to the life even of a
sardonic humorist:

Pity is for the living, envy is for the dead.

All say, "How hard it is that we have to die"—a strange complaint
to come from the mouths of people who have had to live.

Each person is born to one possession which outvalues all his
others—his last breath.

And that paragraph about the death of his daughter, so utterly
inconsistent with the temperament he ascribes to himself: "My life
is a bitterness, but I am content; for she has been enriched with the
most precious of all gifts—the gift that makes all other gifts mean
and poor—death. I have never wanted any released friend of mine
restored to life since I reached manhood. I felt in this way when
Susy passed away; and later my wife, and later Mr. Rogers." Two
or three constructions, to one who knows Mark Twain, might be
put upon that: but at least one of them is that, not to the writer's
apprehension, but in the writer's experience, life has been in some
special way a vain affliction.

Can we, then, accept any of the usual explanations of Mark
Twain's pessimism? Can we attribute it, with Mr. Paine, to the
burdens of debt under which he labored now and again, to the
recurring illnesses, the death of those he loved? No, for these
things would have modified his temperament, not his point of view;
they would have saddened him, checked his vitality, given birth
perhaps to a certain habit of brooding, and this they did not do.
We have, in addition to his own testimony, the word of Mr. Paine:
"More than any one I ever knew, he lived in the present." Of the
misfortunes of life he had neither more nor less than other men, and
they affected him neither more nor less. To say anything else would
be to contradict the whole record of his personality.

No, it was some deep malady of the soul that afflicted Mark
Twain, a malady common to many Americans, perhaps, if we are
to judge from that excessive interest in therapeutics which he
shared with so many millions of his fellow-countrymen. That is an
aspect of Mark Twain's later history which has received too little
attention. "Whether it was copyright legislation, the latest inven-

tion, or a new empiric practice," says Mr. Paine—to approach this subject on its broadest side—"he rarely failed to have a burning interest in some anodyne that would provide physical or mental easement for his species." And here again the general leads to the particular. "He had," says Howells, "a tender heart for the whole generation of empirics, as well as the newer sorts of scienticians." Howells tells how, on the advice of some sage, he and all his family gave up their spectacles for a time and came near losing their eyesight, thanks to the miracle that had been worked in their behalf. But that was the least of his divagations. There was that momentary rage for the art of "predicating correlation" at Professor Loisette's School of Memory. There was Dr. Kellgren's osteopathic method that possessed his mind during the year 1900; he wrote long articles about it, bombarded his friends with letters of appreciation and recommendation of the new cure-all: "indeed," says Mr. Paine, "he gave most of his thought to it." There was plasmon, that "panacea for all human ills which osteopathy could not reach." There was Christian Science to which, in spite of his attacks on Mrs. Eddy and the somewhat equivocal book he wrote on the subject, he was, as Mr. Paine says, and as he frequently averred himself, one of the "earliest converts," who "never lost faith in its power." And lastly, there was the "eclectic therapeutic doctrine" which he himself put together piecemeal from all the others, to the final riddance of *materia medica*.

We have seen what Mark Twain's apparent health was. Can we say that this therapeutic obsession was due to the illnesses of his family, which were, indeed, unending? No doubt those illnesses provided a constant stimulus to the obsession—the "eclectic therapeutic doctrine," for instance, did, quite definitely, rise up out of the midst of them. But it is plain that there had to be an element of "soul-cure" in these various healings for Mark Twain to be interested in them, that what interested him in them *was* the "soul-cure," the "mind-cure." Can he say too much in praise of Christian Science for its "healing of the spirit," its gift of "buoyant spirits, comfort of mind and freedom from care"? In fact, unless I am mistaken, his interest in mental healing began at a time when he and his family alike were free from illness. It was in 1886, when Mark Twain was at the very summit of his fame, when he was the most successful publisher in the world, when he was at work on his most ambitious book, when he was "frightened," as he said, at the proportions of his prosperity, when his household was aglow with happiness and well-being, that his daughter Susy noted in her diary: "Papa has been very much interested of late in the 'mind-cure' theory." It might be added that he was about at the age when, according to his famous aphorism, a man who does not become a pessimist knows too little about life.

In fact, the more one scans the later pages of Mark Twain's history the more one is forced to the conclusion that there was something gravely amiss with his inner life. There was that frequently noted fear of solitude, that dread of being alone with himself which made him, for example, beg for just one more game of billiards at four o'clock in the morning. There were those "daily self-chidings" that led him to slay his own conscience in one of the most ferocious of his humorous tales. That conscience of his —what was it? Why do so many of his jokes turn upon an affectation, let us say, of moral cowardice in himself? How does it happen that when he reads *Romola* the only thing that "hits" him "with force" is Tito's compromise with his conscience? Why those continual fits of remorse, those fantastic self-accusations in which he charged himself, we are told, with having filled Mrs. Clemens' life with privations, in which he made himself responsible first for the death of his younger brother and later for that of his daughter Susy, writing to his wife, according to Mr. Paine, that he was "wholly and solely responsible for the tragedy, detailing step by step with fearful reality his mistakes and weaknesses which had led to their downfall, the separation from Susy, and this final, incredible disaster"? Was there any reason why, humorously or otherwise, he should have spoken of himself as a liar, why he should have said, in reply to his own idea of writing a book about Tom Sawyer's afterlife: "If I went on now and took him into manhood, he would just lie, like all the one-horse men in literature, and the reader would conceive a hearty contempt for him"? That morbid feeling of having lived in sin, which made him come to think of literature as primarily, perhaps, the confession of sins—was there anything in the moral point of view of his generation to justify it, in this greatly loved writer, this honorable man of business, this zealous reformer, this ever-loyal friend? "Be weak, be water, be characterless, be cheaply persuadable" was, he said, the first command the Deity ever issued to a human being on this planet, the only command Adam would never be able to disobey. And he noted on the margin of one of his books: "What a man sees in the human race is merely himself in the deep and honest privacy of his own heart. Byron despised the race because he despised himself. I feel as Byron did, and for the same reason."

A strange enigma! "You observe," wrote Mark Twain once, almost at the beginning of his career, "that under a cheerful exterior I have got a spirit that is angry with me and gives me freely its contempt." That spirit remained with him, grew in him, to the last. The restless movement of his life, those continual journeys to Bermuda, where "the deep peace and quiet of the country sink into one's body and bones and give his conscience a rest," that consuming desire to write an autobiography, "as caustic, fiendish and devilish as possible," which would "make people's hair curl" and get "his heirs and assigns burnt alive" if they ventured to print it within a hundred years, the immense relief of his seventieth birthday, to him "the scriptural statute of limitations—you have served your term, well or less well, and you are mustered out"—how are we to read the signs of all this hidden tragedy? For Mark Twain was right: things do not happen by chance, and the psychological determinism of the present day bears out in certain respects that other sort of determinism in which he so almost fanatically believed. There is no figure for the human being like the ship, he sometimes said. Well, was he not, in the eyes of his contemporaries, just as he proudly, gratefully suggested, in the glory of that last English welcome, the *Begum* of Bengal, stateliest of Indiamen, plowing the great seas under a cloud of canvas? Can we call it merely an irony of circumstance that in his own eyes he was a bit of storm-beaten human drift, a derelict, washing about on a forlorn sea?

No, there was a reason for Mark Twain's pessimism, a reason for that chagrin, that fear of solitude, that tortured conscience, those fantastic self-accusations, that indubitable self-contempt. It is an established fact, if I am not mistaken, that these morbid feelings of sin, which have no evident cause, are the result of having transgressed some inalienable life demand peculiar to one's nature. It is as old as Milton that there are talents which are "death to hide," and I suggest that Mark Twain's "talent" was just so hidden. That bitterness of his was the effect of a certain miscarriage in his creative life, a balked personality, an arrested development of which he was himself almost wholly unaware, but which for him destroyed the meaning of life. The spirit of the artist in him, like the genie at last released from the bottle, overspread in a gloomy vapor the mind it had never quite been able to possess.

Does this seem too rash a hypothesis? It is, I know, the general impression that Mark Twain quite fully effectuated himself as a writer. Howells called him the "Lincoln of our literature," Professor William Lyon Phelps describes him as one of the supreme novelists of the world, Brander Matthews compared him with Cervantes, and Bernard Shaw said to him once: "I am persuaded that the future historian of America will find your works as indispensable to him as a French historian finds the political tracts of Voltaire." These were views current in Mark Twain's lifetime, and similar views are common enough today. "Mark Twain," says Professor Archibald Henderson, "enjoys the unique distinction of exhibiting a progressive development, a deepening and broadening of forces, a ripening of intellectual and spiritual powers from the beginning to the end." To Mr. John Macy, author of what is, on the whole, the most discerning book that has been written on our literature, he is "a powerful, original thinker." And finally, Mr. H. L. Mencken says: "Mark Twain, without question, was a great artist. There was in him something of that prodigality of imagination, that aloof engrossment in the human comedy, that penetrating cynicism, which one associates with the great artists of the Renaissance." An imposing array of affirmations, surely! And yet, unless I am mistaken, these last few years, during which he has become in a way so much more interesting, have witnessed a singular change in Mark Twain's reputation. Vividly present he is in the public mind as a great historic figure, as a sort of archetype of the national character during a long epoch. Will he not continue so to be for many generations to come? Undoubtedly. By whom, however, with the exception of two or three of his books, is he read? Mr. Paine, I know, says that *The Innocents Abroad* sells to this day in America in larger quantity than any other book of travel. But a number of explanations might be given for this, as for any other mob phenomenon, none of which has anything to do with literary fame in the proper sense. Who imagines that without the oxygen of advertising, supplied in almost unlimited quantities, the interest of the great fickle public in this particular idol could ever have been kept alive to such a tune? A great writer of the past is known by the delight and stimulus which he gives to mature spirits in the present, and time, it seems to me, tends to bear out the familiar assertion that Mark Twain's appeal is largely an appeal to rudimentary minds. *Huckleberry Finn, Tom Sawyer,* half a dozen stories like "The Man That Corrupted Hadleyburg," half a dozen sketches like "Travelling with a Reformer," and a few chapters of *Life on the Mississippi,*—these, in any case, can already be said to have "survived" all his other work. And are these writings, however beautiful and important, the final expressions of a supreme artistic genius, one of the great novelists of the world, a second Cervantes? Arnold Bennett, I think, forecast the view that prevails today when he called their author the "divine amateur" and said of *Huckleberry Finn* and *Tom Sawyer* that while they are "episodically magnificent, as complete works of art they are of quite inferior quality."

So much for what Mark Twain actually accomplished: a great deal indeed, but very far from what the eulogists have attributed to him. But if he had not been potentially one of the greatest of men could he have so impressed, so dazzled almost everyone who came into direct, personal contact with him? When his contemporaries compared him with Swift, Voltaire, Cervantes, they were certainly mistaken; but would they have made that mistake if they had not recognized in him, if not a creative capacity, at least a creative force, of the highest rank? Mark Twain's unbounded energy, his prodigal fertility, his large utterance, that "great, burly fancy" of his, as Howells calls it, his powers of feeling, the unique

magnetism of his personality were the signs of an endowment, as
one cannot but think, more extraordinary than that of any other
American writer. He seemed predestined to be one of those major
spirits, like Carlyle, like Ibsen perhaps, or perhaps like Pushkin,
who are as if intended by nature to preside over the genius of
nations and give birth to the leading impulses of entire epochs. "I
thought," said one of his associates in earlier years, "that the noble
costume of the Albanian would have well become him. Or he
might have been a Goth, and worn the horned bull-pate helmet of
Alaric's warriors, or stood at the prow of one of the swift craft of
the vikings." And, on the other hand, hear what Howells says:
"Among the half-dozen, or half-hundred, personalities that each of
us becomes, I should say that Clemens' central and final personality was something exquisite." That combination of barbaric force
and intense sweetness, which so many others noted in him—is
there not about it something portentous, something that suggests
the true lord of life? Wherever he walked among men he trailed
with him the psychic atmosphere of a planet as it were all his own.
Gigantic, titanic were the words that came to people's lips when
they tried to convey their impression of him, and when he died it
seemed for the moment as if one of the fixed stars had fallen in
space.

It was the force, this the energy which, through Mark Twain's
pen, found such a qualified expression. He was, as Arnold Bennett
says, a "divine amateur"; his appeal is, on the whole, very largely,
an appeal to rudimentary minds. But is not that simply another
way of saying, in the latter case, that his was a mind that had not
fully developed, and, in the former, that his was a splendid genius
which had never fully found itself?

It is the conclusion borne out by Mark Twain's estimate of
himself. His judgments were, as Mr. Paine says, "always unsafe":
strictly speaking, he never knew what to think of himself, he was in
two minds all the time. This, in itself a sign of immaturity, serves
to warn us against his formal opinions. When, therefore, one
appeals for evidence to Mark Twain's estimate of himself, one has
in mind no conscious judgment of his career but a far more
trustworthy judgment, the judgment of his unconscious self. This
he revealed unawares in all sorts of ways.

There were times when he seemed to share the complacent confidence of so many others in his immortal fame. "I told Howells," he writes, in his large, loose, easy way, "that this autobiography of mine would live a couple of thousand years, without any effort, and would then take a fresh start and live the rest of the time." And Mr. Paine says that as early as October, 1900, he had proposed to Messrs. Harper and Brothers a contract for publishing his personal memoirs at the expiration of one hundred years, letters covering the details of which were exchanged with his financial adviser, Mr. Rogers. A man who could have proposed this must have felt, at moments at least, fairly secure of posterity, fairly confident of his own greatness. But it was only at moments. Mark Twain was not without delusions of grandeur; otherwise he could not have advertised, as he did, for post-mortem obituaries of himself. But does that sort of megalomania express a genuine self-confidence? Does it not suggest rather a profound, uneasy desire for corroboration? Of this the famous episode of his Oxford degree is the most striking symbol. "Although I wouldn't cross an ocean again for the price of the ship that carried me, I am glad to do it," he wrote, "for an Oxford degree." Many American writers have won that honor; it is, in fact, almost a routine incident in a distinguished career. In the case of Mark Twain it became a historic event: it was for him, plainly, of an exceptional significance, and all his love for gorgeous trappings could never account for the delight he had in that doctor's gown—"I would dress that way all the time, if I dared," he told Mr. Paine—which became for him a permanent robe of ceremony. And Mark Twain, at the age of seventy-two, one of the most celebrated men in the world, could not have cared so much for this degree if it had been a vindication merely in the eyes of others. It must have served in some way also to vindicate him in his own eyes; he seized upon it as a sort of talisman, as a reassurance from what he considered the highest court of culture, that he really was one of the elect.

Yes, that naïve passion for the limelight, for "walking with kings" and hobnobbing with job lots of celebrities, that "reveling," as Mr. Paine calls it, "in the universal tribute"—what was its root if it was not a deep sense of insecurity, a desire for approval both in his own eyes and in the eyes of all the world? During those later years in New York, when he had become so much the professional celebrity, he always timed his Sunday morning walks on Fifth Avenue for about the hour when the churches were out. Mr. Paine tells how, on the first Sunday morning, he thoughtlessly suggested that they should turn away at Fifty-ninth Street in order to avoid the throng and that Clemens quietly remarked, "I like the throng." "So," says Mr. Paine, "we rested in the Plaza Hotel until the appointed hour. . . . We left the Plaza Hotel and presently were amid the throng of outpouring congregations. Of course he was the object on which every passing eye turned, the presence to which every hat was lifted. I realized that this open and eagerly paid homage of the multitude was still dear to him, not in any small and petty way, but as the tribute of a nation." And must not the desire for approval and corroboration, the sense of insecurity, have been very deep in a quick-tempered, satirical democrat like Mark Twain, when he permitted his associates to call him, as Mr. Paine says they did, "the King"? Actual kings were with him nothing less than an obsession: kings, empresses, princes, archduchesses— what a part they play in his biography! He is always dragging them in, into his stories, into his letters, writing about his dinners with them, and his calls upon them, and how friendly they are, and what gorgeous funerals they have. And as with kings, so also with great men, or men who were considered great, or men who were merely notorious. He makes lists of those he has known, those with whom he has spent his evenings—Mark Twain, to whom celebrity was the cheapest thing going! Is there not in all this the suggestion of an almost conscious weakness that sets a premium upon almost any kind of success?

Turn from the man to the writer; we see again this same desire for approval, for corroboration. Mark Twain was supported by the sentiment of the majority, which was gospel to the old-fashioned Westerner; he had the golden opinion of Howells, in his eyes the arbiter of all the elegances; he had virtually the freedom of *The Atlantic Monthly,* and not only its freedom but a higher rate of payment than any other *Atlantic* contributor. Could any American man of letters have had more reason to think well of himself?

Observe what he thought. "I haven't as good an opinion of my work as you hold of it," he writes to Howells in 1887, "but I've always done what I could to secure and enlarge my good opinion of it. I've always said to myself, 'Everybody reads it and that's something—it surely isn't pernicious, or the most acceptable people would get pretty tired of it.' And when a critic said by implication that it wasn't high and fine, through the remark, 'High and fine literature is wine,' I retorted (confidentially to myself), 'Yes, high and fine literature is wine, and mine is only water; but everybody likes water.' " That is frank enough; he is not always so. There is a note of all but conscious guile in the letter he wrote to Andrew Lang, beseeching a fair hearing in England for *A Connecticut Yankee*. He rails against "the cultivated-class standard"; he half poses as an uplifter of the masses; then, with a touch of mock-noble indignation, he confesses to being a popular entertainer, fully convinced at least that there are two kinds of literature and that an author ought to be allowed to put upon his book an explanatory line: "This is written for the Head," or "This is written for the Belly or the Members." No plea more grotesque or more pathetic was ever written by a man with a great reputation to support. It shows how ignorant Mark Twain was of literary values: had he not wished upon literature, as it were, a separation between the "Head" and the "Belly" which, as we shall see, had simply taken place in himself? Out of his own darkness he begs for the word of salvation from one who he thinks can bestow it.

Mark Twain, in short, knew very well—for I think these illustrations prove it—that there was something decidedly different between himself and a writer of the first rank. In that undifferentiated mob of celebrities, great, and less great, and far from great, amid which he moved for a generation, he was a favored equal. But in the intimate presence of some isolated greatness he reverted to the primitive reverence of the candidate for the mystagogue. Was it Emerson? He ceased to be a fellow-writer, he became one of the devout American multitude. Was it Browning? He forgot the man he had so cordially known in the poet whom he studied for a time with the naïve self-abasement of a neophyte. Was it Mommsen? Read this humorous entry in one of his Berlin notebooks: "Been taken for Mommsen twice. We have the same hair, but on examination it was found the brains were different." In fact, whenever he uses the word "literature" in connection with his own work, he does so with a sudden self-consciousness that lets one into the secret of his inner humility. "I am the only literary animal of my particular subspecies who has ever been given a degree by any college in any age of the world, so far as I know," he writes to the authorities of Yale in 1888. A man who freely compared himself with the melodeon, as distinguished from the opera, who, in the preface to *Those Extraordinary Twins,* invited his readers, who already knew how "the born and trained novelist works," to see how the "jackleg" does it, could never have been accused of exaggerating his real importance. "You and I are but sewing-machines," he says in *What Is Man?* "We must turn out what we can; we must do our endeavor and care nothing at all when the unthinking reproach us for not turning out Gobelins."

We are in a position now to understand that boundless comic impudence of Mark Twain, that comic impudence which led him to propose to Edwin Booth in 1873 a new character for *Hamlet,* which led him to telegraph to W. T. Stead: "The Czar is ready to disarm. I am ready to disarm. Collect the others; it should not be so much of a task now"; which led him, at the outset of his career, to propose the conundrum, "Why am I like the Pacific Ocean?" and to answer it thus: "I don't know. I was just asking for information." In a sense, he was tempting Providence; he was trying out the Fates. If he had not had an inner feeling of extraordinary force, it would never have occurred to him, however facetiously, to place himself on an equality with Shakespeare, to compare his power with that of the Czar and his magnitude with that of the Pacific Ocean. On the other hand, it would never have occurred to him to make these facetious comparisons if he had felt himself in possession, in control, of that force. Men who are not only great in energy but masters of themselves let their work speak for them; men who are not masters of themselves, whose energy, however great, is not, so to speak, at the disposal of their own spirits, are driven, as we see Mark Twain perpetually driven, to seek corroboration from without; for something, at these moments, in his inner self, wished to be assured that he really was great and powerful like the Pacific and Shakespeare and the Czar. Even the most trivial jokes have their meaning. He resembled those young boys who have inherited great fortunes which they own but cannot command; the power is theirs and yet they are not in control of it; consequently, to reassure themselves, they are always "showing off." We are not mistaken, therefore, in feeling that in this comic impudence Mark Twain actually was interrogating destiny, feeling out his public, in other words, which had in its hands the disposal of that ebullient energy of his, an energy that he could not measure, could not estimate, that seemed to him simply of an indeterminable, untestable, and above all uncontrollable abundance. Did he not, in this childlike self-magnification, combined with an instinctive trust in luck that never left him, resemble the barbarian conquerors of antiquity? Not one of these, in the depth of that essential self-ignorance, that lack of inner control which makes one's sole criterion the magnitude of one's grasp over the outer world, ever more fully felt himself the man of destiny. All his life Mark Twain was attended by what Mr. Paine calls "psychic evidences"; he never fails to note the marvelous coincidences of which he is the subject; he is always being struck by some manifestation of "mental telegraphy"—he invented the phrase; strange phenomena of nature rise up in his path. Three times, while crossing the ocean, he sees a lunar rainbow, and each time he takes it as a presage of good fortune. Not one of the barbarian conquerors of antiquity, those essential opposites of the creative spirit, whose control is altogether internal, and who feels himself the master of his own fate, could have been more in character than was Mark Twain when he observed, a few months before his death: "I came in with Halley's comet in 1835. It is coming again next year, and I expect to go out with it. It will be the greatest disappointment of my life if I don't go out with Halley's comet. The Almighty has said, no doubt: 'Now here are these two unaccountable freaks, they came in together, they must go out together.' Oh! I am looking forward to that."

A comet, this time! And a few pages back we found him comparing himself with a sewing machine. Which is he, one, or the other, or both? He seems to exhibit himself, on the one hand, as a child of nature conscious of extraordinary powers that make all the world and even the Almighty solicitous about him, and, on the other, as a humble, a humiliated man, confessedly second-rate, who has lost nine of the ten talents committed to him and almost begs permission to keep the one that remains. A great genius, in short, that has never attained the inner control which makes genius great, a mind that has not found itself, a mind that does not know itself, a mind that cloaks to the end in the fantasy of its temporal power the reality of some spiritual miscarriage!

We are in possession now, it seems to me, of the secret of Mark Twain's mechanistic philosophy, the philosophy of that little book which he called his "Bible," *What Is Man?* He was extremely proud of the structure of logic he had built up on the thesis that man is a machine, "moved, directed, commanded by *exterior* influences, *solely,*" that he is "a chameleon, who takes the color of his place of resort," that he is "a mere coffee-mill," which is permitted neither "to supply the coffee nor turn the crank." He confessed to a sort of proprietary interest and pleasure in the validity of that notion. "Having found the Truth," he says, "perceiving that beyond question man has but one moving impulse— the contenting of his own spirit—and is merely a machine and entitled to no personal merit for what he does, it is not humanly possible for me to seek further. The rest of my days will be spent in patching and painting and puttying and calking my priceless possession and in looking the other way when an imploring argument or a damaging fact approaches." You see how it pleases him, how much it means to him, that final "Truth," how he clings to it with a sort of defiant insolence against the "imploring argument," the "damaging fact"? "Man originates nothing," he says, "not even a thought. . . . Shakespeare could not create. He was a machine, and machines do not create." Faith never gave the believer more comfort than this philosophy gave Mark Twain.

But is it possible for a creative mind to find "contentment" in denying the possibility of creation? And why should anyone find pride and satisfaction in the belief that man is wholly irresponsible, in the denial of "free will"? One remembers the fable of the fox and the sour grapes, one remembers all those forlorn and tragic souls who find comfort in saying that love exists nowhere in the world because they themselves have missed it. Certainly it could not have afforded Mark Twain any pleasure to feel that he was "entitled to no personal merit" for what he had done, for what he had achieved in life; the pleasure he felt could have sprung only from the relief his theory afforded him, the relief of feeling that he was not responsible for what he had failed to achieve—namely, his proper development as an artist. He says aloud, "Shakespeare could not create," and his inner self adds, "How in the world, then, could I have done so?" He denies "free will" because the creative life is the very embodiment of it—the emergence, that is to say, the activity in a man of one central, dominant, integrating principle that turns the world he confronts into a mere instrument for the registration of his own preferences. There is but one interpretation, consequently, which we can put upon Mark Twain's delight in the conception of man as an irresponsible machine: it brought him comfort to feel that if he was, as he said, a "sewing-machine," it was the doing of destiny, and that nothing he could have done himself would have enabled him to "turn out Gobelins."

From his philosophy alone, therefore, we can see that Mark Twain was a frustrated spirit, a victim of arrested development, and beyond this fact, as we know from innumerable instances the psychologists have placed before us, we need not look for an explanation of much of the chagrin of his old age. He had been balked, he had been divided, he had even been turned, as we shall see, against himself; the poet, the artist in him, consequently, had withered into the cynic and the whole man had become a spiritual valetudinarian.

✪

The Symbols of Despair

This essay is a chapter, hitherto unwritten, in the biography of Mark Twain. Mr. Paine's *Mark Twain: A Biography* lists some of the manuscripts dealt with here and even devotes a few sentences of description to a few of them. But it is clear that Mr. Paine did not understand their significance and, if he had understood them, I think he would have regarded it as his duty to say nothing about them. Certainly as one reads his *Biography* one gets no proper sense of the effect on Mark Twain of the disasters which these manuscripts deal with.

Those disasters are agonizing as personal history. Our interest, however, is in the manuscripts which came out of them—we are concerned with them as a series of literary episodes. Those episodes occur in the life of a literary genius and by chance, a fortunate chance for criticism, they partly open up an area of literature which is usually closed. They make it possible to document, and so in some small degree to analyze, certain processes of creation. Criticism is usually altogether unable to say how a writer's experience is transformed into works of art. In these manuscripts we can actually see that transformation while it is occurring. We are able to watch Mark Twain while he repeatedly tries and repeatedly fails to make something of experiences that were vitally important to him—and finally we are able to see him fuse and transform them in a work of art. We are able to see the yeasts and ferments actually at work. In the end they do not justify us in saying much about how creative processes may work in other writers. But I think that even a single exposition of how they once worked in one writer is worth making.

One caution. Both psychology and literary criticism are highly speculative fields. This inquiry is more speculative still, in that it is carried on in the no man's land between them. The findings I bring in here are essentially speculative: I cannot prove them. That being said, I may also say that throughout the essay my reference is to demonstrable fact wherever possible. The facts that support my findings are far more numerous, and my argument has a much more solid base, and much stronger links, than there is room even to suggest in the course of a single essay.

A Connecticut Yankee in King Arthur's Court was published in December, 1889. It is the last of Mark Twain's books which we can call certainly of the first rank, and its publication furnishes a convenient date. He was then the most widely known and admired writer in America, and very likely in the world. He was at the summit of his personal happiness. His books had won him not only world-wide fame but a fortune as well. He was the husband of a greatly loved wife, the father of three delightful children, the master of a house famous for the warmth of its hospitality, the center of a small cosmos of beloved friends, an intimate of the famous men and women of his time, courted, praised, sought after, universally loved. His life had a splendor that marked him as the darling of the gods, and that and the splendor of his imagination made more than one person think of him as a mysterious sojourner from somewhere outside the orbit of this earth. The backwoods boy, the tramp printer, the Mississippi pilot, the silver miner, the San Francisco bohemian had become one of the great men of the earth, the hero of a story more romantic than any of Tom Sawyer's dreams.

Our first concern is the series of catastrophes that came in the 1890's. Some years before, he had established his own publishing firm, to publish his books. He had expanded it in order to publish the memoirs of General Grant, and the overextended business required better management than Mark could give it, better management than anyone could give it whom he hired. The firm faltered, the going got worse, and finally, as a result of the freezing of credit in the Panic of 1893, it had to go into receivership. It could have been saved—except that a greater loss had drained Mark's fortune and his wife's as well. Always a speculator, a Colonel Sellers who dreamed of millions but was a predestinate sucker for all salesmen of gold bricks, he had poured nearly a quarter of a million dollars into the development of an invention that was going to make him many times a millionaire. This was the Paige typesetting machine, and his grandiose dream was not absurd, considering the millions which the Mergenthaler Linotype has made. But the Mergenthaler machine succeeded, whereas the Paige machine failed altogether and carried Mark Twain down with it, just at the time when his publishing firm went bankrupt. Furthermore, these same years saw a mysterious alteration in the personality of his youngest daughter, Jean, and finally the terrible mystery was cleared up by the discovery of the still more terrible truth, that she was an epilept. During these years also his capricious but usually exuberant health failed. He was racked by the bronchitis which he was never again to lose, by the rheumatism which was the inheritance of his frontier youth, and by other ailments which were the result of the enormous strain he was under.

So, in 1895, a bankrupt, little better than an invalid, four months short of sixty years old, Mark Twain started on a lecturing tour which was to take him round the world and pay off his creditors dollar for dollar. His wife and one of his daughters went with him, but they left behind them in America their youngest daughter and their oldest one, Susy, the one who Mark felt was nearest him in mind and spirit. Just a year later, the exhausting trip ended in London, and the children were to join them there. They did not. Across the Atlantic from her parents, Susy died of meningitis. And in the months following, Mark's wife began to decline into the invalidism that was to last through the remaining eight years of her life.

The gods had turned against their darling. Such a sequence of calamities might well drive a man mad; there would be little to wonder at if Mark Twain had broken under them. And the truth is that for a time he lived perilously close to the indefinable line between sanity and madness. Passages of his private anguish in the unpublished papers show to what a tautness the membrane of the mind was stretched, and come near breaking the reader's heart. But we are concerned, not with the man's grief but rather with the use the artist made of it.

For, of course, it is obvious that such events as these cannot occur to the man without happening to the artist as well. The rich man had been bankrupted, and the threatened poverty had imperiled his wife and children. The man of great fame had, or so to the tortured ego it must seem, been somehow toppled from his high place, and always thereafter Mark Twain must carry in his heart some remnant feeling of disgrace. Necessarily, his image of himself had been impaired. These blows which had fallen on him, which had been struck at him, had made him something other than he had been—or at least something other than he had believed and seemed. A man's position in the world, his various successes, his public reputation are interstitial with his ego; an injury to any one injures all and so injures his secret image of himself. But also interstitial with that image is a writer's talent. In the deepest psychological sense, even in a biological sense, a man's work is his life. That is to say, the sources of his talent are inseparably a part of his feeling of wholeness, of his identity, and even, quite nakedly, of his power. An injury to the man must necessarily be an injury on this deep level of personal power—a blow at his virility. And equally, an injury to the inner picture of the man by which life is sustained, must be an injury working outward to impair his work as well. In the dark areas where the roots of life go down, the threatened soul cannot easily distinguish among the parts and organs of personality, and if one of them is endangered then the dim mind knows that all have come in peril.

All this is the merest commonplace of experience. Remembering it, we should expect the series of disasters to have a powerful effect on Mark Twain's writing. And also, remembering that it is the nature of writers to forge their art out of the materials of their lives, we should expect to find in his writing some effort to grapple with the disasters. Art is the terms of an armistice signed with fate. Or, if you like the words better, art is experience appraised, completed, neutralized, or overcome. . . . So let us see.

It was July, 1896, when the lecture tour ended in London. The lectures had made almost enough money to clear Mark's debts but not quite, and there remained to write the book about his trip, *Following the Equator,* which was to complete his task. It was in August, 1896, that Susy died. He began the book in October. And he wrote to his friend Twichell:

I am working, but it is for the sake of the work—the "surcease of sorrow" that is found there. I work all the days, and trouble vanishes away when I use that magic. This book will not long stand between it and me, now; but that is no matter, I have many unwritten books to fly to for my preservation; the interval between the finishing of this one and the beginning of the next will not be more than an hour.[1]

Observe that he was relying on work, on writing, to hold his grief at arm's length, the grief of Susy's death. But, besides that pitiful purpose, are we not already entitled to see something else? There seems to me already a hint of what was soon to be plainer, that part of his necessity to write was to vindicate himself as a writer, to restore the image that had been impaired. He had to write: he was compelled to.

Following the Equator is the dullest of his books, and writing it was a laborious and sometimes agonizing task. He rebelled at writing it for money. He rebelled at the meaninglessness of the pursuit, which was part of the meaninglessness of life. For, with Susy dead, life seemed to have no meaning except loss and cruelty. But he kept at work and on April 13, 1897, a notebook entry says, "I finished my book today." But it needed revising and on May 18, the notebook says, "Finished the book again." Several pages of notes follow, some of them for a story I shall be describing in a moment, and then on May 23, five days after the end of the book, the notebook says, "Wrote first chapter of above story today." The

[1] Letter of January 19, 1897.

interval had been a little longer than the hour he predicted to Twichell, but not much.

With that first chapter, Mark had begun the series of experi-ments and failures that are our central interest. And also he began other experiments and other failures not closely related to them. What the next months show is a man writing in the grip of a compulsion, driven to write, flogged and scourged to write by the fierce drive within him—a man under compulsion to write for "surcease of sorrow," but still more to reintegrate a blasted talent, and most of all to restore his image of himself after the intolerable impairment it had suffered. But also this compulsive need to write is constantly blocked, displaced, and distorted. It is so frenzied that it seems aimless—and also it is perpetually frustrated. "I couldn't get along without work now," he wrote to Howells. "I bury myself in it up to the ears. Long hours—8 and 9 at a stretch, sometimes."[2] That shows the compulsiveness, and we get a glimpse of the frustration when he writes to Howells in August, 1898, fifteen months after that confident notebook entry, "Last summer I started 16 things wrong—3 books and 13 mag. articles —and could only make 2 little wee things, 1500 words altogether, succeed—only that out of piles and stacks of diligently-wrought MS., the labor of 6 weeks' unremitting effort." But the truth was more startling and more serious than this glimpse shows, for the inability to make more than on an average two little wee things come out of sixteen starts was to last longer than he thought. It was to last through 1898 and on to 1899, to 1900, to 1904—and in fact the jobs that he completed from 1897 on through the rest of his life represent only a small fraction of the jobs he began. From 1897 on there are scores of manuscripts in the Mark Twain Papers which begin bravely enough and then peter out, some of them after only a few pages, some of them only after many hundred pages of stubborn and obviously heart-wrenching work. Now it is certain that, as Mark grew older, he did not intend to finish some of them—that he began them merely to amuse himself or to jot down a passing observation or perception, or to find release from some

[2] Letter of January 22, 1898.

mood in the only remedy he was able to depend on. But other manuscripts, especially those we are to deal with, he meant and desperately wanted to complete. He was impelled to come back to them time after time, take them up again, try some other beginning or some other set of characters, impose some other form on them or some new outcome or some other meaning or some other moral—but get on with them, sweat them through, mold them to an end. So time after time he came back to them. And time after time he failed. He could not finish them.

Such a frustration is a striking thing. There must be a significant reason for the repeated failure of a practiced literary artist, a man who had been writing all his life with marked success. True, Mark Twain had always been subject to enthusiasms and his enthusiasms were short-lived, so that normally he began a good many manuscripts which he never bothered to finish after the going got hard. But this is something else, a repeated and habitual failure, and he did try to finish them—he tried repeatedly, under the compulsion that had enslaved him. He kept coming back to them—and always he failed. This is no casual or meaningless failure; it is obviously closely interwrought with the fundamental energies of his personality.

The end of our search will come in 1905 but we are most concerned with the two and a half years following that notebook entry of May 18, 1897. During that period he wrote so much that, turning the manuscripts over in my hands and trying to make out their relationships, I have frequently told myself that some of them could not possibly belong to these years, that no man could write so much. But there they are, manuscript after manuscript, a staggering number of them, a still more staggering grand total of words. He actually wrote them during these years. During the same years of course, he also wrote other essays, sketches, reminiscences, newspaper articles, which he succeeded in completing and which were published. But here is a many times greater number of manuscripts which he could not finish.

The force that was impelling him to write was, clearly, both desperate and remorseless. Only a man who was hellridden could write so much. Think of the inner desperation this indicates—and think how that desperation must have grown and spread when time after time he was forced to realize that he could not finish what he had begun. His invention ran out, he could not solve the ordinary problems of structure and technique, he could not overcome the ordinary difficulties of his own intentions, he could not push the thing through to an end. Apart from the manuscripts themselves there is little record of his distress, but surely it was a long agony. Secretly, in the hours of black brooding which had become habitual since Susy died, he must have been forever grappling with the most terrible fear that any artist can feel: the fear that his talent has been drained away, that his spark has been quenched, that his achievement is over forever. It is a poison which acts two ways, spreading back to reinforce the poison that begot it. For the failure of the artist must strike close to the deepest identity and potency of the man—and that identity and potency had already been challenged and grievously impaired by the catastrophes we have glanced at. Of course, it must have proceeded out of those catastrophes, or at least been set in motion by them, and few would doubt that his new impotence was related to the impairment he had suffered or that these literary failures issued from the complex sense of failure that had been created in him.

Much of this heap of manuscript is at random. I disregard that part and consider now only what seems significant in the end. And the first support of what I have just said about impairment comes from Mark's attempts to make use once more of the immortal boys who had conferred immortality on his two finest books—and whom he had called upon again, during the anxieties of the early nineties, for those two lesser stories, *Tom Sawyer Abroad* and *Tom Sawyer, Detective*. So now he put them to work again, involving them in a long conspiracy of Tom's invention more preposterous and much drearier than the one that turns the last part of *Huckleberry Finn* into burlesque. It is a maze of romance and rank improvisation that is trivial to begin with and speedily becomes disheartening. It is wholly without structure and moves without plan by dint of a feverish extemporization which gets more mechanical and improbable as it goes on. It is dull, humorless, without the enchantment of the great originals. Mark's touch is altogether gone from it and, what points most vividly to the truth, even the prose is dead.

It is pitiful to see a great writer turning back, in such a desperate mood, to the works of his greatness. And this effort to repeat what he had done at the height of his power, summoning ghosts from his earlier books, shows the strength of his fear that power had departed from him. It is the more pitiful that the effort to save himself does not save him: the book is a merciless parody of the great books it turns back to. He must have realized the true nature of the effort he was making, and certainly its failure could not be hidden from him. Few more bitter experiences can happen to an artist. Nor is this manuscript the only one in which he tried to use the two boys, as we shall see, nor are *Huckleberry Finn* and *Tom Sawyer* the only earlier books he called on in his need. Through much of the unfinished work of this period runs a diluted strain of other books, *Pudd'nhead Wilson* in particular, and of ideas, devices, stock themes and treatments which he had found effective in his great days but which were not effective now when he needed them most.

It was at this time, also, that Mark began to think seriously about his autobiography. He had written fragments of it before, notably the account of his publication of Grant's memoirs contained in the first volume of the published portions. But now he wrote a number of more or less systematic sketches and planned to buckle down and write the book. He made many pages of notes for it—lists of people, character sketches, memoranda of exciting or important or amusing events. These jottings run through all the notebooks he kept during this period, a long sequence of them in one book shows a comprehensive plan for the book, and there is a forty-page catalogue of Hannibal people which is well along toward actual biography.[3]

Of all this autobiographical material, by far the largest part concerns two periods of his life. Scattering memoranda cover many years, but most of them deal either with the dead child Susy or with the Hannibal of his boyhood. One long section of a

---

[3] "Villagers of 1840–43."

notebook describes the agonizing details of Susy's illness and death, and yearns over the little, trivial, pitiful incidents of her childhood, the promise of her life, the loss and stunning cruelty of her death. These notes he actually worked up into a biographical sketch of Susy; but he could not finish it. He was to come back to it some years later, and to work much of it into the *Autobiography*. But there is even more about Hannibal, and the friends and neighbors of the Clemenses, than there is about Susy.

What is the importance of these facts for our inquiry? Well, it is significant that, in this time of impotence and failure, his mind was constantly turning over not only his memories of his dead daughter, but also his memories of his boyhood. For we know from his books that boyhood was his golden time and that Hannibal was his lost, immortal idyll, not of boyhood only but of home as well. It meant whatever home means of peace, happiness, fulfillment, and especially of security. In the time of desolation whose symbol he was not yet able to forge, he turned back to the years and the place that meant safety. Presently we shall understand why.

Finally, it was at this time that he began to write what he called his Gospel. Twenty years ago or more he had read a paper on philosophical determinism to a club in Hartford, and from time to time thereafter he had shown that the idea was working in him. Now suddenly it began to demand expression—and it was to go on demanding it until he died. A large part of the Mark Twain Papers consists of argumentative or analytical chapters, dialogues, letters, some of them finished, more abandoned, which develop and embroider the twinned themes: man's complete helplessness in the grip of the inexorable forces of the universe, and man's essential cowardice, pettiness, and evil. He went on writing them until within a few months of his death, but actually he began to write them, and wrote the most consecutive of them, in the period we are dealing with. Probably the greater part of those which he privately printed in 1904 as *What Is Man?* were written during these years.

The importance of *What Is Man?* to our inquiry is that it provides the first dependable indication, very possibly the earliest one, of what was going on in the ferments that were at work. We

have asked what was the result on the artist of the calamities that
had all but broken the man, and with this book we may make a
start toward an answer. For *What Is Man?* is not only a treatise on
man's instability, weakness, cowardice, cruelty, and degradation. It
is not only an assault on the illusions of free will, integrity,
decency, and virtue with which mankind makes tolerable its estate.
It is not only an assertion of the familiar logic of determinism, the
fixed universe, the infrangible sequence of cause and effect from
the beginning of time, holding man helpless, and unalterable by
will or wish or effort. If that were all there were to it, surely there
would be significance in its getting itself written at this particular
period. But it is much more than that. For clearly *What Is Man?* is
also a plea for pardon. In describing man's helplessness, it pleads
that man cannot be blamed. In asserting man's cowardice, it
asserts also that man is not responsible. In painting man as
enslaved and dominated by inexorable circumstance, it argues that
the omnipotence of circumstance must answer for what Mark is
inwardly afraid he is being held to answer for. If man is weak,
cowardly, and sentenced to defeat, then one who feels himself
weak, cowardly, and defeated cannot be to blame. If man is not
responsible, then no man can be held responsible. No one, I think,
can read this wearisomely repeated argument without feeling the
terrible force of an inner cry: Do not blame me, for it was not my
fault.

    That theme, which is to be repeated in many forms, is struck
clearly in *What Is Man?* So we may now move on to the three
groups of manuscripts from whose chaos was to be resolved the
answer to that troubled cry. I cannot be sure that my arrangement
is chronological—I cannot date all of them in relation to one
another. But that does not matter much, for they are variations on
themes common to them all, the themes come together in the end,
and I can date most of the significant steps in the evolution that is
really a debate.

    We will follow them rather by idea than by manuscript. A
number of ideas are repeated over and over in the various manuscripts, modulated, changed, adapted, blended, and in the end,
harmonized.

One of these ideas, and probably the earliest, is that of the great stretch of time which may seem to elapse in a dream whose actual duration, in waking time, is only a few minutes or perhaps a few seconds. And mingled with this idea is another one, which holds the germ of the eventual conclusion, the idea of confusing dream with reality. The notebook entry I have quoted, which says that Mark began the "above story" on a certain day, proposes a story in which a man is to nod for a moment over a cigarette, dream a sequence of events which he thinks has lasted for seventeen years, and on waking from his momentary sleep, so have confused the dream with the reality that he cannot recognize his wife. Accompanying this entry is a list of characters for the story which identifies many of them as actual persons from Mark Twain's past. The significance of this is made greater by the fact that, as I have said, Mark was making plans for his autobiography at exactly the same time.

But the story which he actually began to write, though it preserves the framework of the dream, mostly disregards it in favor of another idea, a different theme, whose significance is apparent at sight and which was to arouse, following this story, his most persistent effort. It is the story of a world-famous personage who is cast down from his high estate. The time is shortly after the Mexican War of 1846, and the hero is the youngest major general in the American army, whose heroism and gallantry have made him a world figure and destined him for the Presidency as soon as he shall be old enough to hold that office. He is not only world famous but very rich as well, fortunate and happy, married to a beautiful woman whom he worships, the father of two small girls whom he adores, one of whom is talented and promising. He falls asleep over his cigarette and in his dream the family's magnificent house is burned down and, following that, a greater catastrophe swiftly engulfs them. A trusted relative of the general's wife, who has been trusted with the management of their fortune, proves not only to have dissipated the fortune but to have become involved in widespread chicanery and fraud as well. The general's reputation is blackened, he and his beloved family are plunged not only into abject poverty but into overwhelming disgrace as well, and in all ways he and they are ruined. He sinks into unconsciousness, wakes from that a year and a half later, finds himself and his family living in a squalid log cabin in California, learns the bitter struggle his wife has made to support them—and here the manuscript breaks off. It had broken off before this and been resumed, but this time the break was final. Mark Twain could go no farther.

Already my point must be clear; it hardly needs my assurance that the story is crowded with undisguised autobiographical material—lifelong friends of Mark Twain, members of his family, enemies, incidents that had happened to him, scenes and speeches straight from his life. Notice the starkness of the theme: a great and fine personage of unimpeachable integrity is struck down by catastrophe and disgraced in the eyes of all the world. Notice also how it is made clear that the personage was innocently betrayed, that the catastrophe was not his fault.

Following this story, Mark separated out the dream idea and confined it to a sequence which I will describe in a moment, while proceeding to carry the theme of the virtuous man cast down from his high estate into a series of manuscripts which together represent the strongest and most persistent effort in our whole cycle. He kept coming back to this story not only during 1898 and 1899 but as late as 1904. How many different essays he made I cannot say, I can only say that he made them repeatedly. The thing obsessed him and he must get it out. But time after time he found himself blocked and had to quit.

It is much too long a story and, as his efforts crisscrossed and failed, much too complex a story for me to tell here. It concerns the leading citizen of a town which hardly differs from the St. Petersburg of *Tom Sawyer* and the Hannibal of the *Autobiography,* and not only the squire but another citizen, formerly wealthy, who had suffered the loss of his fortune and is now reduced to poverty but everywhere respected for his virtue and integrity. Through an intricate series of circumstances the virtuous man is led by his own weakness to commit murder, and other intricately wrought circumstances throw suspicion on the squire. The theme is frequently lost sight of in the melodramatic incidents that Mark frantically invented to get it told somehow, or anyhow, and in a flood of other themes from all the other ventures of this period. But the theme is the moral cowardice and hypocrisy of mankind, the liability of everyone, even the most virtuous, to yield to his secret weakness, provided only he is tempted, or there is some seeming necessity, or mere chance comes his way. Back and forth across this theme play related themes from *What Is Man?*

Now see what has happened. The theme of catastrophe has been modulated. The protagonist has been split in two. The victim of catastrophe is no longer innocent, as in the major general's story; he is guilty and knows he is guilty, and a large part of the story is his effort to appease and justify himself. But, though he is guilty, the plea is made for him that he cannot be blamed. In different attempts different reasons are given but they all come to the same thing in the end—that circumstance is omnipotent and what happens must happen, alike to all men. If all men would sin in the given circumstance, then none can be blamed for sinning—the responsibility must be turned back to impersonal fate or to the malevolent God who designed it. But notice that there is here a psychic admission, or an accusation, which the earlier story did not contain. The major general was betrayed by one he had trusted, but the virtuous man of this cycle, though the plea is made that he was not responsible, is cast down by his own act.

This cycle too is crowded with unmistakable portraits and events from the actual world of Mark's own experience. A greater effort is made to transform and adapt them, but they are there. And it should be clear that they are there by the same compulsion that put the admission or accusation there.

Bear in mind that none of the expedients, new starts, or changed devices had worked: Mark had proved unable to bring any version of his story to fruition. Not even when he went back and borrowed from its predecessor. He tried, that is, telling the same story of the virtuous man made murderer and coward and hypocrite by calamity, as something that happened in a dream—in a dream, furthermore, that was to last for a few minutes only, though it seemed to consume many years. So what began as an independent story became essentially the same story, though with the modulation I have pointed out. And that modulation, I think, discloses the

secret self-accusation as it is met by a counterassertion that all
men are guilty as circumstances compel them to be.

We have now got far along in our period and must go back, to
where the idea of the dream began a different evolution. A number
of apparently aimless sketches which have no surface relationship
to our inquiry had dealt with sailors or other people marooned in
the vast Antarctic waste of ice and darkness. In one of these there
had been introduced a legend of an enchanted sea wilderness in the
midst of this eternal winter where ships were caught in a central
place of calm, circumscribed by the ice and snow, and held drifting
forever there with the dead bodies of their crews and passengers
preserved by the unearthly cold. Various components of this idea
run back farther in Mark's thinking than I can trace them here, but
now they have come together in a striking and terrible symbol of
desolation.

Mark had not been able to complete any of these casual
sketches, but, whether consciously or not, they led to a re-entry
and flashed across his mind the bright hope that he had found a
variation of the story that tormented him which, this time, he
would be able to complete. Again we have the happily married
man who is the father of two delightful daughters and again he
falls asleep and is to waken after a few minutes, believing that
years have passed. But this time, before he falls asleep he looks
through a microscope at a drop of water—and that item changes
and immensely deepens the story. For in his dream, he and his
family are on a mysterious ship sailing they know not where in a
perpetual darkness filled with storms of snow and ice. This proves
to be an Antarctic waste in the drop of water which he had looked
at in the microscope, and in that tortured dream the voyage
progresses in mystery and terror—and also in what I feel to be
significance. No one knows where they are, no one knows where
they are going or for what purpose or under whose command, but
they are in the Great Dark at the edge of the microscope's field, a
place of unimaginable desolation, and somewhere far off is the
horror of the Great White Glare, which is really the beam cast
through the microscope's field by the reflector.

Moreover, on this ship there is some recollection of waking

life—the world of reality outside both the microscope and the dream. But this fades, and one comes to doubt it, one comes in the end to believe that the reality one remembers was a dream after all, and that the dream one lives in is the reality. Furthermore, there is a supernatural being on board the ship, the Superintendent of Dreams, who has power over both the ship and the minds of its passengers, who steadily, vindictively, cultivates in their minds the doubt of reality which becomes the belief in dream.[4] And in the terrible darkness, monsters roam the freezing ocean, threatening to snatch victims from the ship and devour them. And finally, there is mutiny and betrayal on this ship, trusted officers who will be untrue and produce catastrophe.

This story also Mark could not finish. He came back to it several times, trying to find an effective outcome for it, trying to give it this slant or that, trying to crystallize round these symbols a coherent expression of the dread they had for him. The frustration still held and he could not do it, but what he did write is markedly superior to anything I have previously mentioned. It is a strange, powerful, and moving story, this uncompleted fragment, which holds you fascinated despite some crudities of construction. There is significance for us in the fact that he was able to make it better literature. And there is more significance in the notes that show how he wanted to finish it. For as the voyage went on, still greater afflictions were to visit the ship. It was to meet other ships caught in the same terrible enchantment. One of them was to contain a fabulous treasure in gold, and this was to madden certain of the already mutinous crew. The baby who had been born to our married couple was to be carried off on another ship, the search for the child was to mingle with the crew's mad lust for the treasure, the wife's heart was to break, her hair was to turn white, and she was finally to go mad with grief, during the ten fruitless years while they tried to find the child. They were to catch up with the other ship at last—but in the Great White Glare, where the child and all the crew and passengers of the second ship were to be

---

[4] I need not point out that the Superintendent of Dreams exactly corresponds to God in *What Is Man?* Watch him become Satan.

killed by the merciless heat. And the Glare was to further madden
the gold-maddened mutineers and to dry up the sea, the monsters
were to gather, and in a final, apocalyptic phantasy of destruction,
the two beloved daughters were to be killed, the grief-crazed wife
was to die, all remaining survivors of the first ship were to die also,
leaving only the helpless narrator and the loyal Negro who was his
servant.

Once more, a great part of the detail of this story was from
Mark's experience. Most of the characters are identifiable from his
life, or correspond to characters elsewhere in our material who
are identifiable. The children's parties, the servants, the arguments
can be annotated. The girl who is so loved and who is killed with
such cruelty dies in exactly the delirium that the faithful notebooks
record of Susy Clemens' fatal illness. And so on.

The pattern had now been repeated many times. We have seen
Mark's compulsion to write it and the inhibition that withheld him
from working it out to an end. So now, I think, we may make some
judgments. We have seen in fiction the shape of the imprint left on
Mark Twain's mind and heart by the series of catastrophes I began
by describing. For essentially they are the catastrophes that obsess
him in these uncompleted stories, nor can there be any doubt what
great personage is cast down from his high place, what beloved
wife is maddened by despair, what beloved daughter dies in agony.
But if we recognize all that, then we must also recognize the
terrible accusation that had risen in his heart. I said, far back, that
he walked the narrow edge between sanity and madness. How
close he came to madness may be understood in this cry, "It must
have been my fault!"

We need neither the anthropology of primitive religions nor the
psychology of the unconscious mind to understand, for in all of us
a similar fear and accusation hover about the margin of the mind,
to come forward a little and lose some of their vagueness in
moments when discouragement is on us or the menace of living
has suddenly sharpened. That primal guilt is of one tissue with our
primal despair, but happily those are brief moments when we are
in health. Yet we all know, of our own experience or experience
near to us, that the shocks of life may sometimes prolong those

moments, bring the accusation into the center of the mind, delay the healthy reaction from it—and then we have at best despair and at worst insanity. This close had Mark Twain come: that there had been set up in him a contention, an accusation he could not bear, a repudiation he could not make. In the yeasty darkness at the mind's base, he had, of his own fault, brought on himself this disgrace and degradation and humiliation. In the phantasy that underlay both his grief and his rebellion, he was the author of his own fall, and the author also of his wife's and daughter's illness, of his daughter's death, of the unabated agony that had come upon his family.

So now he had found the symbols of despair. Through stormy darkness and hemmed in by ice, directed by some unknown and malevolent will, a ship sails a terrible sea where no chart can be had and where monsters lurk that may strike and destroy at any moment. The ship sails there forever, there is no plan or sense to its voyage and no hope that the agony will end, and the helpless passengers are menaced not only by the Great Dark without but by mutiny and greed and maniac revenge within. And quite surely there will come to them bereavement, the death of their loved ones, the triumph of an idle and unmitigated malevolence whose terrible decoys are love and hope and human warmth, to lure humanity to destruction.

The artist is driven to make what he can of experience, and art is the terms of an armistice made with fate. Yet the compulsiveness he shows and above all his frustration make clear that here we are dealing with more than the comparatively simple way of art. The impact of calamity had been too great, he had taken one step too near the edge, and there is evident a struggle not only to make terms with his experience but also to vindicate himself. And not only to vindicate himself but, quite literally, by that vindication to integrate a mind that had been blasted and restore a talent that had been blown asunder.

We have seen his first attempt to still that accusation: the "It was not my fault" of the story where the major general is betrayed by a trusted relative. That would not suffice: the excuse was too transparent. There followed the assertion in *What Is Man?* that no one can be blamed since the chain of circumstance holds him fast in a plan determined by a vindictive God. That would not move the judge's heart, nor could the voice be stilled by the argument of the cycle to which he returned so often (in the stories of the virtuous man turned murderer) that all men are weak and all men fall when tempted.

But important modulations had been made in the dream story. And let me add that at one time, as his notes show, he contemplated going back to the disgraced major general and setting him out also on the dream-bound ship in the eternal ice, together with a company of fellow-victims living out their diverse fates in the same predestined anguish and despair. He did not write it. If he had begun it, he would not have finished it. For though this addition to the idea had hope in it, he had not yet found the reconciliation.

But he had come close to it. There was a grotesque hope, or at least an alleviation, in the position he had now reached. For this dream idea has two parts, one that dreams are brief though their agony may seem to last forever, and the deeper one that the reality may fade into the dream, that one may not be sure, that as one wakes from dream so perhaps one may wake from a lesser to a greater dream. Here the perturbed spirit finds comfort, though not quite enough, in the simple thought, so direct and inevitable, so characteristic of the helplessness of our deepest selves: "It may not be true after all. It may be a dream. Maybe I have dreamed the whole agony. Maybe loss and suffering and despair are false, are only a dream."

Remember that this compulsive writing had produced other manuscripts, apparently at random and without relation to this bitter debate. Among them was a story about Tom Sawyer and Huck Finn, which I briefly described. But that story could not have been altogether aimless and at random. It was, in a way, a premonition. For in his winnowing of his own books and his lost years, he happened upon a mysterious stranger in the town of Hannibal. I do not know much about this man, for he takes various forms, but the important thing is his secret, the fact that there is noble or perhaps royal blood in his veins. This made him kin to Mark Twain, in whose veins ran the blood of an English earldom as well as that of a regicide. And was not Mark, besides, that most mysterious of strangers on this earth, a genius, a man born unlike other men, to a strange destiny? Somehow the image of this unrecognized nobleman blends with another image that has fascinated Mark all his life long, the figure of Satan. And this was a fruitful time to remember Satan, for Satan is an angel and angels are exempt from loss and pain and all mortal suffering; they are exempt from guilt and conscience and self-condemnation also, and temptation has no meaning for them and they have no moral sense, and neither humiliation nor death nor the suffering of anyone affects them in the least. Moreover, of the angels who were all that Mark needed most to be, he felt nearest to Satan, the one who had revolted against the inexorable laws of the universe stated in *What Is Man?* and the one whose insatiable curiosity about the ways of man kept him going up and down on the earth and to and fro therein.

So it is not surprising when, presently, young Satan, a son of the fallen angel, comes to Hannibal and falls in with Tom Sawyer and Huck Finn. This first manuscript is not remarkable, being little more than a succession of marvelous works done by the young angel for the admiration and stupefaction of the village. It was fumbling and tentative and it frayed out. But in it and in the notes made for carrying it on Mark found the vital clues, the seeds that were to bear fruit at last. At first young Satan was no more than a vehicle for Mark's derision of the God whose vengefulness creates human pain and for his scorn of the antlike race pain is inflicted on, and an identification, infantile at base, with a supernatural being who can perform wonders that make him distinguished and envied, a being also of irresistible strength. But he became more than that, and the way out of the basic frustration was his miracles. So another manuscript begins with Tom and Huck and young Satan in Hannibal, but this soon breaks off and a longer, better, and more deeply wrought one begins. The same story has been transferred to Eseldorf, in Austria, centuries ago—but if we needed any clue by now, note that this story includes a print shop such as young Sam Clemens worked in when he was the age of these boys. I will say nothing of this manuscript except that it led directly to the one that came through to triumph at last, the book which, after it had been painfully written over and changed and adjusted and transformed, was to achieve the completion denied its many predecessors, the book which we know as *The Mysterious Stranger.*

In those tortured revisions and adjustments, which are part of the same desperate effort to make the story go somehow that I have traced in other sequences, we see the thing finding expression at last. Or, if I may so phrase it, we see the psychic block removed, the dilemma solved, the inhibition broken, the accusation stilled, and Mark Twain's mind given peace at last and his talent restored. The miracles, which at first are just an idle game for the amusement of the boys and the astonishment of the villagers, become finally a spectacle of human life in miniature, with the suffering diminished to the vanishing point since these are just puppets, unreal creatures moving in a shadow play, and they are seen with the detachment of an immortal spirit, passionless and untouched. And so from a spectacle they become a dream—the symbolic dream of human experience that Mark had been trying to write in such travail for so many years.

So an unrecognized purpose had dominated the chaos of those efforts, after all, and out of it had come *The Mysterious Stranger,* a minor masterpiece, with its clear, subdued colors, its autumnal pity and compassion, its fine, silvery echo of mortality and of hope destroyed and of man's pettiness somehow given the nobility of suffering, the thread of pain binding all living things together. But what is it? Eseldorf—Assville—is just Hannibal, seen far away, softened by the mist of centuries. The boys who are eager and cowardly, aspiring and cruel, are just Tom and Huck once more, which is to say they are what Mark had found best in himself and his long phantasies. The villagers, the human race in little, are just his friends and neighbors, his detractors and enemies and those who had undone him. The deaths died, the injuries suffered and agonies endured—we do not need to inquire what they are, after the innumerable times he had tried to give them meaning in art. Nor can there be any doubt who the immortal Antagonist is, the enemy of God, which is to say the rebel against law—and so against responsibility. Here the dreadful things alleged against mankind, and so made as a confession, in *What Is Man?* are said again, but now they are tolerable, conformable, acceptable, for they have been removed far away, over them broods the peace of distant dream. And now we know that the dream had closed the arc and permitted him to say what he must say and enabled him at last to live at peace with himself.

You perceive, *now* [Satan says, just before he vanishes and the book ends] that these things are all impossible except in a dream. You perceive that they are pure and puerile insanities, the silly creations of an imagination that is not conscious of its freaks—in a word, that they are a dream, and you the maker of it. . . .

It is true, that which I have revealed to you; there is no God, no universe, no human race, no earthly life, no heaven, no hell. It is all a dream—a grotesque and foolish dream. Nothing exists but you. And you are but a *thought*,—a vagrant thought, a useless thought, a homeless thought, wandering forlorn among the empty eternities!

The dream, that is, was the answer and the proof. He had tried to say: it was not my fault, I was betrayed. But the accusation could not be stayed so easily. He had tried to say: it was not my fault, for the fixed universe of inescapable law intended from the beginning that this should happen. But that was too easily exposed as subterfuge. He had tried to say: it was not my fault, for anyone would have done the same, but the remorseless feet that follow, follow after had driven him from that refuge. He had tried to say: it is just a delusion, a dream I will wake from—and that had almost served, but not quite. Susy's delirium was not his delusion and there could be no waking from it—and if that was so, then the terrible accusation still held.

But there was still an answer. If nothing existed but a homeless thought wandering forlorn among the empty eternities, then his smaller agony and his personal guilt were also a dream. If everything was dream, then clearly the accused prisoner might be discharged. The accusation begotten by his experience could be stilled by destroying all experience. It was possible to uproot terror and guilt and responsibility from his little world, by detonating the universe. He could end his contention with the vengeful God and put away remorse forever by reducing all contention, vengeance, pain, degradation, guilt, sin, and panic to a lonely dream.

That was the price he paid for peace. It seems a high price. But art is the terms of an armistice signed with fate, and the terms one makes are the terms one can make. At this cost the fallen angel of our literature, the mysterious stranger who seemed only a sojourner in the cramped spaces of our mortal world, saved himself in the end, and came back from the edge of insanity, and found as much peace as any man may find in his last years, and brought his talent into fruition and made it whole again.

✪

Mark Twain: An Unsentimental Journey

. . . Our national past is now very much in fashion. Not the past of our classical period, the early republic of Jefferson and Madison and Adams, and not the Gilded Age—to use a term coined by Mark Twain—of Grant and Rockefeller and McKinley. Either of these might be instructive, the first as a tradition, the second as a warning. But what is wanted is romance rather than instruction, a past to escape into, not a past to learn from. So the vogue is for the forty-niners, the Civil War, the frontier, the Wild West. The editors of *Life* have celebrated the Winning of the West in seven installments; the most popular television shows are Westerns, and a six-shooter is now as prosaic a utensil as an egg beater; all publishing is divided into three parts—fiction, nonfiction, and Civil War; Carl Sandburg, the good gray laureate of the hinterland, last year intoned a Lincoln's Birthday address, full of piety and glucose, to a hushed session of Congress. Mr. Neider's edition* of the Twain autobiography is conceived in this spirit. "It brings back the tone and flavor of an America which was young and optimistic," he writes in his introduction, "a homespun, provincial America but an America with greatness in its heart. Thoreau's

* *The Autobiography of Mark Twain,* arranged and edited by Charles Neider (New York, 1959) [ed.].

"Mark Twain: An Unsentimental Journey" is from *The New Yorker,* April 9, 1960. Reprinted by permission; © 1960 The New Yorker Magazine, Inc.

America may have contained many lives of quiet desperation. Mark Twain's decidedly did not." We no longer feel very young or optimistic or greathearted, and so we yearn for the myth of the frontier.

Stagehands like Mr. Neider have long been at work on the figure of Mark Twain, turning up the lights to get rid of those frightening shadows—for without such adjustments it is difficult not to see Twain's own life as one of desperation, however unquiet. The strategy is to concentrate on the early Twain. Mr. Neider's edition is almost half over before we have reached *The Innocents Abroad* (1869). He reprints almost all the early material that appears in the Paine and DeVoto editions,* but he has no space for any of the later comments on the Gilded Age—the picture of Teddy Roosevelt ("Hard . . . coarse . . . the worst president we have ever had"), the irreverent descriptions of Gould, Carnegie, and other plutocrats, the indignation at the butcheries of Filipino patriots by American troops. A fourth of DeVoto's edition of the autobiography is taken up with such material, and even the squeamish Paine puts in a lot of it, including fourteen pages on a massacre of Moro tribesmen—and tribeswomen—for which President Roosevelt had congratulated General Leonard Wood. But these earlier editions came out before our national past was thoroughly mythologized; it was still possible then to present Mark Twain not only as a picturesque old party but as a social critic. Writing in the Soviet magazine *Literaturnaya Gazeta,* last August, Y. Bereznitsky charged that Mr. Neider's omission of such material betrayed a political bias. Mr. Neider replied that he had merely omitted "dated, dull, trivial, and journalese sections" and that "for me, Mark Twain is essentially a great fabulist and not a great maker of political utterances." For once, I think the comrades have had the better of a literary argument. Twain's attacks on the oligarchy were much less dated, dull, and trivial than a good deal of what Mr. Neider *has* included, and an autobiography that leaves out

* *Mark Twain's Autobiography,* edited by Albert Bigelow Paine (New York, 1924). *Mark Twain in Eruption,* edited by Bernard DeVoto (New York, 1940) [ed.].

Twain's indignation at what was happening to America in the last two decades of his life does not give a true picture.

But the "fabulist" side of Twain is most certainly now the fashionable one, for reasons that Y. Bereznitsky could analyze, I'm sure, far better than I could. Last spring, a young actor named Hal Holbrook got himself up into a remarkable facsimile of the picturesque old party—the program stated it took him three hours to apply the make-up—and for five months delivered Mark Twain's platform material to enthusiastic New York audiences. Granting all credit to the historical accuracy of Mr. Holbrook's impersonation, for which he studied phonograph records and even motion pictures of Twain, I was disturbed by its reception. It was a strange experience to sit in a house full of contemporary theatergoers who were roaring at witticisms like "Heaven for climate, Hell for company" and arch confessions to such sins as smoking and profanity. It was the ghost of a ghost, a Williamsburgian reconstruction of the twinkling, drawling, cigar-puffing old sinner that even in 1895 was synthetic.

In fairness to Messrs. Holbrook and Neider, it must be said that Twain himself, who, like all actors, was sensitive to the demands of his public, created the part. He stultified his best gifts by playing the provincial iconoclast. It was as if Lincoln had played Raymond Massey. There is a series of photographs in the Neider volume showing Twain lounging in a rocking chair, twiddling his eyebrows and cigar, and ruminating, in captions written in his own hand:

1. SHALL I learn to be good? . . . I will sit here and think it over.
2. There do seem to be so many diffi . . .
3. And yet if I should *really* try . . .
4. . . . and just put my whole *heart* into it . . .
5. But then I couldn't break the Sab . . .
6. . . . and there's so many other privileges that perhaps . . .
7. Oh, never mind, I reckon I'm good enough just as I am.

These were written in 1906, when Twain was seventy-one. But he still played Tom Sawyer, and the farthest reach of deviltry Twain could imagine—or, more accurately, his public image could imagine—was breaking the Sabbath. One of the reasons for Twain's enormous popularity in his lifetime and for his "availability" as a reassuring folk figure today is that he was, like Tom Sawyer, in form a bad boy but in content a good boy, tirelessly mocking a morality that was already, in 1890, decrepit—the morality of his small-town boyhood, before the Civil War—and so allowing his audience to feel broadminded without disturbing any of their real prejudices. With beating of drums and rattle of musketry, he reduced fortresses that had long been abandoned.

If this were all there was to Mark Twain, he would now be forgotten with Petroleum V. Nasby and Artemus Ward. There was, of course, a great deal more. He struck the pose his audience seemed to want, but it didn't satisfy him. The Mark Twain Problem has been copiously explored by two generations of critics; Arthur L. Scott's *Mark Twain: Selected Criticism* (Southern Methodist University Press, 1955) gives a fair sampling of the material, beginning in 1867, long before there *was* a Mark Twain Problem. The Problem is, essentially, the change that took place in the last twenty-five years of his life. Up to then, the line of development is straightforward enough: the boyhood in Hannibal, the young manhood as a Mississippi river pilot, the Western years, the leap into national fame with *Innocents Abroad,* the marriage to the respectable Olivia Langdon, the years of happy family life in respectable Hartford, and the production of most of his best work, culminating in *Huckleberry Finn,* in 1884. Then the complications begin. Twain kept on producing books, he became the beloved sage and humorist, the most eminent American author of his time. But the note of baffled despair sounds more and more even in his published work, while in his unpublished manuscripts it becomes dominant. The amount of this unpublished material is enormous; DeVoto estimates that in his last ten years Twain wrote fifteen thousand pages, almost all for uncompleted projects. He had lost his bearings as a craftsman, he had lost his faith in God and man, his mood was one of neurotic bitterness. It is true he had misfortunes—the failure of his publishing house, his own bankruptcy after spending a fortune on the unsuccessful Paige typesetting machine, the death of one daughter, the invalidism and death of his wife. But are these troubles enough to explain what happened?

A classic controversy arose between Van Wyck Brooks and Bernard DeVoto. It is important because it involves not only two theories about Twain but also two radically opposed interpretations of our culture. "There is no denying that for half a century the American writer as a type has gone down to defeat," Brooks wrote in 1921. He was referring to the desert between the Civil War and the First World War; he wrote at the beginning of the renaissance of the twenties, of which he was a herald. The year before, he had published *The Ordeal of Mark Twain,* presenting Twain as an artist *manqué,* a victim of the forces of Philistinism. The *Ordeal* is still by far the best study of Mark Twain. It is organized emotionally rather than intellectually; it uses much concrete data, but as a poet would—for color and mood. In some ways Brooks is much too "serious"; he insists that Twain's humor was merely an unnatural protective disguise, and he sometimes takes Twain's humorous self-denigration too literally, with disastrous results. But it is an eloquent, imaginative, thorough study, and it has the root of the matter in it—that Twain's genius was perverted by the pressures of his time and place. Twelve years later, DeVoto, then the apostle of middlebrow heartiness and nononsense, reacted with *Mark Twain's America,* which seemed to me a ham-handed celebration of the myth of the frontier. Brooks had taken a dim view of Hannibal and the Wild West as milieus for a developing artist; DeVoto pictured them as just the right background, vital and full of beans, to produce an authentic American writer. Brooks saw Twain as frustrated; DeVoto saw him as fulfilled. They disagreed even on Twain's last, black decades, which Brooks felt confirmed his thesis and DeVoto felt were merely the result of Twain's personal disasters—"I cannot see in what is called his pessimism anything but the fruit of his experience."

The later history of the conflict is strange. DeVoto succeeded Paine as literary executor of the Mark Twain Estate. For the first time, he was able to go through the great mass of unpublished manuscripts; in 1942 he published *Mark Twain at Work,* an unsparing documentation of Twain's dark side. Some of the material seems close to madness, as, for that matter, does some of the published work of Twain's later years. There is, for example, a lengthy fantasia called "A Horse's Tale," which is a peculiar mixture of Kipling, "Black Beauty," Laura Jean Libbey, and Krafft-Ebing. It makes uncomfortable reading, alternately sentimental and sadistic, tedious and grotesque. Twain thought well of it. "I did not tell the 'Horse's Tale,'" he writes in the autobiography. "The horse himself told it through me. . . . When a tale tells itself, there is no trouble about it . . . nothing to do but hold the pen and let the story talk through it." If it really was Twain's unconscious speaking, as he suggests, this bit of automatic writing is an alarming production. It may communicate to horses, since it was told by one, but it makes no contact with a human reader.

Although DeVoto never admitted it, and may never have realized it, reading these manuscripts must have brought him around to Brooks's tragic view of Twain. The contrast between the bombastic swagger of *Mark Twain's America* and the sober mood of *Mark Twain at Work* is striking. On the other hand, Van Wyck Brooks, in the thirties and forties, changed from a critic into a nostalgic impressionist, as his five volumes of American literary history demonstrate. The antagonists neatly exchanged places, DeVoto becoming more precise and rigorous, Brooks becoming vague, euphoric, seeming to feel a personal need to be positive about the cultural past he had once seen largely in negative terms. Now Twain strikes him not as a crippled genius but as "an American legend," the authentic voice of "this old primitive Western world, its first pathfinder in letters, its historian and poet." Now the Gilded Age becomes solid gold. *Innocents Abroad* (of all books!) had "somehow struck the keynote of his epoch, the boisterous geniality and self-confidence of the triumphant nation, unified by the Civil War, aware of the resources it was rapidly exploiting, good-naturedly contemptuous of the Europe it had once revered. . . . In his large, loose easygoing way, he seemed to speak for the pioneer West. . . . Mark Twain was a symbol of the new America." Or of the new Van Wyck Brooks.

Popular and academic interest in Mark Twain today is greater than it has been at any time since his death, and this interest is in the spirit of the new, rather than of the old, Van Wyck Brooks. In the pantheon of our folk heroes, Twain now occupies a niche little lower than that of Lincoln himself. On the popular side, there is to be, in addition to the Neiderized *Autobiography* and the Holbrook impersonation, a Metro-Goldwyn-Mayer version of *Huckleberry Finn*. On the academic side, no less than four new Twain items have come to hand in the last six months: *Mark Twain and Southwestern Humor* (Little, Brown), by Kenneth S. Lynn, of Harvard; *Mark Twain & Huck Finn* (California), by Walter Blair, of the University of Chicago; *Mark Twain-Howells Letters* (Harvard), edited by Henry Nash Smith, of the University of California, and William M. Gibson, of New York University; and *The Art, Humor and Humanity of Mark Twain* (Oklahoma), an anthology edited by Minnie M. Brashear, a pioneer Mark Twain student, and Robert M. Rodney. Except for the last, these are all substantial works. Professor Lynn makes an interesting and, to me, novel point—that the pre-Civil War dialect humorists of the Southwest were conservative Whigs who wrote from "the gentleman's point of view" about illiterate clowns, and that it was Mark Twain's originality that made the clown (Huck) the point-of-view character, a reversal that had enormous significance for our literature. Professor Blair traces in minute detail the personal and literary sources Twain drew on, between 1874 and 1884, in writing *Huckleberry Finn*. The book is one of those accumulations of data, presented without much style, that are typical of our scholarship. It has some interesting information but it fails to answer what seems to me to be the crucial question (a speculative one, and hence not real in the academic canon), which is how did Twain leap from *Tom Sawyer* to the heights of *Huckleberry Finn,* just as Professor Lynn (whose book is much better written) fails to explain the miracle of a Mark Twain emerging from the dreary unfunniness of his Southwestern predecessors. The Twain-Howells letters (two volumes, at twenty dollars) are a moving record of a long and generous friendship, but most are trivial and none struck me as distinguished. These two volumes are strictly for scholars; the editing is superb, the factual notes are often more interesting than the letters—this is what our scholars are good at. *The Art, Humor and Humanity of Mark Twain* is an all too reverent collection of extracts, including sixty painful pages from *A Connecticut Yankee,* addressed to those who "feel that Mark Twain and his writings are a vital part of the American experience." A small part of the writings are such indeed, but unless a good deal more critical discrimination and a good deal less piety are exercised toward both Twain and our national past than is now the fashion, we may find ourselves more impoverished than enriched by the American Experience.

What is striking about all four of these books is that the critical note is hardly ever sounded. The authors seem to accept Twain's work more or less as a whole, assuming that he was a major writer instead of—a very different thing—the author of one truly major work. Professor Lynn compares the tragic sense of life in *The Education of Henry Adams* to that in *A Connecticut Yankee.* He also finds amusing the Southwestern humorists who created Simon Suggs, Sut Lovingood, and other such exponents of brutal practical jokes and even more brutal dialectese; this has been the fashion since the publication, in 1931, of Constance Rourke's *American Humor.* Professor Blair is impressed by the extent of Twain's reading and even by the results ("This man with little formal education was fiercely determined to wrest from books and from life a philosophy"); one agrees that Twain read a lot and that he was fiercely determined, etc., but one would welcome some evaluation of this reading and of its results. Professors Smith and Gibson write that Howells' favorable review, in the *Atlantic,* of *Innocents Abroad* "for perceptive, forthright praise of an unconventional and apparently unliterary work . . . will bear comparison with Emerson's letter to Whitman praising *Leaves of Grass.*" But how could even Mark Twain specialists not see that *Innocents Abroad* encouraged precisely those Philistine attitudes of new-rich America that prevented *Leaves of Grass* from achieving recognition? Howells' praise of it was perhaps courageous—considering he wrote in the *Atlantic*—but surely not perceptive.

I must admit that for me the great bulk of Mark Twain's work is no longer readable. No other major nineteenth-century author, not even Balzac, produced so much that was so markedly inferior to his best. One thinks of the coarse-grained journalese (*Innocents Abroad*), the all too fine respectablese (*Joan of Arc*), the painful burlesque (*A Connecticut Yankee* when it isn't moralistic melodrama), the simplistic philosophizing (*What Is Man?*), the grotesque extravaganzas ("The Stolen White Elephant," and half a dozen other examples collected in a current Bantam paperback by the devoted Mr. Neider), and the extraordinary amount of just plain trivia. The miracle, and the puzzle, are that such a writer should have produced one great book and several books that are still fresh. For we are still left with *The Mysterious Stranger,* that oddly perfect late fruit of a tree that had seemed long past bearing, the first half of *Life on the Mississippi,* some excellent yarns in the vernacular, a little of *Pudd'nhead Wilson* (*pace* F. R. Leavis, who, it seems to me, reads it intellectually rather than aesthetically), more of *Tom Sawyer,* and almost all of *Huckleberry Finn.* A few miscellaneous items might be added—"Fenimore Cooper's Literary Offenses," some chapters from *Roughing It,* and several satirical pieces, like "The War Prayer" and "To the Person Sitting in Darkness." But, by and large, this is all that I can still read with pleasure.

Tom Sawyer is his "best-loved" book—for poor reasons, I think. Tom is the matrix from which such later stereotypes as Penrod, Andy Hardy, and Henry Aldrich were stamped—the kind of boy that adults like to imagine they once were and the kind of boy they like to deal with. He is swaggering, "full of mischief," but for all that he is basically "just a real boy" (alternatively, "all boy"), which is to say he is a Fifth Columnist in the juvenile world, his rebellion is phony, and when the chips are down he is amenable to adult control. Huck Finn has produced no stereotypes, partly because he is a real rebel, quite outside society, but chiefly because, while Tom is a sentimental abstraction, Huck is Huck.

Tom is the All-American Boy. He tries to avoid washing, he resists medicine, he plays hooky, he teases the cat, he patronizes the old (ole) swimming (swimmin') hole (hole), he squirms in church, he wriggles in school, he is ritualistically absurd in love, he is fertile in mischief. By page 2, Aunt Polly is saying, "I never did

see the beat of that boy!" By page 3, she is saying, "He's full of
the Old Scratch!" The first chapters are fascinating, for here, as in
the first glimpses of Sherlock Holmes in *A Study in Scarlet,* we can
see a mass-culture hero taking form. The sureness with which
Twain builds up the cliché is something to be admired (or de-
plored). One of Tom's most endearing (or irritating) qualities is
his love of romantic mystification. He is a general, a Robin Hood,
a pirate: "There comes a time in every rightly constructed boy's
life when he has a raging desire to go somewhere and dig for
hidden treasure. This desire came upon Tom one day. He sallied
out. . . ." Tom can't even lose a tooth without adding to the
cliché: "But all trials bring their compensations. As Tom wended
to school after breakfast, he was the envy of every boy he met
because the gap in his upper row of teeth enabled him to expectorate in a new and admirable way." There is a lot of "fine"
writing in *Tom Sawyer.* Sometimes, as in "sallied out," "wended,"
and "expectorate," it is ironic; describing boyhood trivia in inflated
language is, or was, a reliable comic device. More often, it is the
kind of stylistic lapse one often finds in Whitman, another self-
taught folk writer. The folk tradition had become feeble by the
second half of the nineteenth century, and naïve geniuses were
more open to corruption by the elegant rhetoric of their time than
they would have been a century earlier. So one gets sentences like
"The two boys flew on and on, toward the village, speechless with
horror. . . . The barkings of the aroused watchdogs seemed to
give wings to their feet."

But *Huckleberry Finn* is a masterpiece of style from its first
sentence: "You don't know about me without you have read a
book by the name of The Adventures of Tom Sawyer; but that
ain't no matter." By speaking through Huck, Mark Twain solved
the problem of style; he knew how Huck talked and so the tone is
always right. He was able to raise the vernacular into a great style,
no small feat if one recalls what even a Kipling perpetrated in
Soldiers Three. It was an achievement comparable to Words-
worth's revival of common speech after the artificiality of eighteenth-century verse. I think this is what Hemingway had in mind
when he made his famous statement that "All modern American

literature comes from one book by Mark Twain called *Huckle-berry Finn.*" Twain felt comfortable inside the skin of Huck, the outcast. The problem that James worried so much about and that Twain didn't but should have—namely, the point of view—was perfectly resolved by letting Huck tell the story. Even more important, all those worries about gentility that bothered poor Twain so much vanished once the speaker was a real bottom dog. "Judge Driscoll could be a free-thinker and still hold his place in society," we read in *Pudd'nhead Wilson,* "because he was the person of most consequence in the community, and therefore could venture to go his own way and follow out his own notions. [Pudd'nhead Wilson], the other member of his pet organization [The Free-thinkers' Society], was allowed the like liberty because he was a cipher in the estimation of the public, and nobody attached any importance to what he thought or did. He was liked, he was welcome enough all around, but he simply didn't count for any-thing." So, too, with Huck—"I was so ignorant, and so kind of low-down and ornery." For the first and last time in his life, Twain had found a point of view from which he could speak with moral and artistic freedom. In *Tom Sawyer,* written in his own voice, he couldn't venture beyond local color and conventional humor; Jim is just a superstitious darky, Huck is a picturesque genre figure. They become people in *Huckleberry Finn.*

It is interesting that Twain originally tried to write *Tom Sawyer,* too, in the first person. In *Mark Twain at Work,* DeVoto prints a very early draft, twenty pages long, which he found among the Mark Twain Papers. It is first-person and it makes dreary reading, "cute" and contrived; Twain just didn't feel at home inside a middle-class boy. He was quite right to do *Tom Sawyer* in the third person. For Tom is too respectable, too close to what Twain had become after his literary success and his marriage to the daughter of the leading coal dealer of Elmira, New York. "Mark Twain was a man who . . . never became in all respects mature," T. S. Eliot writes. "We might even say that the adult side of [Twain] was boyish, and that only the boy in him, that was Huckleberry Finn, was adult. As Tom Sawyer grown up, he wanted success and applause. (Tom himself always needed an audience.) He wanted prosperity, a happy romantic life of a conventional kind, universal approval, and fame."

And yet even *Huckleberry Finn* seems to me to be marred by its last hundred pages, in which the insufferable Tom Sawyer reappears to carry out one of his foolish and boring mystifications. Jim has been captured and is imprisoned in a flimsy hut until he can be returned to slavery. Tom and Huck could free him easily, but Tom insists on pretending he is a prisoner in the Bastille and on doing it all "in style," with rope ladders smuggled in pies, letters written in his blood, rats and spiders tamed by him—but one really cannot go on. Then, almost on the last page, Tom reveals that Jim has been free all the time, Miss Watson having emancipated him on her deathbed, so the masquerade is doubly pointless. Both Mr. Eliot and Lionel Trilling have taken a genial view of this ending, arguing that Twain was simply rounding off his tale by returning to the Tom Sawyerish mood of the opening chapters. But the point is precisely that the fake "adventures" initiated by Tom in the opening chapters yield to the real adventures of Huck and Jim, and a corresponding deepening of their characters. (Tom Sawyer is constitutionally incapable of experience, since he is a professional Small Boy.) To return to the mode of the opening is, in my opinion, to falsify and not to round out the artistic logic. The true novel begins when Old Man Finn suddenly comes back into Huck's life; he is a real villain, not a melodramatic one like Injun Joe in *Tom Sawyer,* and his appearance liberates Huck from his role of straight man for Tom. I agree with Leo Marx's "Mr. Eliot, Mr. Trilling, and 'Huckleberry Finn,' " in the Autumn, 1953, issue of the *American Scholar.* Mr. Marx points out that the farcical ending is out of key with what has gone before, and that it is not reasonable to suppose that Jim, who rebukes Huck for a minor practical joke during the trip down the Mississippi and who has slowly turned into the moral hero of the book, would submit to being the passive butt of Tom, especially in anything so vital to him as his freedom. Or that Huck, who, just before the arrival of Tom, has reached his greatest moral development with his decision to try to free Jim even if it is a sinful act ("All right, then, I'll *go* to hell"), would become again an ally in the most tedious—and tasteless—of Tom's "tricks."

This dismaying change of key—as if Siegfried were to start singing falsetto—is characteristic. *Tom Sawyer* begins as a humorous idyll and ends as Victorian melodrama; *Life on the Mississippi* begins as a poem and ends as a travelogue; *Pudd'nhead Wilson* teeters crazily back and forth between realism, melodrama, and burlesque. And it could have been much worse with *Huckleberry Finn.* DeVoto quotes one of Twain's working notes: "Farmer has bought an elephant at auction. Gives him to Tom, Huck and Jim and they go about the country on him making no end of trouble." "That elephant," adds DeVoto, "might easily have wandered into *Huckleberry Finn.*" It might indeed. Arnold Bennett called Twain "the divine amateur." Becky Thatcher, of *Tom Sawyer,* becomes Bessie Thatcher when she reappears in *Huckleberry Finn* because Twain didn't bother to check back, and he thanked his literary mentor, William Dean Howells, for relieving him of "the dreary and hateful task of making final revision of *Tom Sawyer.*" He didn't even read all the final proofs of *Huckleberry Finn,* but just gave Howells carte blanche.

"The writing of books and magazine matter was always play, not work," Twain says in the autobiography. "I enjoyed it; it was merely billiards to me." There is bravado here, not to be taken at face value. But he may be telling us more than he intended, for in his unhappy last decades billiards was for him what drugs, liquor, and gambling are for others; he played for hours, often till dawn, walking around the table like a bear shuffling around his cage, always willing to postpone his re-entry into reality for "just one more game." The endless writing of his later years, most of it uncompleted and inchoate, had a similarly compulsive quality. But whether he used writing as a diversion or as an escape, the notion of literary effort was foreign to Mark Twain. In a way, he wasn't a writer at all. He was a speaker, an actor, who paid much more attention to the niceties of delivering a lecture than to literary technique. He says nothing on the craft of writing to match the subtle analysis, in the autobiography, of the timing of The Pause, as illustrated in his platform experiences with the "Grandfather's Old Ram" monologue and the Negro ghost story "The Golden Arm." He gave Browning readings at his home in Hartford. "It is very enjoyable work," he wrote a friend, "only it takes three days to prepare an hour's reading." There is no record of such effort being spent on anything he *wrote*. Twain's prose style has often been praised, perhaps too often. He wrote an easy, fluid, idiomatic English, but it is a spoken English that gets its effects the way a raconteur does. The texture is coarse—the ear accepts things the eye rejects—and the individual phrases are rarely memorable and often infected with cliché. But when he is going right, they fall together to convey the general sense. Most of the time he wasn't going quite right, and the result is watery and verbose; squads of adjectives and platoons of subordinate clauses could be mustered out without altering the line of march.

"As long as the book would write itself," he says in a celebrated passage in the autobiography, "I was a faithful and interested amanuensis and my industry did not flag, but the minute that the book tried to shift to *my* head the labor of contriving its situations, inventing its adventures, and conducting its conversations, I put it away and dropped it out of my mind. Then I examined my unfinished properties to see if among them there might not be one whose interest in itself had revived through a couple of years' restful idleness and was ready to take me on again."

This happened to *Huckleberry Finn,* which he laid aside after the first dozen chapters, returning to it a year or two later, laying it aside again, and so on, so that it took him ten years to finish it. In that time, he also wrote a pleasant travel book, *A Tramp Abroad;* an insipid historical novel for boys, *The Prince and the Pauper;* and a number of stillborn tales, including "The Loves of Alonzo Fitz Clarence and Rosannah Ethelton," a spoof of majestic ineptitude about a courtship by long-distance telephone. And when he was finishing *Huckleberry Finn,* he was also working on a project that interested him much more—"1002," a lengthy burlesque of the Arabian Nights that DeVoto thinks "probably the dullest of all Mark's work . . . almost lethal." Fortunately, Howells didn't like "1002," and it was never completed. Of all his books, the two Mark Twain thought the most highly of were just the ones entirely lacking in his special qualities—*The Prince and the Pauper* and *Joan of Arc,* genteel excursions into pseudohistory that could have been written by dozens of hacks of the period. Looking back on his lifework at the age of seventy-three, he said, "I like *Joan of Arc* best of all my books; and it *is* the best; I know it perfectly well. And besides, it furnished me seven times the pleasure afforded me by any of the others: twelve years of preparation and two years of writing. The others needed no preparation, and got none." Perhaps it was just as well that he *was* so careless. Perhaps the divinity was inseparable from the amateurishness.

Writers are often poor judges of their own work, but Mark Twain's obtuseness reached the pathological. Not only did he share his present editor's illusions about the autobiography—he boasted it "would live a couple of thousand years without any effort and would then take a fresh start and live the rest of the time"—but he insisted it was precisely the kind of book it was not. He pictures all other autobiographers, with the possible exception of Cellini, as sitting at a window and commenting on the famous people who pass by. "This Autobiography of mine is a mirror and I am looking at myself in it all the time. . . . I rejoice when a king or a duke comes my way . . . but they are rare customers. . . . For real business I depend upon the common herd." The psychological phenomenon of easing one's conscience about one's failings by projecting them onto others has seldom been more neatly illustrated; Twain dearly loved a lord. The common herd is here represented by a few picturesque "characters," but eminent persons abound. He dwells in detail on his dinner with the Kaiser, his honorary degree from Oxford, his oratorical triumphs at great banquets, his contacts with authors like Kipling and Stevenson, generals like Grant and Sherman, businessmen like H. H. Rogers.

As for the mirror simile, it is safe to say that no autobiography is *less* inward-looking. The tone is that of the public performer; the mirror is used not for introspection but to put on the make-up. Twain's strategy for avoiding self-examination was the platform humorist's trick of accusing himself of vanity, ignorance, cowardice, and laziness, but always in stock situations that avoid the concrete personal note and seduce the sympathy of the audience by suggesting "I'm no better than you." Yet Twain was convinced that for the first time in human history a man was putting down his real thoughts and feelings. Only Paine was naïve enough to print his "Preface, as from the Grave":

In this Autobiography I shall keep in mind the fact that I am speaking as from the grave . . . because I shall be dead when the book issues from the press.

I speak from the grave rather than with my living tongue, for a good reason: I can speak thence freely. When a man is writing a book dealing with the privacies of his life—a book which is to be read while he is still alive—he shrinks from speaking his whole frank mind; all his attempts to do it fail, he recognizes that he is trying to do a thing which is wholly impossible to a human being.

But the promised record of a soul laid bare reads as impersonally as, and very much like, one of those after-dinner speeches Twain was so good at.

His accounts, for instance, of his mother and his wife, two strong-willed and proper ladies who there is reason to believe had even more influence on his development than mothers and wives usually do, are not revealing. One gathers he loved and admired them, but he hardly needed to hide in the grave to say that. Of his mother he writes, "I knew her well during the first twenty-five years of my life, but after that I saw her only at wide intervals, for we lived many days' journey apart. . . . She had a character, and it was of a fine and striking and lovable sort." Some anecdotes support this characterization, but it still seems undernourished. And one wonders *why* he saw his mother "only at wide intervals." The "many days' journey apart" isn't very convincing, for Twain was a great traveler. The mists are even thicker about his wife:

Under a grave and gentle exterior burned inextinguishable fires of sympathy, energy, devotion, enthusiasm, and absolutely limitless affection. . . . Perfect truth, perfect honesty, perfect candor were qualities of my wife's character. . . . Her judgments of people and things were sure and accurate. In her judgments of the characters and acts of both friends and strangers there was always room for charity, and this charity never failed. I have compared and contrasted her with hundreds of persons and my conviction remains that hers was the most perfect character I have ever met. And I may add that she was the most winningly dignified person I have ever known. Her character and disposition were of the sort that not only invite worship but command it. No servant ever left her service who deserved to remain in it.

One begins to detest poor Olivia Clemens, one even suspects that she fired at least one servant unjustly, because one knows she couldn't have been as good as all that. Twain was a devoted husband and father, but the quality of his devotion was false, like the loving pride of the mother who sees her darling as the brightest star in the seventh grade. In sexual love, this attitude can produce literature because there really is something mythological, something absolute, about Eros. But in the prose of family life it comes out wrong. The chapters written after the deaths of his wife and of his daughters Susy and Jean move one humanly but not imaginatively. On Christmas Eve, 1909, a few hours after the sudden death of Jean by epileptic seizure, he writes:

I lost Susy thirteen years ago; I lost her mother—her incomparable mother!—five and a half years ago . . . and now I have lost Jean. How poor I am who was once so rich! . . . She lies there, and I sit here—writing, busying myself, to keep my heart from breaking. How dazzlingly the sunshine is flooding the hills around! It is like a mockery!

Seventy-four years old, twenty-four days ago. Seventy-four years old yesterday. Who can estimate my age today?

I have looked upon her again. . . . The sweet placidity of death! It is more beautiful than sleep.

This might have been written by any bereft father with a knack for the banal. Not that he is overstating his feelings; he simply lacks the vocabulary for this kind of writing. Even here, "as from the grave," he cannot drop the public mask, even here he conceals his grief beneath the standard jargon of bereavement.

The tragedy of Mark Twain, I think, is this peculiar inability to speak in his own voice. "The frankest and freest and privatest product of the human mind and heart is a love letter," he writes in the autobiography. "The writer gets his limitless freedom of statement and expression from his sense that no stranger is going to see what he is writing. . . . It has seemed to me that I could be as frank and free and unembarrassed as a love letter if I knew that what I was writing would be exposed to no eye until I was dead, and unaware, and indifferent." This is interesting because of the hostility it assumes between the writer and his readers, who are thought of as Peeping Toms, with no right to share one's "private" thoughts. It is a notion that could not have existed before the end of the eighteenth century, when the rise of a mass market for culture introduced a novel division between creator and consumer. Up to then, the artist or writer had worked for his peers, a small upper-class group who were sophisticated enough to know what he was doing. He could "be himself"—to use a significant idiom—because they "spoke his language," to use another. But as the Industrial Revolution, democracy, and popular education brought ever larger masses of people into the cultural market, expanding and adulterating it, the writer was forced to choose between addressing this vast new public and speaking in his own voice. Some deliberately ignored the market (Stendhal), some deliberately wrote for it (Scott), some straddled the issue without being conscious of it, producing work that fluctuated between *Kitsch* and genius. The novels of Balzac and Dickens are unstable compounds of originality and cliché. Byron wrote romantic best sellers like *Manfred* and *Childe Harold*. He also wrote *Don Juan,* which satirizes precisely such romantic posturing and which is still readable because it expresses his (so to speak) personal personality, as against his public personality.

Mark Twain was one of these two-level writers, and the least conscious of all. While he appeared never to know when he was being himself and when he was manufacturing for the market, he sensed that something was wrong. "Writers are manacled servants of the public," he admitted in *Life on the Mississippi.* "We write freely and fearlessly, but then we 'modify' before we print." Perhaps "admitted" is not the word. So deeply had he accepted the necessity, so unaware seems he to have been of any alternative, that he probably thought of his statement as a mere truism. In the autobiography, he records at length a talk in 1907 with Elinor Glyn, whose erotic best seller *Three Weeks* was the *Lady Chatterley's Lover* of the period. The topic was "free love," and Twain apparently sympathized with Mrs. Glyn's advanced views, though, even writing from the grave, he found it inadvisable to state just what they were: "Take it all around, it was a very pleasant conversation and glaringly unprintable, particularly those considerable parts of it which I haven't had the courage to more than vaguely hint at in this account of our talk." She "implores" him to let her publish his endorsement of her views. "But I said, 'No, such a thing is unthinkable.' I said that if I, or any other wise, intelligent, and experienced person should suddenly throw down the walls that protect and conceal his *real* opinions on almost any subject under the sun, it would at once be perceived that he . . . ought to be sent to the asylum. I said I had been revealing to her my private sentiments, *not* my public ones; that I, like all other human beings, expose to the world only my trimmed and perfumed and carefully barbered public opinions and conceal carefully, cautiously, wisely my private ones."

But the most remarkable statement of this theme is another preludial note to the autobiography, which appears only in Paine:

What a wee little part of a person's life are his acts and his words! His real life is led in his head and is known to none but himself. All day long, and every day, the mill of his brain is grinding, and his *thoughts,* not those other things, are his history. His acts and his words . . . are so trifling a part of his bulk! a mere skin enveloping it. The mass of him is hidden—it and its volcanic fires that toss and boil, and never rest, night nor day. These are his life, and they are not written, and cannot be written.

What a curious conception of a writer—that his thoughts, which "cannot be written," are his real history and not "those other things" (i.e., his writings); that what is written is "a mere skin" over inarticulate volcanic depths. In short, that the writer is just like everybody else. He keeps himself *to* himself, and he is not such a fool as to chatter in public about what goes on in the privacy of his head. But the writer is *not* like everybody else, and his specialty is just to make his private thoughts public. Only a writer who felt profoundly alienated from his public would express himself in these terms.

Mark Twain's was a peculiarly difficult period for a writer who wanted to strike his own note. The old New England tradition, already enfeebled, was submerged by the materialistic expansion, one might almost say explosion, that followed the Civil War, and it was not until the First World War that there were signs of a literary renaissance. The half-century between the wars, when Twain wrote, was a bad time for the arts. A provincial society of merchants and small farmers was changing into a cosmopolitan one of mass industry and finance capital. Great cities were arising (Chicago had three hundred thousand inhabitants in 1870 and a million seven hundred thousand thirty years later), the West was being settled, our imperialistic adventures were beginning overseas, and —possibly the most important change from a literary viewpoint— the needs of industry were attracting vast numbers of immigrants, most of whom didn't speak English. Standards, cultural as well as ethical, were simply swept away in the rush. Everybody was making money or dreaming of doing so. The common man was entering his kingdom; "America from about the middle of the last century," observes an English critic, A. C. Ward, "experienced the most extraordinary spate of professional funny men ever known in any country. The success of the dialect humorists depended chiefly upon the fact that their sayings and writings were a subtle if unconscious flattery of the great unlettered American public, which was tickled to death to find literary gentlemen speaking a language every one could understand and cracking jokes comprehensible to the most unassuming intelligence." Mark Twain was one of these funny men, and while he was above the crude dialect and grotesque misspellings the others relied on, his spirit was often theirs.

The Philistinism of *Innocents Abroad* was to remain with him all his life. Although he was an ardent traveler and lived abroad almost continuously from 1890 to 1900, remarkably little rubbed off on him. The forty-odd pages of the autobiography devoted to his years in Florence are almost all about the plumbing, heating, and other aspects of the domestic economy of his villas there. There is nothing on art, nothing on architecture, and the only passage on the city is a banal set piece that begins, "To see the sun sink down, drowned on his pink and purple and golden floods, and overwhelm Florence with tides of color that make all the sharp lines dim and faint and turn the solid city to a city of dreams, is a sight to stir the coldest nature and to make a sympathetic one drunk with ecstasy." This Burton Holmes Kodachrome, which misses the point that it is the sharp lines and the solidity that are the city's distinctive quality, is all we get about Florence, but there are five glowing pages on a parade in Vienna: "All the centuries were passing by; passing by in glories of color and multiplicities of strange and quaint and curious and beautiful costumes not to be seen in this world outside the opera and the picture books. . . . I have been looking at processions for sixty years, and, curiously enough, all my really wonderful ones have come in the last three years." Parades were the one art form Twain responded to; he might have written more about Florence had there been some really good parades while he was there. One is reminded of Roger Fry's comment on the elder J. P. Morgan's feeling for art: "A crude historical imagination was the only flaw in his otherwise perfect insensibility." One imagines that Morgan would have relished Twain's historical romances.

Writing to Andrew Lang in 1889, Mark Twain formulated a literary credo:

> The critic assumes every time that if a book doesn't meet the cultivated-class standard, it isn't valuable. . . . The critic has actually imposed upon the world the superstition that a painting by Raphael is more valuable . . . than is a chromo . . . and the Latin classics than Kipling's far-reaching bugle-note. . . . If a critic should start a religion, it would not have any object but to convert angels, and they wouldn't need it. It is not that little minority who are already saved that are best worth lifting up, I should think, but the mighty mass of the uncultivated who are underneath! That mass will never see the old masters—that sight is for the few; but the chromomaker can lift them all one step upward toward appreciation of art. . . .
>
> I have never tried . . . to help cultivate the cultivated classes. I was not equipped for it either by native gifts or training. And I never had any ambition in that direction but always hunted for bigger game—the masses. . . . I have always catered for the Belly and the Members but have been . . . criticised from the culture-standard—to my sorrow and pain; because, honestly, I never cared what became of the cultured classes; they could go to the theatre and the opera; they had no use for me and the melodeon. . . .

My audience is dumb; it has no voice in print, and so I cannot know whether I have won its approval or only got its censure.

Like most of Mark Twain's thinking, this is not substantial. If standards are a "superstition," what can the masses be "lifted up" *to?* And were chromos a step toward Raphael or a substitute for Raphael? It is also characteristically *ad hoc.* If consistency be the bugbear of little minds, Twain's intellect was of Goethian proportions. His actor's sensibility led him to play wildly different roles at different times. When he wrote to Lang, he was in his "Connecticut Yankee" phase, as the tribune of the American common man against the aristocratic privilege of the Old World—and, besides, Lang had not liked "Yankee." But fifteen years earlier Twain had expressed himself in just the opposite way. When his friend Howells had told him reassuringly, as editor of the *Atlantic,* apropos of his first efforts for that awesome journal, "Don't write *at* any supposed *Atlantic* audience, but yarn it off as if into my sympathetic ear," Twain had replied, "It isn't the *Atlantic* audience that distresses me; for *it* is the only audience that I sit down before in perfect serenity (for the simple reason that it don't require a 'humorist' to paint himself stripèd & stand on his head every fifteen minutes)."

But the letter to Lang did express an important truth about Mark Twain—his feeling of identity with the masses rather than with the classes. He was, at his best, a folk writer. "Our one American example of the bardic type of artist and sayer," Ludwig Lewisohn calls him, adding, "He was not essentially divided from the folk for which he wrote . . . by any difference of *vision,* only by genius—like the tribal bards of old. . . . In his small and homespun way Mark Twain is related to Homer . . . A poor relation, a late descendant, but of the authentic lineage and blood." Yet despite the laughter of his lecture audiences, despite the sales figures on his books, Twain felt out of touch: "My audience is dumb; it has no voice in print, and so I cannot know whether I have won its approval." By his time, the folk audience had become as inflated and corrupted as the aristocratic audience. It was no longer a specific group with certain values and standards in common; it had been absorbed into the mass audience, an abstract, heterogeneous crowd whose tastes were those of everybody in general and nobody in particular. This was the audience before whom Twain postured as the frontier humorist and crackerbarrel philosopher, for whom he wrote his endless journalese. His genius led him to create a folk epic in *Huckleberry Finn,* but neither he nor his mass audience realized it. They preferred the mechanical jocosity of *Innocents Abroad*—as late as 1908 it was still outselling *Huckleberry Finn*—and he preferred the synthetic romance of *Joan of Arc.*

There was an alternative to the mass audience, and it had an even worse effect on Mark Twain's work. This was the genteel school that arose after the Civil War as a rear-guard defense of the New England tradition against the vulgarity of the new-rich and the ignorance of the immigrants. Rear-guard actions can only delay the defeat, but this one failed to do even that. It was like a proper Bostonian spinster in charge of a class of slum kids. The cultural values became desiccated, and the kids didn't get educated, either. Twain was very much under the influence of such genteelists as Thomas Bailey Aldrich (whom he unrecognizably described as "always brilliant . . . a fire opal set round with rose diamonds"), Edmund Clarence Stedman (who complained that the word "sewer" appeared three times in *A Connecticut Yankee*), Richard Watson Gilder (who represented bohemian avant-gardism on the *Century* and who, when *Huckleberry Finn* was serialized in his magazine, deleted "I was in a sweat," "Dern your skin!," "We was always naked," and several dozen other low-class expressions), and the most sophisticated of them all, William Dean Howells (who wrote Twain that the description, in *Tom Sawyer,* of a dog who had sat down on a pinchbug sailing up the church aisle "with his tail shut down like a hasp" was "awfully good but a little too dirty"; the impropriety was deleted). But Twain himself was always prudish, and he did a lot of self-bowdlerizing. It really took considerable ingenuity to find anything to clean up.

What was more important was that Mark Twain's genteel tutors bowdlerized his talent, diverting it into flaccid historical pageants and away from American themes, where it could be dangerous.

They also discouraged his natural tendency toward satire. The age of Grant and McKinley could have done with a Swift, but, except for a few flashes like that mordant bit of pacifist irony "The War Prayer," Twain prudently confined himself to making fun of the Sabbath. Had not Howells, for all his realistic doctrine and his Socialist sympathies, pronounced "the more smiling aspects of life . . . the large cheerful average of health and success and happy life" to be "the more American"?

In compensation, Mark Twain went far toward pessimism in anonymous works like *What Is Man?* and posthumous ones like the autobiography. In fact, much too far. It isn't that, as he fondly imagined, his ideas are particularly shocking. His surviving daughter still refuses to release five chapters of religious speculation from the autobiography. "Not to be exposed to any eye until the edition of A.D. 2406—S.L.C.," he solemnly scrawled at the head of two of them. However, judging by Mr. Neider's description of their content, they would cause no seismic upheavals if they were published five minutes instead of five hundred years hence. No, this is village-atheist stuff that goes too far emotionally and not far enough intellectually. In its frantic overstatement, denying any value to God, to man, to life itself, it is like a severely compressed spring that leaps back when it is released, reminding one of those Twain curiosa like the skit about the court of Queen Elizabeth called *1601,* in which repressed sex explodes into scatology. And just as *1601* was written specially for his pastor, so, one imagines, the schoolboy nihilism was directed at Howells, Aldrich, Stedman, and his other tutors. That Twain felt the need for such defiance was to his credit, yet if only he had realized that the most effective riposte would have been not cosmic rebuttal—for which he had no gift and which absurdly inflated the issue, since these opponents based their position on nothing more profound than provincial convention—but merely to write in his own natural vein! This would have been more difficult, and Twain was not a man to seek out difficulty. Also, he was never clearly aware that his genteel mentors *were* his opponents. Much easier to muffle his bitterness in slashing generalities not to be exposed to any eye until A.D. 2406.

Mark Twain's difficulty was a peculiarly modern one—he was damaged by success, as, later on, Fitzgerald and Hemingway were to be. He was simply too popular for his own good, with both of the important publics of his time—the masses and the genteel school. He was overfed with praise and starved for understanding; the ponderous machinery of exploitation drew him in and he was processed. A generation earlier, Melville had failed in the old-fashioned way. His early books of exotic adventure (*Typee, Omoo, Mardi*) and straightforward reportage (*White Jacket, Redburn*) had been successful, but when he at last spoke out fully in his own voice, *Moby Dick* sold less than a thousand copies, and he entered on the obscurity that lasted till his death, forty years later. Twain's only important contemporaries, James and Whitman, also experienced the old-fashioned kind of failure. Like Melville, James was reasonably popular in his early decades, but he lost his audience when he began to extend his range and to reflect stylistically his maturing sense of the complexity of human relations. *The Bostonians,* published in 1886, the year after *Huckleberry Finn,* was the turning point. It was his best up to then, but it was too "difficult" for the general public—Twain, who as a reader was a part of that public, said he would rather be consigned to the Puritan heaven than read it—and it also managed to offend the genteel with its satire of New England provincialism. The same year, *The Princess Casamassima,* with its anarchistic background, hardly improved matters, and James slowly resigned himself to writing for a small audience and sometimes, he felt, for no audience at all. He gave up the hope of popularity with reluctance—the stillborn plays he wrote after these two failures were pathetic efforts to regain it—but he did give it up. He also gave up his country, living abroad and finally becoming a British citizen. Like Twain, he wanted popularity, but he was unwilling to pay the price. He paid a good deal for his isolation—the sometime eccentricity of his later style, for instance—but it was less than Twain paid for success.

Mark Twain had little in common with James—except, as F. W. Dupee has acutely noted, humor—but much with Whitman. Both were folk writers, identifying themselves with the people in their

diction, their defiant innocence of higher education, and their
personal "style"—Whitman's open-collared flannel shirt, prospector's beard, and slouch hat, Twain's Western drawl, unruly mop of
hair, gambler's mustache and cigar. Both shared with their fellow-
Americans two deep and inconsistent faiths, in democracy and in
the technological progress that was its executioner. Twain had the
first private telephone and was the first literary man to use a
typewriter; Whitman's apostrophes to Progress were a poor man's
substitute for such equipment. But Whitman resembled James in
being unwilling—or, rather, unable—to make important conces-
sions for the sake of popularity. His shabby little house in Camden
was as isolated from American life as James's country place in
Sussex. His poetry was more appreciated in England than here—
the genteelists rightly thought it barbarically improper (though
Emerson upheld the honor of the older New England tradition
with his "I greet you at the beginning of a great career"), while
the masses he addressed with unfaltering democratic faith paid
no attention to him, finding Ella Wheeler Wilcox and James Whitcomb Riley more to their taste. Whitman thought he was a bard—
"essentially not divided from the folk for which he wrote . . . by
any difference of *vision,* only by genius"—but he was in fact an
avant-gardist. He yearned to be one with the common people, but
his vision was incomprehensible—even worse, boring—to them.
They couldn't see why he thought they were so exciting. Twain
would have guffawed if anyone had called him a bard, which was
one reason why, in that period, he was. That Whitman was poor and
of simple tastes while Twain was rich and lived in princely style
is beside the point; the one was hopelessly recherché, for all his
bardic aspirations, while the other was a bard—at times—in
spite of his keen sense of the literary market place.

In 1887, Twain attended a lecture by Whitman on, of all
appropriate subjects, Lincoln. There is no record of his reactions,
but, as a master of the platform, he must have been distressed by
Whitman's inept performance. Not that Whitman was at all averse
to appearances of this sort. On the contrary, he sought them out as
assiduously as Twain came to avoid them. But he was as stiff and
self-conscious as Twain was easy, his bardism being as theoretical

as Twain's was spontaneous, and he got pitifully few invitations. Perhaps his major public appearance was in New York, at the fortieth National Industrial Exhibition, in 1871. Horace Greeley usually gave the opening address, but he was out of town that year and the committee offered Whitman a hundred dollars and expenses to write and recite an ode for the opening. He accepted with delight; the fee was, for him, munificent, and the poem would be published in the newspapers. Whitman wrote some verses celebrating industrial progress; he urged the Muse to emigrate to the United States and he ended with a spread-eagle salute to the flag. "It was more like an oration than a poem," writes Gay Wilson Allen in his biography. "It is difficult to understand how a poet who had recently written 'Passage to India' could have composed so bad a poem as 'After All, Not to Create Only.' Yet this is what the desire to be topical and *popular* could bring him to." Whitman, who promoted his works with a shamelessness that would have appalled Twain, sent out fulsome press releases, but only two or three hundred people came to listen. Even these faithful few were frustrated, for by one of the ironies of literary history, Whitman's delivery, which was ineffectual to begin with, was drowned out by proletarian static—the hammering and sawing of workmen making last-minute installations. Although twelve of the seventeen daily papers the city then boasted (*eheu, fugaces*) printed the poem, their reaction was largely hostile. "The vacancy caused by Mr. Greeley was regarded with painful emotion," observed the *World,* while the *Tribune* printed a savage parody by Bayard Taylor, beginning:

Who was it sang of the procreant urge, recounted sextillions of subjects?
Who but myself, the Kosmos, yawping abroad, concerned not at all
    about either the effect or the answer.

Whitman tried to repair the damage by planting anonymous articles in out-of-town papers. These gave a flattering account of the proceedings—the workmen laid down their tools, spellbound, to listen; the audience (multiplied by ten) interrupted with applause; most pathetic of all, his delivery was admired ("His gestures are few, but significant. . . . He was perfectly self-possessed. . . .

The main impression was markedly serious, animated, & earnest.
. . . All the directors & officers of the Institute crowded around
him & heartily thanked him"). This face-to-face meeting with the
American common man—and with the press that spoke for him—
was a traumatic experience for Whitman. "He made himself ridiculous with his poem and mannerisms," Mr. Allen says in concluding
his account of the episode, "and the resulting travesties on him and
his poetry left wounds that would continue to fester until the end
of his life." The subtler wounds that Mark Twain suffered from his
adoring public were more paralyzing to him as an artist. Perhaps
Whitman had the better of it, after all. Acceptance can be worse
for a writer than rejection.

The question of Mark Twain is the question of America. Was the
Hannibal of his boyhood idyllic or squalid? Was the West of his
young manhood Mr. Brooks's vision of it (as of 1920) or Mr.
DeVoto's (as of 1932)? Was the Gilded Age of his maturity a
degeneration from the past or was it merely the growing pains of
progress? And which Mark Twain are we to believe, the cocksure
American jingo of *Innocents Abroad* or the disillusioned cynic of
"Pudd'nhead Wilson's Calendar"?
    Mark Twain's life spanned the Great Divide in our history, the
Civil War. The period from which all his significant work came
was his boyhood; he returned to it again and again, compulsively,
in abortive gropings like *Tom Sawyer Abroad* and *Tom Sawyer,
Detective,* and even in *The Mysterious Stranger,* like a dog returning to a bone he has buried too deeply. He was never at home in
the postwar period. He felt that a money-grubbing age, conformist
and corrupt, had replaced what he remembered as a larger, more
innocent time. ("You feel mighty free and easy and comfortable
on a raft," Huck says.) At the same time, he was an ardent
believer in Progress. *A Connecticut Yankee* is a how-to-do-it
book, demonstrating the superiority of advanced technology; the
triumphs of Sir Boss over Merlin and other feudal reactionaries
suggest our own Point Four program in their more benevolent
aspects and, in their more severe, what is now going on in Tibet.
"All you men," orated Mark Twain to a dinner party of prosper-

ous fellow-citizens who had assembled to celebrate his sixty-seventh birthday, "all you men have won your places not by heredities and not by family influence or extraneous help, but only by the natural gifts God gave you at your birth, made effective by your own energies. This is the country to live in." Some years earlier, in 1889, he had written, on behalf of a committee of literary men, a curious letter to Walt Whitman, for his seventieth birthday. It is curious because there is no reference to Whitman's poetry—which Twain very likely had never read—and because, instead of congratulating the age on Whitman, it congratulates Whitman on the age. It is also curious, and significant, as a full-blown expression of that religion of Progress in which both sender and recipient believed—or, more accurately, wanted to believe:

To WALT WHITMAN:

You have lived just the seventy years which are greatest in the world's history and richest in benefit and advancement to its peoples. These seventy years have done much more to widen the interval between man and the other animals than was accomplished by any of the five centuries which preceded them.

What great births you have witnessed! The steam press, the steamship, the steelship, the railroad etc. etc. . . . Yes, you have indeed seen much—but tarry for a while, for the greatest is yet to come. Wait thirty years, and *then* look out over the earth! You shall see marvels upon marvels! . . . man at almost his full stature at last! . . . Wait till you see that great figure appear, and catch the far glint of the sun upon his banner. Then you may depart satisfied, as knowing you have seen him for whom the earth was made, and that he will proclaim that human wheat is more than human tares, and proceed to organize human values on that basis.

MARK TWAIN

So one true believer reassured another, and it was perhaps merciful that both were dead before the thirty years ended with a war that destroyed the historical base for the doctrine of Progress.

Like Twain, Whitman had lived on both sides of the Great Divide; he, too, felt that the quality of American life had changed for the worse. But he was more optimistic than Twain—perhaps because his contacts with the great world were so much slighter—

and, for all his misgivings, he died in the faith. It was the avant-garde poet who struggled to believe in Progress and Democracy, while it was the popular entertainer who was profoundly disillusioned.

There is something heroic about those last black years of Mark Twain's life. His personal disasters coincided with his growing pessimism about America. "He had no philosophy, no values . . . with which to face [these problems]," Lewisohn observes. "Nor did he seek in books or converse any knowledge of the thoughts whereby men in the past have sought to wring from the stubborn universe a triumph for the spirit of man. He knew neither Plato nor Spinoza nor Kant; there is no evidence that he had ever read Emerson. He sat down to develop out of his own head, like an adolescent, like a child, a theory to fit the facts as he seemed to see them, and the only influence discernible in his theory is that of Robert Ingersoll!" (This is an overstatement, but a slight one; Twain also was influenced by Lecky's nineteenth-century *History of Morals*.) But he did insist on facing the bleak reality. He lacked the equipment to cope with the theme, but it was a great one, nothing less than the breakdown of the American dream, and he wouldn't settle for less. As Henry Nash Smith has demonstrated in *Mark Twain's Images of Hannibal* (University of Texas *Studies in English*, 1958), there is a significant change in Twain's concept of his boyhood town, so important throughout his creative life, from the idyllic St. Petersburg of *Tom Sawyer,* through the more realistic river towns of *Huckleberry Finn* to the folly and cruelty of the Eseldorf ("Asses' Town") of *The Mysterious Stranger*. Professor Smith's conclusion is not overdrawn:

Mark Twain came nearer registering in fiction the death of nineteenth-century culture than did such contemporaries as Howells, whose remarkable gifts as a novelist could not in the end overcome his intellectual confusion, or James, who created the technique of the modern novel but paid the price for his single-minded devotion to art by failing to recognize the countenance of the twentieth century until the outbreak of the First World War. From the 1890's onward Mark Twain was struggling with his perception that democracy had been corrupted by money and that war was the normal behavior of modern as well as of ancient nations. When he tried to ignore these insights his work had no vitality, yet he could not devise a form to embody them. "The Mysterious Stranger," his nearest approach to such a feat, was left unfinished at his death. He had bet too much on the doctrine of Progress and the belief in an orderly benign universe to be able to emulate the younger writers who in his old age were finding literary capital in the master image of the Waste Land and were beginning to produce a whole literature of alienation.

Unfinished *The Mysterious Stranger* may be, yet it is more of a piece than any other work of Mark Twain. It is not his highest flight, but it is the only sustained one; there are none of those changes of key, those unfortunate improvisations that mar all of Twain's other books. There is a miracle here, especially since the book was written in his final decade, when nothing seemed to come together, artistically, for him. It is as if Twain's personal griefs and his anxiety about America were compacted, as a diamond is formed under pressure, into this sad, hard little fable. The style is simple and muted, quite different from the unbuttoned journalese of his other late works. Of course he didn't dare have it published while he was alive, of course he stipulated that it be excluded from any collected edition of his works, and of course Harper brought it out as a boy's book, with illustrations by N. C. Wyeth in his most romantic vein.

One suspects that the juvenile format and the Wyeth illustrations would have tickled Mark Twain's sense of irony. *Gulliver's Travels* has been defused in the same way. *The Mysterious Stranger* is an even grimmer parable than *Gulliver,* whose satire was restricted to mankind. Twain's target is cosmic. Satan is the book's hero, and God, with his "moral sense," which always seems to produce even greater cruelties than uninstructed human nature could think up by itself, is the villain. There is no afterlife and there is considerable doubt even about this life. Satan, who manifests himself as Philip Traum (Philip Dream), tells the boy narrator at the end, "Life itself is only a vision. . . . Nothing exists save empty space—and you! . . . I myself have no existence; I am but a dream—your dream. . . ." Lewis Carroll's Alice is told she exists only because the Red King is dreaming her, a sufficiently disturbing idea. But little Theodor Fischer, of Eseldorf, is the solitary dreamer who has the nightmare responsibility of creating the Red King (or Satan) himself. In Philip Traum's world, the *summum bonum* is death, which is at least a release from the sordid agony of living. "He did not seem to know any way to do a person a kindness but by killing him," the boy Fischer wonderingly observes.

As for Progress, that last refuge of the noblest spirits of his age, Mark Twain, speaking through Satan, is explicit:

You perceive that you have made continual progress. Cain did his murder with a club; the Hebrews did their murders with javelins and swords. . . . The Christian has added guns and gunpowder; a few centuries from now he will have so greatly improved . . . his weapons . . . that all men will confess that without Christian civilization war must have remained a poor and trifling thing. . . . In five or six thousand years five or six high civilizations have risen, flourished, commanded the wonder of the world, then faded out and disappeared; and not one of them except the latest invented any sweeping or adequate way to kill people. They all did their best—to kill being the chiefest ambition of the human race . . . but only the Christian civilization has scored a triumph to be proud of. Two or three centuries from now it will be recognized that all the competent killers are Christians; then the pagan world will go to school to the Christian.

When he wrote this, Mark Twain was thinking of such toys as the Gatling gun and the Maxim rifle. And his prediction that it would take "two or three centuries" for Christian civilization to perfect its mass-killing techniques was just ten times too optimistic. Before Twain had finished *The Mysterious Stranger*, Albert Einstein had published the equation from which the atomic bomb was to be created. It would be an interesting exercise in historical imagination to think of what he and Mark Twain might have had to say to each other if, by some odd chance, they had ever met— perhaps at a parade in Vienna. The mere notion is enough to discourage a satirist.

KENNETH S. LYNN

❁

Huck and Jim

By his own account, Mark Twain's career as a writer began on the
fateful day when a young printer's apprentice named Sam Clemens
read a page torn out of a book that he had found lying in the dust
of a Hannibal street and for the first time understood what a power
there was in words. The story is charming, and may even be true,
although it is perhaps wise to remember that as compensation for
our lack of a literary tradition American writers have always
tended to enlarge their own personalities into archetypes, and that
as a self-mythologizer Mark Twain ranks with Benjamin Franklin,
Edgar Poe, and Ernest Hemingway. However, what is significant
about the anecdote is not its veracity, but the fact that the page
which Twain said changed the whole course of his life was a
description of Joan of Arc in the cage at Rouen. Twain is by no
means the only comic writer of modern times who has found the
Maid a compelling figure, yet there was a special urgency about
Twain's fascination with Joan's captivity not to be found in Shaw's
or Anouilh's interest in this aspect of her career. For the image of
an abandoned youngster, locked up and forgotten, haunted
Twain's imagination from childhood to death; by saying that the
description of Joan in the cage made him a writer, Twain offers us
one of the master keys to his life and work.

This selection is reprinted from Kenneth S. Lynn, "Huck and Jim," *Yale
Review*, Vol. XLVIII, No. 3 (Spring 1958), pp. 421–431. Copyright Yale
University Press.

The fantasy of being locked up and forgotten was deeply rooted in Twain's experience of growing up in the Clemens household. Although Twain's mother was warmhearted, the family atmosphere was dominated by the personality of his father. Thanks to this strange, austere, loveless man, the Clemenses were reserved and formal with one another at all times; at night, they shook hands before going to bed—a warmer gesture would have been unthinkable; indeed, Twain could only remember one occasion (the death of one of his brothers) when a kiss was ever exchanged between members of his family. The story that Mrs. Clemens married her husband out of spite and was not in love with him has never been satisfactorily verified, but there is no doubt as to the nature of the relationship between father and sons. Twain spoke for his brothers as well as himself when he wrote, "My father and I were always on the most distant terms when I was a boy—a sort of armed neutrality, so to speak."

In such an atmosphere, Twain must have suffered almost daily from rejection, but the instance that seemed to him to epitomize all his experiences of neglect was the time when his family, moving from Florida, Missouri, to a new home in Hannibal, drove off without him. Writing an article in later years for the *North American Review,* Twain could still remember the "grisly deep silence" that fell upon the locked house after his family had gone, and the terrible darkness that descended as the afternoon waned into evening. As the late Dixon Wecter has pointed out, the story is engrossing, but untrue, for Twain was here describing as a personal experience something that in fact had happened to his older brother Orion. So acute, apparently, was Twain's sense of rejection and of isolation from his father that in looking back on his early life he was convinced that it was surely he who had suffered the agony of being locked up and forgotten.

The loneliness of Twain's childhood is reflected everywhere in his work. As has often been observed, loneliness is the peculiar quality of a great deal of American writing and comes out in many forms—one thinks of Melville's renegades and castaways, the solitary men in the stories of Hawthorne and Poe, the sense of "otherness" in Henry James and Henry Adams—but in Twain, loneliness almost without exception takes the form of alienation from the family. In *The Innocents Abroad* Twain describes himself as a "helpless orphan"; Tom Sawyer has lost his father and mother; the prince and the pauper, like the protagonists of *Huckleberry Finn* and *Joan of Arc,* are runaways; the "aristocratic" Tom Driscoll in *Pudd'nhead Wilson* makes the nightmarish discovery that his real mother is a Negro mammy. And for all these orphans and runaways there exists the horror of incarceration. The solitary confinement cells in the Chateau d'If have a fearful fascination for the narrator of *The Innocents Abroad* (indeed, in all of his travel books, prisons, dungeons, tombs, and catacombs are the sights that Twain is most powerfully attracted to); death in a cave lies in wait for Tom Sawyer and for the boys in *A Connecticut Yankee;* Huck's equivalent of Joan's cage is the cabin in the woods where his Pap locks him in while he goes off for days at a time. With the possible exception of Poe's fantasies of being buried alive, there is no other corpus of American writing that reverts so often as does Twain's work to the nightmare of being utterly cut off.

But the obverse of the nightmare of being locked up and forgotten is the dream of release and recognition, of power and glory. Henry James considered that only primitive persons could be interested in Twain, but James's belief in the supremacy of the artist has a great counterpart in Twain's conception of the role of the humorist. The nihilistic vision of *The Mysterious Stranger* is perhaps a strange place to look for affirmations, but that book was for Twain what *The Tempest* was for Shakespeare, a valedictory, and the Stranger is as bold as Prospero in asserting the glory of his creator's life. The human race, says the Stranger, for all its grotesqueries and absurdities and shams, has one really effective weapon—laughter. "Power, money, persuasion, supplication, persecution—these can lift at a colossal humbug—push it a little— weaken it a little, century by century; but only laughter can blow it to rags and atoms at a blast. Against the assault of laughter nothing can stand." For Twain, the humorist was above all else a moralist, in whose hands the ultimate weapon of laughter might conceivably become the means of liberating mankind from its enslavement to false ideals.

Over and over again in his work, Twain plays with phantasies of power that express the scope of his ambition. In *Life on the Mississippi,* he apotheosizes Mr. Bixby, the pilot who reigns over the titanic river that had conquered even La Salle. The hero of *A Connecticut Yankee* doesn't amount to much in nineteenth-century America, but in the world of King Arthur he becomes "the Boss." The pauper from Offal Court becomes the heir to the English throne. Like Poe's Dupin, the detective heroes of *Pudd'nhead Wilson* and *Tom Sawyer, Detective* are the indispensable agents of social justice. Richard Watson Gilder might assure the readers of the *Century* that Twain was not a "giber at religion or morality"; Howells might call him "a humorist who never makes you blush to have enjoyed his joke . . . [and] whose fun is never at the cost of anything honestly high or good"; all America might regard him as a funny man; but for Twain, the humorist was not only a giber, but a destroyer, a Jeremiah preaching the corruption of the state. When he described his books as "sermons," America took it as just another joke—his agnosticism, after all, was notorious—but Twain was in dead earnest. (Perhaps the people who best understood him were not his admirers and friends, but the librarians who banned his books as subversive.) Like Joan of Arc, Twain dreamed of purging society of its pettiness in order that it might become great, and if in the end it was safer to burn Joan, it was manifestly more convenient to regard Twain as a joker who never made fun of anything high or good. Given what society did to him, it is no wonder that the most memorable of Twain's phantasies of power are also prophecies of tragedy and defeat.

Today we lament Twain's taste when he asserted that *Joan of Arc* was his favorite of all the books he wrote. Yet by now it should be as easy to understand this judgment as it is to comprehend why he should wish to have it believed that reading about her was the turning-point of his career. For in a sense, Twain spent his lifetime writing about Joan; the tension between the nightmare of being locked up and forgotten and the dream of liberation is in all his best work. The most exquisitely poised expression of this tension is, of course, *Huckleberry Finn.* If Twain never fully recognized the book's greatness, we nevertheless have him to thank for knowing that we should call it a sermon.

The first episode from *Huckleberry Finn* to appear in print was the chapter about Huck and the raftsmen that Twain casually excised from the still-uncompleted novel and threw—as he phrased it—into *Life on the Mississippi*. The purpose of the transposition was to illustrate "keelboat talk and manners" as they had existed in the 1840's, but Twain could hardly have chosen a more significant chapter for introducing what he liked to call "Huck Finn's Autobiography" to the world, because in his prodigally wasteful American way, Twain improved a good book at the cost of looting his masterpiece of an episode of extraordinary richness, of great beauty and humor, which sets forth in a parable the two major themes of the novel.

The chapter begins immediately after Huck and Jim's terrifying experience of getting lost in the fog. Drifting down an unfamiliar and "monstrous big river," the boy and the Negro decide that Huck should find out where they are by swimming over to a huge raft they have seen in the distance and gathering the information by eavesdropping. Under cover of darkness, Huck reaches the raft, climbs on board without being noticed, and settles down to listen to the talk of the raftsmen, to their colossal boasting, their roaring songs, and above all, to the fantastic tall tale about a man named Dick Allbright and the mysterious barrel that followed him on the river wherever he went rafting, bringing terror and death to his companions. Nothing, the teller of the tale assures his audience, could keep the barrel off Dick Allbright's trail or mitigate its inexorable fatality, until finally a raft captain swam out to the barrel and hauled it aboard. Inside its wooden walls, the captain and his men found a stark-naked baby—"Dick Allbright's baby; he owned up and said so. 'Yes,' he says, a-leaning over it, 'yes, it is my own lamented darling, my poor lost Charles William Allbright deceased,' says he—for he could curl his tongue around the bulliest words in the language when he was a mind to. . . . Yes, he said, he used to live up at the head of this bend, and one night he choked his child, which was crying, not intending to kill it—which was prob'ly a lie—and then he was scared, and buried it in a bar'l, before his wife got home, and off he went, and struck the northern trail and went to rafting; and this was the third year that the bar'l had chased him."

Crouched in the darkness, naked and afraid, Huck seems utterly apart from these coarse, rough men, but the phantasy of violence and terror which the raftsman has spun for the scoffing delight of his fellows nevertheless vitally involves the runaway boy, for the story tells, after all, of a man who locked up his son, and of a naked child floating down the river in search of its father. That Huck has escaped to his fabulous voyage by making his Pap think he has been murdered only completes his identification with the dead baby who was somehow "reborn" in the river, an identification which he makes explicit when, suddenly seized from his hiding-place and surrounded by strange men demanding to know his name, Huck jokingly replies, "Charles William Allbright, sir." Always in Twain the best jokes reveal the profoundest connections, and with the release of laughter triggered by Huck's superbly-timed joke the chapter not only reaches its humorous climax, but we are suddenly made aware that through Huck we have been eavesdropping on a parable of the search for the father and of death by violence and rebirth by water which takes us to the very heart of the novel.

Yet even this awareness does not exhaust the richness of the riverman's story. The symbolic connection between Huck Finn and the tall tale beautifully exemplifies how Mark Twain could exploit for the purposes of high art the tradition of Southwestern humor; but it also reveals that behind the novel there stands the Bible. A baby in a barrel afloat on a great, continental river: beyond a raftsman's phantasy we discern the infant Moses in the ark of bulrushes hidden in the Nile. Through that association we can understand that Twain was doing a great deal more than simply setting up a magnificent joke when he began *Huckleberry Finn* with a chapter entitled "I Discover Moses and the Bulrushers"; for although Huck soon loses all interest in Moses, "because I don't take no stock in dead people," the humorous introduction of the

Biblical story effectively announces the somber theme of death and rebirth, with its attendant implications of slavery and freedom, and inextricably associates Huck with the Mosaic saga of an infant who "died" and was reborn in the river, and who grew up to lead an enslaved people to freedom.

The Moses theme unfolds in a series of initiations. A new life, a fresh start, is constantly being attempted by Huck; in the course of his journey down the river he assumes a dazzling variety of roles, becoming by turns George Peters, George Jackson, a young girl, an English valet, and finally, Tom Sawyer. But just as Pap's spiritual rebirth culminates in a quite literal fall from grace (dead drunk, off a porch roof), so Huck's initiations run a cycle from birth to death. His "new life" at the Widow's terminates with his simulated murder in the cabin where Pap has locked him up; his identity as George Jackson is concluded by the bloodbath at the Grangerford's; his masquerade as an English valet is abandoned in a graveyard. The same cyclical movement marks the drama of liberation. From the time that Tom and Huck tie up Jim "for fun" at the beginning of the novel until they make a game out of liberating him from the cabin on the Phelpses' farm at the very end of the book, Jim moves in and out of one bondage after another. But these sine wave movements from birth to death and from freedom to slavery that give the novel its characteristic rhythm take place within the framework of a larger movement that carries Huck and Jim simultaneously toward triumph and tragedy. When Moses led the Israelites to freedom he also moved toward his prophesied appointment with death; the great paradox of *Huckleberry Finn* is that Huck and Jim's voyage toward freedom takes them due south, into the very heart of the slave country, and that the triumphant liberation of Jim inexorably enforces the tragic separation of the boy and the Negro. As W. H. Auden has observed, the final meaning of *Huckleberry Finn* is that freedom and love are incompatible, which is another way of saying that the liberation theme and the search for the father theme are tragically at odds.

The search theme is officially introduced when Judge Thatcher and the Widow Douglas go to court to get permission to take Huck away from his Pap. Who should be his parents, the respectable aristocrats who are no blood relation to Huck, or his violent, drunken father? Nothing less than a human life is at stake; the decision would seem to call for the wisdom of Solomon. Echoing Huck's judgment of Moses, Nigger Jim "doan' take no stock" in the wisdom of Solomon, yet in the chapter entitled "Was Solomon Wise?" our laughter at Jim's stupidity carries with it the realization that the search theme also has a connection with the Bible. Jim regards it as utter foolishness that Solomon should have attempted to settle the parenthood dispute by offering to cut the child in two—"De 'spute warn't 'bout half a chile, de 'spute was 'bout a whole chile; en de man dat think he kin settle a 'spute 'bout a whole chile wid a half a chile doan' know enough to come in out'n de rain." As well as being marvelously funny, the speech throws into Biblical perspective the entire problem of parenthood with which the novel is concerned.

Like Solomon, Huck listens for the voice of truth and the accents of love as a means of identifying the true parent he seeks, but neither side in the legal contest so identifies itself, and therefore when Huck escapes to the river he is fleeing, as Twain once pointed out, both a "persecuting good widow" and his "persecuting father." Encountering Jim, Huck is at first amused and exasperated by the black man's ignorance, but part of the great drama of their relationship is Huck's gathering awareness that Jim is always right about all the things that really matter, about how certain movements of the birds mean a storm is coming, about the dangers of messing with snakes, and the meaning of dreams. But if Jim's relationship to Huck is fatherly in the sense that he constantly is correcting and admonishing the boy, forever telling him some new truth about the world, he is identified even more unmistakably as Huck's father by the love that he gives him. Just as Huck is searching for a father, so Jim is attempting to rejoin his family, and he lavishes on the love-starved river waif all of his parental affection, calling Huck honey, and petting him, and doing "everything he could think of for me." Jim's ludicrous horror at Solomon's apparent willingness to split a child in two is, as it turns out, a humorous statement of his loving care for the integrity of his white child.

The moral center of the novel focuses in the intense relationship between Huck and Jim, but as in Gogol's *Dead Souls,* the panoramic sweep of Huck's journey in search of his father also opens to view a whole civilization, and the wrath of Twain's judgment of that civilization is the novel's most Biblical quality. Entering many houses in his quest for truth and love, Huck calls only the raft his home, a fact which symbolizes at the broadest reach of social implication Twain's massive condemnation of the society of the Great Valley as he knew it in the tragic quarter of a century before the Civil War.

When, at the beginning of the novel, Huck is sworn into Tom Sawyer's gang and introduced to Miss Watson's piousness, he is thereby initiated into the two mysteries of the society which offer—respectively—an institutionalized version of truth and love: romanticism and religion. For Tom, life is a circus, a romantic adventure story. Turnips are "julery" and Sunday school picnickers are "Spanish merchants and rich A-rabs," and Tom denounces Huck as a "numskull" for his literal-mindedness about these marvels. Huck, however, who understands that the fine spectacle of lights twinkling in a village late at night means that "there was sick folks, maybe," knows that romanticism is a way of faking the nature of reality, and when he temporarily forgets this, when he disregards Jim's warning and boards an abandoned steamboat to have an adventure of which Tom Sawyer would have approved, he comes close to losing his life. (The fact that the steamboat is named the "Walter Scott" is scarcely accidental, for in *Life on the Mississippi* Twain had already blasted the Scott-intoxication of the South as "in great measure responsible" for the Civil War.) But the novel's bitterest attack on the romantic imagination occurs in two interrelated and successive chapters, 21 and 22. In the latter chapter, Huck goes to a circus, sees a drunken man weaving around the ring on a horse, and is terribly distressed, although the crowd roars with delight. But it is not Huck's charming naïveté in not recognizing that the drunkard is a clown that Twain condemns, it is the callousness of the crowd. For this circus scene depends upon the preceding chapter, which really does involve a drunk, the drunken Boggs, who weaves down the street on horseback, shouting insults at Colonel Sherburn. When Sherburn mortally wounds Boggs, a crowd gathers excitedly around the drunkard to watch him die. Everyone is tremendously pleased—except Huck, and the dying man's daughter. Thus by this juxtaposition of episodes, each of which contrasts the boy's sympathetic concern with the gleeful howling of the crowd, does Twain lay bare the depravity of a society that views life as a circus, as some kind of romantic show.

For Miss Watson, life is a moral certainty. Bible readings and daily prayers fill her smug world with assurances. She tells Huck that if he will pray every day he will get whatever he asks for, and when he prays for fish hooks without being able to "make it work," she calls him a fool, just as Tom had called him a numskull. Yet it is Miss Watson, prattling of Providential mercy, who treats Nigger Jim severely, who despite her promise to him that she would never sell him away from his wife and children, can't resist the sight of a stack of money and agrees to sell him down the river. If romanticism is a lie, religion is a monumental lovelessness, a terrible hypocrisy. When Huck goes to church with the Grangerfords, the minister preaches a sermon on brotherly love to a congregation made up of men armed to the teeth and panting to kill one another; when the King pretends he is infused with divine grace in order to con the camp meeting, he is only acting out Miss Watson's hypocrisies on the level of farce. But once again, as in his attack on life as a circus, Twain's most withering blast at lovelessness and hypocrisy is delivered by juxtaposing two chapters with a vengeance.

The last paragraph of Chapter 23 is perhaps the most poignant moment in the entire novel, for it is here that Jim relates to Huck how his daughter, after recovering from scarlet fever, became a mysteriously disobedient child. Even when Jim had slapped her and sent her sprawling she refused to obey his orders, but just as he was going for her again, he realized what was wrong: "De Lord

God Amighty fogive po' ole Jim, kaze he never gwyne to fogive hisself as long's he live! Oh, she was plumb deef en dumb, Huck, plumb deef en dumb—en I'd ben a-treat'n her so!" On the last page of Chapter 24, the King and the Duke launch their scheme for robbing the Wilks girls of their inheritance, with the King pretending to be a parson and the Duke acting the part of a deaf mute. When viewed beside Jim's sorrow and compassion for his deaf-and-dumb daughter, the spectacle of the two frauds talking on their hands is sickening—"It was enough," says Huck, "to make a body ashamed of the human race."

In the end, Huck turns his back on the corruption of society, but his tragedy is that in the very moment of doing so he loses Jim. In one of the numerous sequels to the novel that Twain obsessively sketched out in his later years, Jim has somehow been caught again and Huck fantastically plans to free him by changing places with him and blacking his face. But the sad reality of the novel is that such a masquerade is an impossible dream; once Jim has reached the promised land of freedom, Huck is forever separated from his black father by the tragedy of race. It is scarcely necessary to know that in still another contemplated sequel Twain envisioned Huck as a broken, helplessly insane old man in order to sense that at the conclusion of the novel Huck's voyage has become as doomed in its way as Captain Ahab's, and that in lighting out for the Territory without Jim beside him he flees with "all havens astern."

LESLIE A. FIEDLER

Duplicitous Mark Twain

Duplicity is the most notable, perhaps the essential characteristic of the greatest American novelists; and surely the most duplicitous of all is Mark Twain, precisely because he wears the mask of straightforward simplicity. The notorious "Notice" affixed to *Huckleberry Finn* reads: "Persons attempting to find a motive in this narrative will be persecuted; persons attempting to find a moral in it will be banished; persons attempting to find a plot in it will be shot." This apparently bluff warning, however, comes to us not directly from "the Author," but "Per G. G. Chief of Ordnance"; it is, that is to say, proffered as a joke, a piece of fiction. And who is "the Author," anyhow? Huckleberry Finn, who purports to tell the story which follows? "Mr. Mark Twain," who, Huck informs us in his first paragraph, told a few "stretchers" in *Tom Sawyer?* Or Samuel Langhorne Clemens, who lurks somewhere behind the Mark Twain who looks over the shoulder of Huck. If he is Huck or Mark, he is only a character speaking inside a story or a lifelong impersonation, not very different from the "Ishmael" who ironically warns us against taking Melville's account of the whale hunt as a "hideous and intolerable allegory." And if he is Samuel Clemens, who likes to boast of how he took his readers in, he can scarcely be trusted!

Reprinted from *Commentary,* by permission; copyright © 1960 by the American Jewish Committee. The selection appeared in the March 1960 issue of *Commentary,* pp. 239–248.

But who is the *persona* called Mark Twain and loved alike by lovers of literature and those who sincerely hate it? He is, first of all, a funny man, but more particularly, one who is funny at the expense of culture: an antiliterary writer, whose best books are travesties of others—of the Arabian Nights, the romances of Walter Scott, the tales of King Arthur. When he was not writing burlesques, he was mocking the piety of tourists before old masters, getting the goods on Shelley, exposing the absurdities of James Fenimore Cooper, being snide at the expense of Jane Austen, mocking the New England Brahmins in a speech which he hoped vainly they would take for a good-natured joke, or (over and over!) revealing how romantic literature had corrupted the American South! The self-distrust of the American writer, projected ambiguously in such authors as Poe and Hawthorne, he worked into an open attack on the artist as the Other. It is Twain's contempt for culture which won him quite early the kind of popular acclaim never accorded in his lifetime to an American writer of equal merit. No literate Philistine could help feeling at home with his apparent espousal of experience over sensibility, truth over elegance, simplicity over sophistication, artlessness over art.

In some quarters, his pose has been hypostatized into a position, and he is spoken of as the founder of a school which descends via Dreiser to Hemingway and James Jones: an Americanist or Redskin (the term is Philip Rahv's) school opposed to the Europeanizers or Palefaces. Twain is markedly different, however, from most other writers put in the Redskin camp. Like Whitman or Dreiser or Hemingway, he deals with native materials and relatively simple people, using colloquial speech; but unlike them, he is not an open rebel, a self-declared enemy of society. His avoidance of sex, for instance, betrays the sense in which he is, however crude in his manners, basically genteel: at worst, a genteel Noble Savage, the friend of enlightened clergymen. Even his pornographic *1601* was written for the bland approval of the Congregational minister, Joseph Twichell, who enjoyed condescending to the author, in whom, for all his "coarse spots," he found the heart of a conformist.

Just once in his writing career, Twain seemed to have made an error in judgment—with the publication of *Huckleberry Finn*. He had, as was his practice, read the manuscript to his wife and sent it off for approval to his moral arbiter and friend, William Dean Howells; then had censored it to meet all their objections, as well as his own more finicky ones. Yet his book was banned by the committee of the Public Library of Concord, Massachusetts, who found it "rough, coarse, inelegant, dealing with a series of experiences not elevating. . . ." and concluded that "it is the veriest trash." Newspapers all over the country joined in the chorus of disapproval, extending their disapproval to *Tom Sawyer,* and declaring of both that "they are no better in tone than the dime novels which flood the blood-and-thunder reading population." The polite reviewers were frightened into silence, even Howells, who had applauded in private, not daring to write his usual adulatory notice; but no one, least of all Twain, was prepared to defend the book on the grounds that it was, indeed, "irreverent . . . irreligious . . . inelegant," truly "subversive." The single review of *Huckleberry Finn* to appear was published as a letter to the *Century Magazine* and insisted upon Huck's "courage" and "manliness," as well as "the total absence of morbidness in the book."

Perhaps the main function of *Tom Sawyer Abroad,* the first of two published sequels, was to try to put *Huckleberry Finn* in a favorable perspective, make it seem good, clean, quite undangerous fun; yet Twain never was wholly at ease with his greatest work. He certainly ranked it below the obviously uplifting *Joan of Arc,* and even agreed with his wife in her preference for the more vapid *The Prince and the Pauper.* To Twain, an unqualified national acceptance was as necessary to his concept of his role as failure and rejection had been to Poe. It is not merely that Twain was a successful writer, or that he was interested in making money; the essential point is that he could not abide any hint that he was not loved and trusted by the great audience which despised and distrusted other first-rate art. For him, literature was a way of arriving: the sole method of social climbing capable of winning him the approval of the moral arbiters of elegant society, without losing him the affection of the scarcely educated general public.

It is tempting to label him the Philistine as artist and let it go at that—attributing his triumphs to a grace which he did nothing to deserve. Yet it is evident that he had values and standards, for all his show of artlessness, and that he distinguished among his own books between those which he wrote merely for money and those he wrote for posterity. It is, perhaps, better to think of him as the artist as Philistine, as one who, half deliberately at least, assumed a disguise in which he could penetrate into the midst of a populace grown restive under the pressure to love culture. In this sense, he plays the role of the stereotypical Westerner opposing the condescension of the East, the stereotypical husband resisting the demands of a culture-hungry wife, the stereotypical American tourist rising in resentment against the guides and tour books, the steamship companies, and the vast, commercialized museum of Europe itself!

Toward the end of the nineteenth century, American tourism began in earnest; and upon the ambivalence of the New World tourist to the Old World, source of his religion and his high culture, a long line of American writers commented, beginning tentatively with Cooper, and reaching a first climax with Henry James, Henry Adams, and Mark Twain. Though Twain had begun to break through to national recognition with the reworking of a Western tall story, his real entry into literature is made with *Innocents Abroad* (1869). It is worth remarking, precisely because it is so easy to overlook, that Twain is, with the possible exception of James, the most Europe-oriented, Europe-obsessed of our late-nineteenth-century novelists. After the *Innocents Abroad,* he turns eastward again and again, confronting the Old World in *A Tramp Abroad, The Prince and the Pauper, A Connecticut Yankee in King Arthur's Court, Tom Sawyer Abroad, Personal Recollections of Joan of Arc, 1601, Following the Equator, The Mysterious Stranger;* and the last posthumous collection of his stray pieces is called *Europe and Elsewhere.*

Whenever, as a matter of fact, Twain dreamed of producing "literature" rather than "entertainment," like a good, genteel American of his period, he looked across the Atlantic for his subject matter and techniques, producing such stiff costume dramas, moistened with tears, as *The Prince and the Pauper* and *Joan of Arc.* The beginnings of his career as a writer Twain liked to date from the moment when a stray leaflet telling the story of Joan had blown against him in the streets of Hannibal. Yet he produced nothing of real merit out of his piety toward the European past, despite the time and energy he invested in research, writing, and revision. The other side of his ambivalence is more fruitful; and his only "Eastern" novel to approach in zest and inventiveness his great "Western," *Huckleberry Finn,* is *A Connecticut Yankee,* in which he plays the Philistine as self-satisfied boor rather than the Philistine as tremulous worshiper at the shrines of history. Yet even *A Connecticut Yankee* does not quite come up to the freshness and vigor of the nonfictional *The Innocents Abroad.*

Already in *The Marble Faun,* the subject matter of *The Innocents Abroad* is implicit; but it is a comic subject matter, which cannot really define itself in the Gothic ambience of Hawthorne's melodrama. Hawthorne's boredom as he tagged along behind his wife through the picture galleries of Europe, his sneaking conviction that the clean copies of the old masters made by American art students are superior to the cracked and dirty originals, reappear in Mark Twain, turned into frank and ribald jests. The comic cliché of the child-husband (stanchly American and honest) revolting against his mother-wife (Europeanizing and pretentious) is by no means the invention of Twain. As a matter of fact, he embarked on his actual first voyage to Europe without any wife at all, making do with a substitute "mother" picked up on the cruise: a Mrs. Fairbanks, to whom he read his mildly blasphemous articles, checking all questions involving "good taste."

His blasphemy is finally no more than pseudoblasphemy: not a denial of, but a complement to the culture-religion of the American female, another aspect of our national sexual division of labor!

In the end, though, Twain was only kidding, pretending to be a more hopeless boor than he in fact was, in order to provide for himself and Mrs. Fairbanks the special American *volupté* of intersexual acculturation. Twain in *The Innocents Abroad* has assumed the role not of the rebel but the Good Bad Boy; and the clue is there all the time in his calling Mrs. Fairbanks "Mother"— in his being bad just for her!

Almost everywhere in his work, Twain writes as a boy for a world accustomed to regarding the relations of the sexes in terms of the tie that binds mother to son. Not only does he disavow physical passion, but he downgrades even the Faustian role incumbent on American authors. In him, the diabolic outcast becomes the "little devil," not only comical but cute, a child who will outgrow his mischief, or an imperfect adult male, who needs the "dusting off" of marriage to a good woman. Twain's typical fictional devices were contrived at a time when everywhere in the popular American novel the archetypes were being reduced to juveniles. As Clarissa becomes a small girl in *The Wide, Wide World,* so Werther becomes a child in Twain's total work, turns into the boy-author Mark Twain; and not only the American women who made Susan Warner a best seller approve, but their husbands, too, who laughed at their wives' taste. Even dirty, tired adult Europe approves, finds no offense in *The Innocents Abroad* itself, since Twain was playing a role that European self-hatred and condescension to the United States demanded, acting the Good Bad Boy of Western culture. For everyone, male and female, European and American, he represents the id subverting tired ego-ideals, not in terror and anarchy, but in horseplay, pranks, and irreverent jests.

There is notoriously a price for assuming a mask, indeed, always a suspicion that what the mask hides is no face at all! And certainly one senses in Twain the insecurity of a man never quite sure of what he had to believe to survive: that somewhere beneath the high jinks of Twain, there was a real and quite serious Sam Clemens: with serious ideas, too dangerous to utter; and serious ambitions, too lofty to risk in the market place—even a serious vein of bawdry, too masculine and broad for the general reader. But his serious ideas eventuate in the sophomoric cynicism of *What Is Man?*, his serious aesthetics in the sentimental banalities of *Joan of Arc,* his serious bawdry in the pseudoarchaic smutty jokes of *1601.*

Finally, Twain is betrayed not by his contempt for culture, which is involved, ironical, and sometimes wickedly witty, but by his pretensions to culture. He was a man fitfully intelligent when he did not know he was thinking, a spottily skillful stylist when he was not aware he was writing artistically; but he lacked critical judgment completely (his notion of criticism was a hunt for boners in the Leatherstocking Tales), and was tormented by an urge toward self-parody that verged on self-punishment. He is, therefore, an embarrassment to admiring critics, who tend either to swallow whole his dishearteningly uneven achievement; or to admire him only for the bitter wisdom presumably concealed from the vulgar beneath the hilarious surfaces of his work. There are corresponding traps for dissenting critics, who may find Twain the beneficiary of a cult of native humor finally more deadly than the cult of museums which he exposed; or cry out that his "philosophe" is the product of a childish mind, and his dissembling of it for popularity's sake shameful.

To make of Twain either a cult or a case, however, is finally to lose the sense of him as a poet, the possessor of deep and special mythopoeic power, whose childhood was contemporaneous with a nation's; and who, remembering himself before the fall of puberty, remembered his country before the fall of the Civil War. The myth which Twain creates is a myth of childhood, rural, sexless, yet blessed in its natural Eden by the promise of innocent love, and troubled by the shadow of bloody death. The world in which his myth unfolds is one in which passion is less real than witchcraft, ghosts more common than adulterers; but it is also one in which a pure love between males, colored and white, triumphs over witches and ghosts and death itself. It is, of course, a world already dreamed in the fiction of Cooper and Poe, Dana and Melville, but never before labeled: "For Children Only!"

It is hard to say whether the fear of sex, a strange blindness to its manifestations, or the attenuation of sexuality itself drove the

American novel back over the lintel of puberty in the declining years of the nineteenth century. Twain himself seems to have believed that it was the last; in *1601,* he suggests, in the guise of a joke, that genitality itself had withered to the vanishing point in America: "Then spake ye damned wyndmill, Sir Walter, of a people in ye uttermost parts of America that copulate not until they be five-and-thirty years of age, ye women being eight-and-twenty, and doe it then but once in seven yeares." In the mouth of "ye damned wyndmill," this is spoken contemptuously, but in his own voice, Twain makes a similar assertion about the young people of his childhood community, with a certain amount of pride: *"Chastity.* There was the utmost liberty among young people—but no young girl was ever insulted, or seduced, or even scandalously gossiped about. Such things were not even dreamed of in a society, much less spoken of and referred to as possibilities."

The dream which Twain dreamed, at any rate, did not include such possibilities; and *his* memories of the past, at least, were duly expurgated, though just once in *Tom Sawyer* his censorship relaxes. For a single moment, we see Becky caught out peeking at the dirty picture in the teacher's anatomy book, and for that moment we are reminded of the living flesh beneath the pinafores and roundabouts. But it does not finally matter; since Twain will not let his protagonists over the borderline of adolescence, playing such games with their ages that the reader cannot tell from page to page whether they are barely out of kindergarten (in *Tom Sawyer,* Tom is just losing his baby teeth) or on the verge of manhood (in *Huckleberry Finn,* one summer later, Huck, Tom's apparent coeval, is fourteen). Yet Twain's dream of boyhood begins with a dream of love in a sexless world; and, indeed, the "Boy's Manuscript," which he wrote in 1870, and which is the seed of all the later books about Huck and Tom, is an account of a love affair between eight- or nine-year-olds—involving flirtation, jealousy, and reconciliation, though not, of course, passion.

Demoted year by year, love in the United States comes to sit at last in the kindergarten, final refuge of innocence. Yet for all its sexual purity, Tom's childhood world is intimately acquainted with death.

Violence is omnipresent, yet somehow is never considered to impugn innocence, so long as it does not involve concupiscence. The plan of Injun Joe in *Tom Sawyer* to take revenge on the Widow Douglas was apparently based on an actual case involving the threat of rape, which Twain bowdlerized to a mere slitting of the nostrils and notching of the ears—thus apparently making it suitable for child readers.

There is the sense everywhere in Twain that *violence doesn't count,* the muting of sensitivity which is always demanded by slapstick and the more brutal forms of farce; and it is this which the earliest review of *Huckleberry Finn* applauded as "a total absence of morbidness in the book," a proof that "the *mal du siècle* has not reached Arkansas." But this is scarcely the whole story; for concurrent with such acceptance of terror in Twain, is a guilt-ridden obsession with it, an inability to let it alone. Twain's attitude toward violence is finally as complicated, subtle, and deliberately ambiguous as his attitude toward sex is naïve, senti-mentalized, and hopelessly evasive. He is not only the creator of childhood idylls but a great poet of violence; and, indeed, his very humor depends upon a world in which there is neither a stable order nor civil peace.

His hope for order and peace he invested in the genteel Atlantic seaboard society into which he married, after years of drifting from job to job through West and East and South, looking for these qualities especially in his wife, whom he drafted as a superego, a living conscience. "I would . . . quit wearing socks if she thought them immoral," he said of his Livy. The society which had made him the untidy boor he always felt, he recalled as a world of violence and horror. Missouri he remembered as a slothful subfrontier, in which the fathers no longer had any authority, and the mothers sought in vain to assert certain simple-minded standards of piety and decorum. Certainly, his own father had died in Twain's childhood, crying despairingly, "Let me die!"; while his mother, in fact, had pleaded with him at the deathbed, "Only promise me to be a better boy. Promise not to break my heart."

Yet to Twain, Missouri was also a world of innocence and

freedom and joy, a world in which *he,* at least, had been innocent and free and joyous, a naked boy, swimming and fishing and smoking on Jackson's Island. To the idyllic era of his childhood, Twain's mature mind reverted over and over, only to discover there certain nightmare images of violence: the dead man he had discovered after breaking into his father's office; the vagabond shot down in the street and gasping for breath beneath the heavy Bible laid on his chest; the hellish storm that had broken the night Injun Joe died, and had left Twain whimpering for the salvation of his soul; the tramp who had burned himself to death in the local jail, setting himself on fire (perhaps!) with matches the boy Twain had smuggled to him. Each terror brought with it the shadow of guilt: he should not have been sneaking into his father's office after dark; he should have been good enough to regard the crash of thunder with equanimity; he should have protested against laying so heavy and pious a burden on a dying man's chest; he should not have passed contraband through the bars.

Twain began to feel after a while that he carried with him the infection of death out of the world he had left into the new world in which he sought peace. The death of his father, perhaps, and certainly that of his brother Henry (whom he pilloried later as Sid all the same), he felt as somehow his responsibility; but these at least belonged to the life he had led before meeting Livy. When his son died, however, after an act of carelessness on his part, his favorite daughter, Susy, while he was absent in Europe, "died where she had spent all her life till my crimes made her a pauper and an exile"; when his daughter Jean developed epilepsy, and his wife ailed, he was more than ever ridden by a guilt which he could not allay, except by trying to persuade himself that death was a final good. "She has found," he said of Susy, "the richest gift the world can offer." Yet the books in which he tried, toward the end of his own life, to express his dark despair are flat and unconvincing or shrill and sophomoric.

His most profoundly sad books are the most mad and idyllic, his wisest those he wrote dreaming, not thinking: dreaming the golden dream that threatens momentarily to turn into nightmare: and the wisest and saddest of them all, as it is also the craziest and most euphoric, is, of course, *Huckleberry Finn*. Indeed, to turn from *Huckleberry Finn* to the rest of Twain's work is disheartening; for there are only portions of other books which approach it; most of the first part of *Life on the Mississippi*, a good deal of *Pudd'nhead Wilson;* and to a lesser degree, *The Innocents Abroad, A Connecticut Yankee in King Arthur's Court, Tom Sawyer*. Beyond this, there is much that is merely occasional, even trivial; much that is without passion or point; much that is highfalutin' or absurdly noble; much that is terrifyingly unfunny and empty. After a while, the reader who has made the mistake of reading too much Twain begins to feel that even the books he has liked cannot possibly be as good as he has thought them; that what Twain has left behind is not so much a real *oeuvre* as a bag of tricks.

And then one reads *Huckleberry Finn* again, hears—intermittently at least—a voice which is neither Clemens' nor Twain's but genuinely Huck's, which is to say, not the voice of a genteel sentimentalist or a clown in full make-up, but of a boy-Ishmael: "the juvenile pariah of the village . . . idle, and lawless, and vulgar, and bad. . . ." The phrase is out of *Tom Sawyer,* of course, and it is with that earlier book that any discussion of *Huckleberry Finn* must begin; for it is Tom who discovers Huck and discovering him discovers also a great mythic theme. That theme succeeds in time in overwhelming the love story of Tom and Becky, which was the first inspiration of the book, and even thrusts aside the kind of genre picture ("Whitewashing the Fence" —the illustrator's dream!) which was its second. Of Tom Blankenship, the original of Huck, Twain writes in the *Autobiography:* "He was the only really independent person—boy or man—in the community . . ."; and in *Tom Sawyer,* adds that all the children "wished they dared be like him." The memory of "all the boy" Twain was or dreamed himself afterward is Tom; the memory of all he was not and only wished he dared aspire to be is Huck; and it is fitting that they be companions, the books named after each, sequels.

"Mark Twain's next book will bear the title of 'Huckleberry Finn, A Sequel to Tom Sawyer,' " a puff in *The Dial* for February,

1884, announced; but Twain was unwilling to depend on advertising alone to make his point. "You don't know about me," the first sentence of the new novel reads, "without you have read a book by the name of *The Adventures of Tom Sawyer.* . . ." And it is well, for once, to take Twain at his word, though there intervened between the publication of the first book (in 1876) and the second eight years, nearly seven of which Twain spent bogged down and unable to write a line, once his first impetus had taken him through the fifteenth chapter of the book as it presently stands. The point was, though it took Twain seven years to find it out, that his new book had ceased to be a continuation of the old, developing a much more complex relationship to it than that of a mere sequel.

Though *Huckleberry Finn* begins in the same idyllic summer of which *Tom Sawyer* had already consumed more than the normal number of weeks, and comes to a close in the following year, both boys have grown older by perhaps five or six years. And the author, too, has matured, is only *playing* now at producing an entertainment for children. If *Tom Sawyer* was always a boy's book, even when Twain thought he was writing for adults, *Huckleberry Finn* is on one of its levels at least, not merely an adult but a subversive novel.

The language of Huck is a function of Twain's understanding of his character and role, and varies in authenticity with the author's sense of what both he and his character are doing. In all three Tom Sawyer stories, Huck is Tom's Noble Savage, a sentimentalized id-figure representing the Good Bad Boy's dream of how bully life might be without parents, clothing, or school; and in those books, Huck is more condescended to than admired. In *Huckleberry Finn,* however, Huck does the condescending toward Tom, who represents his misguided ego-ideal, the embodiment of a "literary" style which he cannot really afford. When he is truest to himself, Huck respects, in the teeth of all he has been taught, Nigger Jim, which is to say, an even more ultimate id-figure; in his weaker moments, he joins Tom in relegating the surrogate for the instinctive life to the world of make-believe, which is also a prison.

In general, the two boys represent to each other the writer's conception of "experience" and the nonreader's conception of "art." It would be pleasant to say that they fuse finally into a single figure: but in Twain, and in American life as a whole, the two are notoriously disjoined: the artist and the naïf, the man who has made it and the man who never knew it was there to be made. It is all very well to tell us that Huck's original ended as "a good citizen and greatly respected." This, we know, is not true of the fictional Huck, who is finally lost to Tom and respectability alike, though in boyhood, Mark-Tom and Tom-Huck (surely, the inversion of the names is a deliberate joke!) were permitted to play hooky together; it is clear that once Mark-Tom decides to be good, to marry Livy, he will never again answer Tom-Huck's meow. Only in phantasy will he slide down the lightning rod again; but even his phantasy will end on a note of separation, not really belied by the desperate attempts, published and unpublished, to continue beyond *Huckleberry Finn* his childhood alliance with the village pariah.

If we think of the two books not as sequels but as alternative versions of the same themes, those themes will reveal themselves in their mythic significance. Stripped of incidental ornaments, *Tom Sawyer* and *Huckleberry Finn* are seen as the same dream dreamed twice over, the second time as nightmare; though the terror of the second dream is already at work in the first, whose euphoria persists strangely into the second. In both books, there is a pretended, quasi-ritual death to the community and its moral codes; though in *Tom Sawyer* that "death" is a lark, undertaken in childish pique, while in *Huckleberry Finn* it is a last desperate evasion, an act of self-defense. In both, there is a consequent spying on the community from cover to watch the effects of that death, the aftermath of regret: the childish dream of the suicide, who longs to be present at his own discovery, come true. In the one case, however, the spying is a prelude to a triumphant return, in the other, to further concealment.

In both, there is an escape to an island. But in one case, the natural Eden is a boys' paradise, from which one returns as from a picnic; in the other, it is an asylum not only from "sivilization" but from pursuit, enslavement, and death; and leaving it, the refugee plunges into further flight. The good companions, in the one case, are other boys, homesick almost from the start; in the other, the sole companion is a runaway slave, whose home is nowhere. In both, there is a night journey across the river back into the abandoned world of obligations and restraints, a scouting foray into what has become enemy country; but in the one case, the scouting prepares for a return, in the other, a more desperate withdrawal.

In both, the escapee and presumed ghost watches from a place of concealment (how much in both books is peeked at, witnessed, overheard!) a sentimental Pietà, the sorrow of the "mother" over her mischievous and presumably lost boy. But how different is Huck's witnessing of Aunt Sally's tears, which are not even shed for him, from Tom's watching Aunt Polly cry. Tom is already prepared for his reconciliation with the offended mother while Huck is already incubating his great refusal. In Tom's pocket all the time is the message, *"We ain't dead—we are only off being pirates";* while Huck is preparing inwardly for the moment when he will declare: "But I reckon I got to light out for the territory ahead of the rest, because Aunt Sally she's going to adopt me and civilize me, and I can't stand it."

In both books, there is a terrorized flight from a threatening Satanic figure, also outside of the community from which the boy-protagonist tries to escape in earnest or in play; and in each case, the outlaw figure represents a grotesque travesty of the boy himself, his innocence distorted into an image of guilt. Tom plays the robber, the pirate, which Injun Joe is in fact; Huck yearns in Widow Douglas' house for the life of ignorance and sloth, which his Pap actually lives. But in *Tom Sawyer,* the shadow of the protagonist is represented as utterly alien, a melodramatic half-breed out of a dime novel; in *Huckleberry Finn,* Huck's shadow is his own father: no creature of melodrama, but the town drunk—a vision of what he himself may well become!

In both books, the shadow figure controls or threatens a treasure which can be possessed in peace only after he has died; and in both, the plot involves a simultaneous revelation of that death and

the protagonist's deliverance: his coming for the first time or
again, into a fortune. In both cases, the death of the demonic
guardian of the hoard is rendered with special horror: Injun Joe at
the cave's stony sill, a broken case-knife in his hand and the
gnawed claws of bats beside him; Pap, naked and stabbed in the
back, in the floating house of death, its walls scribbled with
obscenities. But only in *Huckleberry Finn* is the full Oedipal
significance of their deaths revealed, the terrible secret that the
innocent treasure can be won only by destroying the Bad Father!

   In both books, there is a good angel, too, a redemptive *anima*
figure, contrasted with the threatening shadow. In *Tom Sawyer,*
that figure appears in the form of Becky Thatcher, juvenile version
of the snow maiden: "a lovely little blue-eyed creature with yellow
hair plaited in two long tails, white summer frock." She is called
Tom's "new angel," and, for all her peeping at the forbidden
picture in the teacher's book, will obviously grow up to be just
such a good woman as Twain himself married. Meanwhile, she
scarcely knows which she admires more in the Good Bad Boy
Tom, his badness ("Oh, you bad thing!"), which it will give her
pleasure to subdue, or his goodness ("Tom, how *could* you be so
noble!"), which she calls forth and will sustain. It is of marriage
with her that Tom dreams; for, as he explains to Huck, she is a
"girl" not a "gal"! But marriage, to Huck, means only domestic
strife and the abandonment of the world in which he is at home.
Wistfully and a little jealously, he remarks, "Only if you get
married I'll be more lonesomer than ever."

   Yet Huck has his good angel, too, appropriately enough as
black as Becky Thatcher is white: not a future good woman but a
runaway slave, who represents his aspiration toward a deeper level
of the primitive, even as Becky represents Tom's yearning for a
"higher" level of civilization. Miss Watson's Jim is the Becky
Thatcher of *Huckleberry Finn*. They cannot be present in the same
book; Jim does not appear in *Tom Sawyer;* and when he enters the
sequel she withdraws, making even her brief farewell bow under
the name of Bessie Thatcher. With Jim, of course, Huck does not
dream of any sexual relation, any more than Tom does with
Becky; nor does he think of their union in terms of a marriage. Yet

they pet and sustain each other in mutual love and trust; make on their raft an antifamily of two, with neither past nor future, only a transitory, perilous present of peace and joy.

Like Tom and Becky, Huck and Jim triumph over the petty pride that threatens to separate them in the midst of horror and pursuit, declare their affection without shame or fear of ridicule in the face of death; yet, like Tom and Becky, they seem to be already drifting apart after their moment of deliverance. For Huck and Jim, there is no possibility of a continuing love; Jim has a family, which will presumably claim him, and Huck must follow the centrifugal impulse which has made and will keep him the "only independent person . . . in the community." Moreover, he and Jim are separated not by the schoolyard code which forbids the fraternizing of boys and girls, but by the profound social gulf between black and white in ante-bellum Missouri. Huck knows that the talk of another lark involving Jim, the outing to the Indian Territory, will not really materialize. The prospect of "howling adventures amongst the Injuns" is merely another of Tom's artistic lies, a forecast as vain as his assurance in the earlier book that Huck will come and live with him after he and Becky are married.

Tom and Huck had, in fact, already stood alone at the close of both *Tom Sawyer* and *Huckleberry Finn;* for each book tries to end with a pact in which the Good Bad Boy and the juvenile pariah come to terms: the juvenile pariah agreeing to accept an adoptive mother, and the Good Bad Boy agreeing in return to accept the pariah into his world of make-believe—the robber gang or the expedition to the territory. Both the integration into the family and the playing of terror in the place of living it stand for a surrender of independence, since Tom, who thinks he wants to be like Huck, secretly wants Huck to be like him. In *Tom Sawyer,* the melancholy happy ending works; but *Huckleberry Finn,* which begins with the collapse of that first happy ending, closes with the hint it will not hold the second time either.

All of which means, finally, that *Huckleberry Finn* is a true book, *Tom Sawyer* only "mostly a true book" with "some stretchers," one of which is its ending. Huck can tell the truth about Tom, for though he lies by preference almost always, he *knows* when he is lying; but Tom is incapable of telling the truth about Huck, because he does not ever know when he is lying. From time to time, Huck sees quite clearly what Tom is like: "So then I judged that all that stuff was only just one of Tom Sawyer's lies. I reckoned he believed in the A-rabs and the elephants, but as for me I think different. It had all the marks of a Sunday-school." Toward the end of this book, however, when he has *become* Tom, Huck seems to lose this insight, and submits himself to the hoax of trying to steal Jim in fiction as he has already tried in fact; but at this point the book has become Tom's, not his.

By and large, it is possible to say that *Tom Sawyer* is a fable of lost boyhood written by Tom, while *Huckleberry Finn* is that same fable transcribed by Huck. Somewhat misleadingly, Tom's version does not appear in the first person, though Twain considered telling it that way. But its third-person narrative is finally even more right; for Tom is always an actor in a fiction of his own making. One of the chief functions of its style is to make the events it describes seem less real. The reality of the emotions it evokes is deliberately called into question by overwriting which verges on burlesque: "Life to him seemed hollow, and existence but a burden" or "He thought he loved her to distraction, he regarded his passion as adoration; and behold it was only a poor little innocent partiality." The characters described so solemnly are eight- and nine-year-old kids!

Toward the book as a whole, Twain adopts the same ironical tone, closing it with the words: "So endeth this chronicle. It being the history of a *boy,* it . . . could not go much further without becoming the history of a man." "So endeth this chronicle. . . ." It is at once a confession of falseness and an attempt to evade it, utterly different from the conclusion of *Huckleberry Finn:* "so there ain't nothing more to write about, and I am rotten glad of it. . . ." *Tom Sawyer* is the first of a long line of books intended to be read by a boy with his father looking over his shoulder, and thus to perpetuate for a new generation the legend of an older one. From it descends a tradition, which passes via Booth Tarkington to the creators of Henry Aldrich and the Good Bad Boys of contemporary comics: the praise of good-badness as the true Americanism.

Huckleberry Finn, however, is not the progenitor of anything, because it is written neither by Tom nor Mark Twain, but by the evoked Huckleberry himself, who makes it quite clear at the end that he intends to write no more: "and if I'd 'a' knowed what trouble it was to make a book I wouldn't 'a' tackled it, and ain't a-going to no more." Nor could Twain himself make him change his mind, though he tried to call him up over and over for an encore. Only once did Huck really possess his presumable author, speak through him in his authentic voice. In the book called by his name, Huckleberry Finn exists, dictates his own style, his own moral judgments, his own meanings, which neither Twain nor the reader has to understand to experience. Tom Sawyer notoriously enters the book before it is finished, not letting Huck speak for himself again until the very last pages; but though he can counterfeit Huck's style, he cannot make him live, only move woodenly through the howling farce—which reveals the poverty of Tom's values and imagination, and exposes the falsity of his role.

Tom Sawyer's imagination, whose compass spans only what is in Twain's everyday power, takes over at precisely the point where Huck's sense of reality can no longer function, where "life" yields to art, strategy to style. Though both are liars, Huck lies to stay alive, while Tom lies for the glory of it; the modest dream of Huck is survival, the less modest vision of Tom heroism. That is why *Tom Sawyer* is a book about glory, in which even Huck is persuaded to play ineptly a heroic role, while *Huckleberry Finn* is an account of staying alive, which Tom cannot be persuaded to take seriously. Even as the bullet enters him, crossing the border between his world of idyllic make-believe and the adult world of slaveholding reality, he is already planning to wear that bullet on a string around his neck, swagger with it down the main street of Hannibal.

✪

Hannibal and the Bones of Art

> . . . there ain't anything that is so interesting to look at as a
> place that a book has talked about.
>
> —Huckleberry Finn in *Tom Sawyer Abroad*

> I have yet to see more than one of the places in which he lived
> —including that most important of all, his boyhood village on the
> Mississippi River, Hannibal, Mo. But no doubt thousands of his
> readers feel exactly as I do: I feel that I have been in Hannibal.
> Not perhaps Hannibal as it is today, but Hannibal as it is forever.
>
> —W. T. Scott in the Providence *Journal,* 1952

It was a hot afternoon in mid-July (1959), when I took a cab
from the airport in Quincy, Illinois, to cover the twenty miles to
Hannibal, Missouri. The rural Illinois landscape, now no longer
quilted country far below me, seemed familiar; without the stone
walls or the occasional abruptness of New England, yet like New
England in its barns and farmhouses and its fields of brown-eyed
Susans and Queen Anne's lace. But then within half an hour we
came to the great river and sight of the town on the other side and
with, for me, a tremendous sense of adventure we crossed, so it
seemed, from Midwestern America to the South, from the present
to (as I supposed) the past, from a lifetime of anticipation to a
complex of two days' experience which was bewilderingly riddled
with both past and present. I longed for the sentimental surge of

---

Reprinted from *New Mexico Quarterly,* Vol. XXX, No. 4 (Winter 1960–
1961). Copyright © 1961 by The University of New Mexico Press.

feeling that I had been in Hannibal before, that in some blood-stirring way I "remembered" it. No, the two days were instead a kind of rambling amongst an archeology of toys, a blundering grasp to equate the everyday reality of streets and houses with the towering reality of art.

So I arrived at the town which Dixon Wecter called Mark Twain's "predestined great good place." One hundred and twenty years before, the Clemens family had moved there from the village of Florida, Missouri, where Mark was born. At the time of their moving he was four years old. For fourteen years he grew up there, acquiring the material of his most enduring work. After 1853 he returned only as a visitor—from his tramp printing days, from his gaudy years as a pilot, later from his Western mining and news-paper-writing adventures, but always on the move; and still later there were infrequent visits over the many years of his titanic fame, last of all as a white-haired man in 1902, eight years before his death. He was obsessed with his childhood. He mourned his exile from youth, out of it he assembled his finest fabrications. It is testimony to the world-altering changes of the nineteenth century that in so young a country the greatest of our writers should be also the most nostalgic.

I had planned my stay of two nights and days because I wanted the sense of *being there,* unhurried, loafing. This is not customary. That July afternoon, Hill Street, where the Clemens—or Tom Sawyer—house stands, was thronged with a continual replenish-ment of tourists; they parked their luggage-topped cars; they got out—fathers and mothers and children, everybody in shorts and cameras—and did the house and the Mark Twain Museum and the Becky Thatcher house across the street; they bought souvenirs, they took photographs, then they drove away: many, no doubt, two miles south to the Mark Twain Cave, but all of them in and out of town in a couple of hours. According to that excellent newspaper, the Hannibal *Chronicle,* which runs a daily box score, over fourteen hundred had registered at the Museum on the previous day. And so it goes all summer, the mass invasion of a little town of twenty thousand population.

The winter months must be quiet. But winter? There is no

winter in the St. Petersburg of *Tom Sawyer* and *Huckleberry Finn;* nor in the Dawson's Landing of *Pudd'nhead Wilson;* nor in the Hadleyburg that got corrupted. Whatever its names in literature, Hannibal drowses always in the summer sun athwart the river. Not until the last transformation does snow fall upon it, when it becomes the Austrian Eseldorf in *The Mysterious Stranger* and when we are deep in the winter of Mark Twain's discontent. And even then, we are told, the town "was a paradise for us boys." But how interesting it is that Hannibal in its own locale exists in the unsuccessful drafts of the *Stranger:* as though Mark Twain had to move the town from the idyllic pastures of his childhood before he could focus and perfect that bitter, final masterpiece of renunciation of all life's values excepting only death. As Mark Twain declared, *Tom Sawyer* is a hymn, and although it shares with *Huckleberry Finn* a God's plenty of fright and horror, of murder and mayhem, it nonetheless remains a preserve of amber in the summer sun. This is Hannibal as it is forever.

In a way it is there. I climbed Cardiff Hill—Holliday's Hill—at the north end of Main Street and sat for an hour on the ground at the foot of the lighthouse where I could look steeply down at the town and the river. This of course is the world of the boys' Robin Hood play and other adventures, and the edge of it, where I sat, the site of Widow Douglas' house. There are houses here and there, but the hill is fairly wooded still. A wild rabbit hopped past me, descendant of those that ran the forest when Sam Clemens rushed by in his shirttails. Nobody but myself came there that afternoon. There were the silence and the sense I wanted. I would have welcomed only a doodlebug—and a few young ghosts.

In the town, as abruptly below one as though at the foot of a long flight of stairs—as in fact it is: there are wooden steps built all the way up the hillside—the streets were crowded with traffic, the sidewalks with shoppers; it was any American town busy in its shirt sleeves on a hot afternoon. Nevertheless a size is recapturable from the past: only ten blocks or so south, Main Street comes abreast of Lovers' Leap, an even more sudden bluff than Cardiff Hill. Westward the town slopes uphill to more shops and a residential district, but this is no matter to the Twain enthusiast; *his* town is all there within a small compass by the river, all there within one lift of the eyes. Although a literary map of it has in many instances to note only "the site of" this and that vanished structure—Huck Finn's house, Joe Harper's, the jail where Muff Potter was held—this is the heartland.

Over toward Lovers' Leap, Bear Creek still runs into the Mississippi. Close by the foot of Cardiff, I could see the roof of the Clemens house. Of course, moving past it all as always, the broad, magnificent river, and out on the river the silent islands: Jackson's Island, and others, wooded, mysterious. It was unimportant—on Cardiff Hill—that the ascending whistles were not from steamboats but from the incessant shifting, siding, shunting, and bucking of freight trains on the tracks which now make a wide iron belt between the streets and the riverbank; it was even amusing that the only activity out on the simmering water that afternoon was one wildly swerving skier at the tail of a zippy motorboat off the Illinois shore. What seemed to happen was a rise of essence, from the river most powerfully, from the remainders of Tom Sawyer's village, that was held in a suspension of dream within a heat-misted, lovely stillness. And I think the hill itself was the compellent agent. So much there below had vanished, was altered, was buried beneath a century of paving. But on Cardiff Hill the trees smelled thickly of summer, caught the odors of the everlasting river; and here against my hands was the earth where boys race barefoot through an eternal summer.

There were a few comparable moments, the others having to do with darkness, one of them in the Mark Twain Cave.

I cannot care for caves, whether in Bermuda or Virginia or New Mexico or wherever. They are freaks, and freaks are not seriously interesting. No mere oddity is seriously interesting. (I am not forgetting that Mark Twain seemed incapable of recovering from a fascination with Siamese twins. But he was prone to a lifelong, Tom Sawyerish beguilement by anything weird in the line of medicine or invention, or just some natural outcropping of rock which resembled Napoleon. His era, after all, was also P. T. Barnum's.) Even to lovers of caves, the famous one in Hannibal cannot rate highly. It is unbeautiful. Its narrow passages of murky limestone open to no breath-taking palaces and towers. Its walls are smoky from the candles of the past and are scratched with uncounted names—among them Laura Hawkins (the original of Becky Thatcher) and Mark Twain's one grandchild, Nina Gabrilowitsch. No Sam Clemens.

But of course you have to go there. The interest of the cave is altogether literary, and that is vibrant enough. Along the electric-lighted, guided tour, half the "attractions" are blobs of limestone alleged to look like an ape, an Indian, an old man, Adam's footprint, and similar stupidities. Yet the cave is one of the stage sets of a great book and it has its authenticity. Here Tom and Becky were lost. Here (though filled in) was the dip where Tom reached to find a way out and saw Injun Joe. Here, that book aside, Sam Clemens and his chums played and hid and hollered, and many a generation of Hannibal youngsters after them. Simply—as Huck is made to say in that observation which alone demonstrates how literary a man, after all, Mark Twain was—it is "a place that a book has talked about."

The guide did an imaginative, fetching thing. In one of the wider passages, first warning us of his intent, he doused the electric lights, and our tourist group stood speechless in black darkness, utter darkness, unmitigated darkness. That is how it is to be lightless in an underground cave. And then the guide lit a candle, and we knew what it was like to be so faintly, so closely lighted by one candle in an underground cave. Specifically, in *that* cave. Pages in literature that we all knew and loved (I suppose) had been suddenly personified, ourselves—no less—within the drama. I wondered what stage director *manqué* first thought of intruding into the usually shallow world of tourism so deeply graceful a gesture as momentarily to bless it.

Outside the cave the land is unchanged. There too is a nearness with the past if you sight above the souvenir stand and the parked cars to the old entrance in the hillside and over it all the woods that so thickly range the sky. There is a quietness, as though it were the past.

One touches the limestone in the cave—touches the balustrade in the house at 206 Hill Street—because one has to. The determined chastity of our contemporary literary criticism, however admirable for scholarship and the classroom, cannot obviate the passionate concern of the common reader for the biographical associations of the authors he reveres.

The Clemens house has a pretty setting, for down the hill between it and Main Street other structures have been removed and the lot planted with a rose garden. The white-clapboarded house is such a little house, so frail and thin-walled, and inward-leaning, with its tiny el to the rear, that all-important el where Sam and his brother Henry slept—Henry doing the bulk of the sleeping, and Sam skinning out into the night. Mark Twain in 1902, like any old man returned to his childhood home, thought it astonishingly small and that, if he should return after ten years, it might by then have shrunk to a birdhouse. And indeed it seems a toy compared to the ornate monstrosity he created at Hartford, or his tall brick house on Fifth Avenue, or that last house of all, Stormfield, that spread so handsomely over a hillside in Connecticut.

The cat and the painkiller, the spilled sugar and the whack with the thimble, Aunt Polly and Joe Harper's mother tearfully talking by the bedside when they thought their boys were drowned in the river: these scenes throng in the head in the rooms of the little house. Here is the stage, but it is an empty stage: touching, if one imagines it to be so, and yet incomparably diminished beside what came from it.

Mark Twain himself is all around one in the museum, a stone building which serves also as entrance to the house. (The whole thing, by the way, is maintained by the City of Hannibal, is uncommercial, and thus has a memorial dignity. Souvenir sales go on at Becky Thatcher's house, opposite.) The museum contains a typical proportion of extraneous exhibits, era stuff; stills from various Twain movies which were better filed; a loan exhibit of Norman Rockwell's paintings for *Tom Sawyer* and *Huckleberry Finn* which are shallow shadows of the true depth of Mark Twain's prose. Nevertheless, and overwhelmingly, hundreds of priceless mementos: photographs, newspapers, letters; one of Mark's pipes, and his high-backed cane chair; a cast of his right hand, wrinkled, delicately tapered, not large; startlingly, a death mask of his baby son Langdon; a white jacket from one of those suits; his gray and scarlet Oxford gown which he flagrantly wore at his daughter Clara's wedding to Ossip Gabrilowitsch; the table he used at Quarry Farm while writing much of *Tom Sawyer;* his antique typewriter; the fantastic orchestrelle which he so expensively had lugged from New York to New Hampshire to Connecticut, and the three rolls of music which Albert Bigelow Paine played on the orchestrelle that last Christmas night at Stormfield while Mark at an upper window watched through lantern light in thickly falling snow his daughter Jean's body being taken away to Elmira.

Although it was for me a secondary question as I walked back and forth on Main Street or tried to find a patch of shade in the baking hot park by the river's edge, I found myself wondering what it is like to live in Hannibal. That is, what is it like to live always in the glare of a great memory? I had just spent a day in Springfield, Illinois, but despite the supreme greatness of Lincoln, with whom a visitor is bound to be preoccupied, a visitor is aware that Springfield is a big modern city with infinite preoccupations of its own. But Hannibal is a small town, looking like thousands of its size all over America. Yet it is known for one reason, mobbed by tourists for one reason; and besides the actual shrines it has a statue of Mark Twain in Riverview Park, a statue of Tom and Huck at the foot of Cardiff Hill; and there are the Tom Sawyer Movie Theater, the Mark Twain Produce Company, the Mark Twain Beauty Shop, the Mark Twain Hotel; the bridge linking its shore with Illinois is the Free Mark Twain Memorial Bridge, and the bridge sweeps west into Route 36/61, Mark Twain Avenue. I omit a few samples, but these are testimony enough that here is no ordinary city—it bears the scar of greatness, it has been everlastingly injured with immortality.

Maybe the inhabitants, if not sometimes bored by this or even resentful of it, can ignore it. Bankers, lawyers, newspapermen, teachers, shopkeepers and clerks, waitresses, housewives, gas station attendants have their own lives to lead. And the children— let's not forget—have theirs. And everybody looks like their own kind all over America. But to the visiting spy they dwell, all the same, in a special light; and when assembling Rotarians fill the hotel lobby right after twelve noon and they greet each other with "Good evening!" the visiting spy—no matter what *they* are thinking—thinks, "Ah, just as people do in the book."

The Mark Twain Hotel stamps its drinking glasses "America's Stratford-on-Avon." That is all right with me as far as hotel business is concerned. But the comparison is totally erroneous. The thing about Hannibal, to Mark Twain's readers, is that it is deeply involved in his work. There is no such association in Stratford, where one goes because Shakespeare was born and grew up there and after a life elsewhere returned, died, and is buried there. But Stratford is not the locale of his plays. Here in Hannibal, on the contrary, are the river and its islands, the woods and streets and alleyways and, even, three or four still-standing houses which figure in our greatest literature. (One should add, it is the only place in America that could get away with the comparison.)

Hannibal was for decades in my mind the place above all others in America that I wanted to see. At last to be there was a contentment, more vivid at moments (as on Cardiff Hill) than at others, but still a sort of completion: to touch the (substitute) whitewashed fence, the (I suppose original) doorways in the Clemens house, to walk its rooms.

I was not moved as I had expected to be.

Here was the town. It was not the village. Yet it contained artifacts, reminders, the very bones of art. Then that was it: the bones of art. A closet of some of the actual costumes, some of the actual props. But such actuality is not the play. I had walked head on into untheorized proof that the reality of art transcends the reality of everyday life. My two days, however beautiful, were vague shadows on the river water of the thing that had mattered: the thing of imagination. What else could cause the dimness I felt? I had been closer when I was not here. To be in Hannibal made for both a nearness and a new distance. Here change and emptiness puzzled me with interpenetrations of resemblance to what I had long known; this town has been used and it exists more powerfully elsewhere, on a higher dimension than here. So in a sense it cannot be here. It died into art. It is immortally alive in the one great good place capable of perpetual renewal.

I walked the streets again at night. There is so much night in *Tom Sawyer*. And the streets were quiet, the lamplight dim on the side streets such as Hill. On the corner of Hill Street and Main—across from the rose garden—is the Levering house which, with its elegance of Greek pilasters, little Sam Clemens thought the loveliest house he had ever seen. It is being restored now as an old-fashioned apothecary shop, such as occupied it when Sam was a boy. It is an important building, among our props: on that ground floor Uncle Sam Smarr breathed his last, shot down in the street outside just as it was all to be described years later when Colonel Sherburn shot down old Boggs in *Huckleberry Finn*. Upstairs the Clemenses, in their most impecunious straits, had lived for a while and Mark Twain's father died there and Sam witnessed through a keyhole a secret post-mortem; there he did his nightmarish sleepwalking and there by his father's coffin took his pledge to his mother to try to be a better boy. It is an important house.

Behind it is the tiny building which was John Clemens' law office. A short way above that, Becky Thatcher's house. I crossed the street to walk once more past the museum, past the little white-clapboarded house. Thus in real life do we settle for coffins, whether in the snow upon Stormfield or as tourists on a literary pilgrimage—touching the doorknob, touching the stone. The smell of the river dampened the night air on Hill Street. Off in the night a dog howled—I had seen many complacent mongrels, sleeping by day in shady doorways, under parked cars in the street: throwbacks to the town I had known since I was ten and used to feel I had been in. He howled, so far away as to sound lonesome. And then, somewhere toward the riverbank, just for a miraculous moment, a whippoorwill called. Those two haunted sounds of dog and bird so dread with fatal portent to Tom and Huck. Who's going to die?

✪

Mark Twain's Nom de Plume

In a letter of 1877 Mark Twain thus explained the origin of his pen name:

"Mark Twain" was the *nom de plume* of one Captain Isaiah Sellers, who used to write river news over it for the New Orleans *Picayune:* he died in 1863, and as he could no longer need that signature, I laid violent hands upon it without asking permission of the proprietor's remains. That is the history of the *nom de plume* I bear.[1]

By 1888 he said that he had given three thousand explanations of these "facts," which were among the few things he was sure of. Hence the story became established and has been generally accepted, though by Twain students with reservations, to this day.

The story is dubious. Paine remarks that "Captain Isaiah Sellers had used and dropped the name," but offers no support for that statement.[2] On the other hand, Ernest E. Leisy says:

I have examined the files of the New Orleans papers during the period when Clemens was a pilot on the Mississippi, but I find no evidence of anyone's using the sobriquet "Mark Twain."[3]

[1] Samuel L. Clemens to John A. McPherson, May 29, 1877, San Francisco *Daily Alta California,* June 9, 1877.

[2] Albert Bigelow Paine, *Mark Twain: A Biography* (New York, 1912), I, 222.

[3] "Mark Twain and Isaiah Sellers," *American Literature,* XIII (May 1942), 399.

This selection originally appeared in *American Literature,* Vol. 34, No. 1 (March 1962), pp. 1–7, and is reprinted with the permission of the author and Duke University Press.

Ivan Benson, who read Sellers' journal (from February, 1825, to November 22, 1862), concludes:

it is doubtful . . . that Captain Sellers ever used the nom de plume "Mark Twain." Neither the name "Mark Twain" nor a single reference to Samuel Clemens occurs in the log.[4]

Considering Sellers' humdrum Mississippi River data—which Sam Clemens burlesqued for the New Orleans *Crescent* over the name of "Sergeant Fathom" in 1859—and Benson's surmise that the captain was too inept a writer to produce news stories unassisted, the invention of an imaginative pen name seems unlikely. Benson also gives Sellers' vital statistics: October 5, 1803—March 6, 1864.[5] Mark Twain was using his pen name by February, 1863; therefore his explanation of its origin is wrong on one count and, in the light of testimony given above, probably wrong on the other.[6]

If the nom de plume did not derive from Sellers, how did it originate? A credible explanation comes from one of the publishers of the Eureka, Nevada, *Sentinel,* in 1877. "We knew Clemens in the early days," he said,

and know . . . how he came to be dubbed "Mark Twain." John Piper's saloon . . . used to be the grand rendezvous for all . . . Virginia City Bohemians. Piper conducted a cash business, and refused to keep any books. As a special favor . . . he would occasionally chalk down drinks to the boys on the wall back of the bar. Sam Clemens, when localizing for the *Enterprise,* always had an account with the balance against him. Clemens was by no means a Coal Oil Tommy, he drank for the pure . . . love of the ardent. Most of his drinking was conducted in singlehanded contests, but occasionally he would invite Dan De Quille, Charley Parker, Bob Lowery or Alf. Doten, never more than one of them . . . at a time, and whenever he did his invariable parting injunction was to "mark twain," meaning two chalk marks.

[4] Ivan Benson, *Mark Twain's Western Years* (Stanford, 1938), p. 81.
[5] *Ibid.,* p. 82.
[6] Henry Nash Smith and Frederick Anderson, eds., *Mark Twain of the Enterprise* (Berkeley, 1957), p. 47, cites a letter to the Virginia City *Territorial Enterprise* "on or about" January 31, 1863, as the earliest use yet discovered of the name "Mark Twain."

. . . in this way . . . he acquired the title which has since become famous wherever . . . English . . . is read or spoken.[7]

The *Sentinel* was published by A. Skillman and George W. Cassidy. The latter, a quondam resident of Washoe, was well enough known on the Comstock to merit an editorial welcome from *The Gold Hill Daily News* on his return from the Reese River diggings in 1863.[8] He could many times have seen and talked with Sam Clemens in John Piper's popular place, known as "Old Corner Saloon," at B and Union Streets, Virginia City. The Local of the *Enterprise,* labeled a conspicuous bohemian by his contemporaries, was almost certainly a frequent visitor there; so too were such cronies as Dan De Quille (William Wright), his best friend on the paper, and Alf Doten, another good friend of the Virginia City *Union.*

A variant of the Eureka *Sentinel's* story comes from the Nevada City, California, *Transcript,* February 22, 1866:

A Washoe genius thus explains the origin of the *nom de plume* "Mark Twain." "Wall now, d'ye see," says he, " 'Mark'—that is Sam, d'ye see—used to take his regular drinks at Johnny Doyle's. Well, 'Mark' that is Sam, d'ye see, used to run his face, bein' short of legal tenders. Well, 'Mark,' that is Sam, d'ye understand, always used to take two horns consecutive, one right after the other, and when he come in there and took them on tick, Johnny used to sing out to the barkeep, who carried a lump of chalk in his pocket and kept the

---

[7] Eureka, Nevada, *Sentinel,* May 8, 1877. The name "Coal Oil Tommy"—properly "Coal Oil Johnny"—came, according to one story, from John W. Steele, of Oil City, Pennsylvania. One of a large poor family, he was adopted when a young boy by wealthy neighbors named McClintock, who became more wealthy when they struck oil. After the death of the foster parents, Johnny set out with plenty of money, and in a year or so squandered about two million dollars in a prolonged spree: giving ten-thousand-dollar diamonds to favored ladies; leasing an entire hotel and footing all bills for everybody in it; organizing a minstrel troupe and outfitting each member with wardrobe, diamond ring, gold watch, and chain; bucking dealers at faro, at which he was said to have lost $50,000 in one night—all of these escapades accompanied by grand drinking bouts. When the money ran out, he got a job hauling barrels of oil at fifty cents a barrel.

[8] October 31, 1863. "Mr. G. W. Cassidy, formerly of Dutch Flat, made us a short call yesterday, and having just returned from Reese River . . . gave us some information. . . ."

score, 'mark twain,' whereupon the barkeep would score two drinks
to Sam's account—and so it was, d'ye see, that he come to be called
'Mark Twain.' "

Charles Collins' 1864–1865 *Mercantile Guide and Directory for
Virginia City, Gold Hill, Silver City and American City* lists John
E. Doyle as barkeeper in the Bank Exchange Saloon, Main Street,
Gold Hill. In J. Wells Kelly's *Second Directory of Nevada Territory, 1863,* a John Doyle appears as proprietor of Doyle's Saloon
on Main Street near River, Dayton. The restless Sam Clemens,
who was often in nearby Gold Hill—including the Bank Exchange—frequently visited other towns in the district. He could
have known either or both of these Johnny Doyles. The date of the
Transcript story is close enough to Twain's Nevada days to merit
consideration; the story suggests, also, that if he had begun the
custom of calling out "Mark twain"—in, say, Piper's place—
other barkeepers quickly caught on and saved him the trouble.

Contemporary evidence attests Mark Twain's stamina in a
rugged society that displayed little enthusiasm for temperance,
none for prohibition. When the famous Austin flour sack was
auctioned in Washoe towns for the benefit of the Sanitary Fund in
1864, the parade that accompanied it with band music, whoop and
halloo, and a carriage load of reporters, including Mark Twain,
invariably stopped before the principal saloon in every town, the
place being immediately jammed while the proprietor handed out
free drinks all around.[9] The Western code of the gentleman,
though it might make fun of the overpersistent toper, did not
ostracize him, and it condemned the insult of refusing to drink
with a man. As Mark Twain himself put it:

Etiquette varies according to one's surroundings. In the mining
camps of California, when a friend tenders you a "smile," or invites
you to take a "blister," vulgarly called a drink, it is etiquette to say:

[9] *The Gold Hill Daily News,* May 17, 1864, quipped: " 'Tone' was given
to the procession by the presence of Gov. Twain and his staff of bibulous
reporters, who came down in a free carriage, ostensibly for the purpose of
taking notes, but in reality in pursuit of free whiskey." Nevertheless Mark
Twain did not shirk his reportorial duty; he wrote two long, detailed stories
of the occasion for the *Enterprise* of May 17 and 18.

"Here's, hoping your dirt'll pan out gay." In Washoe, when you are requested to "put in a blast," or invited to take your "regular poison," etiquette admonishes you to touch glasses and say: "Here's, hoping you'll strike it rich on the lower level."[10]

Among numerous items illuminating vinous prowess, we have Mark Twain's own story of the riotous ten days—roof-walking antics and so forth—spent with Artemus Ward and other revelers in December, 1863. *The Gold Hill Daily News* reported on October 26, 1863, that

Mark Twain, Jim Hardy, Judge Leconey, See-Yup, and a lot of other Chinamen at Virginia, are having a series of "high old" drunks, making as an excuse for their debauchery, the presentation of "Stars" to Policemen.

Paine tells of Mark Twain and Alf Doten on the trail of a news story at Como, but not going after the story because every morning for three days Mark Twain led his partner into a brewery, where they stayed all day.[11] Over a year after he had left the West Coast for good, the Grass Valley, California, *Daily National* observed, September 7, 1869:

Mark Twain is writing a drama which will appear soon, entitled "One Night in Ten Bar-Rooms." No doubt it will have a successful run, as Mark understands that subject to a dot.

In the San Francisco *News-Letter* of February 19, 1870, that caustic contemporary, Ambrose Bierce, remarking upon the recent marriage of Mark Twain, not only contributed a comment on inebriety, but also underlined the barroom method of totting up drinks:

Mark Twain, who, whenever he has been long enough sober to permit an estimate, has been uniformly found to bear a spotless character, has got married. . . . Well, that genial spirit has passed away;

[10] Downieville, California, *Mountain Messenger*, September 28, 1867.
[11] See Paine, *Mark Twain: A Biography*, IV, Appendix C, II, 1599–1600. Perhaps this episode was responsible for an item in the Como *Sentinel* of June 4, 1864; it said that Como lager was "the best in the Territory, as we can prove by 'Mark Twain,' who has sat in the brewery and drank 'gallons and gallons' of it without arising from his seat."

that long, bright smile will no more greet the early bar-keeper, nor the old familiar "Chalk it down" delight his ear.

The nautical "Mark twain," said to have been sung out to and by bartenders, is plausible, considering that the former Mississippi pilot was not long off the river. Since he used sailors' lingo occasionally in his writing, probably he also spoke it.[12] According to Paine, when Sam Clemens arrived at the *Enterprise* office in September, 1862, after purportedly hiking some 135 dusty miles from Aurora, his first words were:

> My starboard leg seems to be unshipped. I'd like about one hundred yards of line; I think I am falling to pieces.[13]

Those words may be only the fanciful creation of Mark Twain's unreliable memory, evoked late in life for the benefit of his biographer, but they are true to the spirit of the ex-riverman in 1862. The river was in his blood then, and it was still there when, in 1864, he told John McComb that he had applied to Washington for an appointment as government pilot on the Mississippi, and had been accepted.[14] On February 13, 1866, the Virginia City *Union* announced his departure "for the East in a few days to pursue his old calling of piloting on the Mississippi river." In August of the same year he concluded, as he told a correspondent, that he was too old for piloting but was still interested in boats and, if younger, would go back to relearn the river.[15] Since the river had so prominent a place in his mind, a reasonable assumption is that river language flavored his talk as much as his writing, if not more.

[12] To mention a few examples of nautical terms in writing: two from *The Golden Era,* September 27, 1863, in "All About the Fashions," remark upon "a superb speckled foulard, with the stripes running fore and aft"; and in "The Lick House Ball" upon "a square pelerine of solferino *poil de chevre* amidships." In " 'Mark Twain' in the Metropolis," *The Golden Era,* June 26, 1864, he calls a circus performer the "charming, clipper-built Ella Zoyara."

[13] Paine, *Mark Twain: A Biography,* I, 205.

[14] Will M. Clemens, *Mark Twain: The Story of His Life and Work* (San Francisco, 1892), pp. 57–58.

[15] Samuel L. Clemens to "Bill," August 25, 1866, Mark Twain Papers, University of California, Berkeley.

On the basis of facts and inferences discussed here, the origin of the famous nom de plume in an atmosphere of bonhomie, redolent of malt and brandy, is more consistent than the Sellers story with Washoe ways, and with the life and character of the Western Mark Twain. Why did he industriously promulgate the Sellers version? Possibly because, never good at recalling facts, he somehow pulled this conglomerate out of the haze of memory and by frequent repetitions convinced himself; possibly because, in pursuit of affluence and respectability in New England, he was well aware that association with a saloon would be damaging in a region less tolerant than the Far West of barroom peccadilloes.

An analogous example of probable concern for propriety was his indignation over the resurrection, in 1906, of the Thomas Jefferson Snodgrass letters, written for the *Keokuk Post* in 1856–1857. When Thomas Rees of the *Illinois State Register* correctly identified the author and proposed to publish these letters, together with others written later for the Keokuk *Gate City,* Mark Twain blew up. He dictated a blistering condemnation of Rees, and denied having written any "literature" between 1859 and 1866. Professing not to remember the Snodgrass letters and wishing to suppress them, he nevertheless did not specifically repudiate them.[16] As Franklin R. Rogers observes, some of the spleen and confusion may have been the result of faulty memory, but reluctance to acknowledge the letters

must be attributed in part to his conscious desire to gloss over what he had come to consider the indiscretions of his youth.[17]

The barroom origin of his nom de plume could have been a more glaring indiscretion had Mark Twain not forestalled disclosure by putting his explanation firmly on record and sticking to it. It is significant that he readily produced the Sellers story when asked—if not three thousand times, as he said, yet a good many times, one of the last of multiple repetitions being in that 1906

---

[16] See "The Snodgrass Letters (September 10, 1906)," Bernard DeVoto, ed., *Mark Twain in Eruption* (New York, 1940), pp. 228–239.

[17] Franklin R. Rogers, ed., *The Pattern for Mark Twain's Roughing It. Letters from Nevada by Samuel and Orion Clemens, 1861–1862* (University of California English Studies 23; Berkeley, 1961), p. 2.

dictation—as if determined to fix it indelibly in the public mind as well as his own. Indicative of his tendency either to believe something that was not so or to gloss over is his remark in 1882: "I have not had a large experience in the matter of alcoholic drinks."[18] Western friends, Western newspapers, and the Mark Twain of Nevada tell a contrary tale.

Mr. Leisy's conjecture that the "Sergeant Fathom" of Sam Clemens' 1859 burlesque naturally suggested the other and racier sobriquet may be accepted if it be extended to include the originator's typically Twainian method of putting the name into circulation. A final surmise is that, for those Washoe barkeeps, he drawled it like a Mississippi leadsman: "M-a-r-k twain!"

[18] Samuel L. Clemens to A. Arthur Reade, March 14, 1882, A. Arthur Reade, ed., *Study and Stimulants* (Manchester, England, 1883), p. 120.

✪

The California Bull and the
Gracious Singers

In the summer of 1876, when Mark Twain plunged into the opening sequence of *Huckleberry Finn* while he was reading proof for *Tom Sawyer,* his conception of his role as a writer was in some ways even more ambiguous than it had been eight years earlier when he began composing *The Innocents Abroad.* He was still considered to be primarily a humorist, a disciple of Artemus Ward; yet he had also displayed a surprising ability to hold his own in the *Atlantic Monthly,* which Howells accurately characterized as "the most scrupulously cultivated of our periodicals."

Since its founding in 1857, the *Atlantic* had served as the principal organ for the literary culture of New England, and its best-known contributors—Emerson, Longfellow, Whittier, Holmes, Motley, Lowell—embodied for the general public the ideal of the man of letters. Such authors were regarded with a veneration now hardly conceivable. Rebecca Harding Davis said that when she first visited New England as "a young woman from the backwoods" (that is, West Virginia), she considered Emerson "the first of living men," "the modern Moses who had talked with

Reprinted by permission of the publishers from Henry Nash Smith, *Mark Twain: The Development of a Writer* (Cambridge, Mass.: Harvard University Press). Copyright, 1962, by the President and Fellows of Harvard College.

God apart and could interpret Him to us." "When I heard him coming into the parlor at the Wayside," she continued, "my body literally grew stiff and my tongue dry with awe." In a celebrated passage in his *Literary Friends and Acquaintance*, Howells recounts his similar pilgrimage from the backwoods of Ohio to Boston and Cambridge and Concord.

It was Howells, of course, who had brought Mark Twain into the *Atlantic*. Howells had been appointed to the staff of the magazine in 1865 because he seemed "alert to new developments in literature." An equally important qualification was his respect for the New England literary tradition. His dislike of tension and controversy led him to minimize the differences between old and new attitudes; throughout his long life he continued to venerate the famous writers of an earlier generation, especially Emerson. Yet he realized that they belonged to the past. His own interest in the novel was basically foreign to their world. His doctrine of "realism" in literature owed much to Emerson's ideas, but nothing to his practice. In the 1870's Howells knew better than most Americans that a new era in literature was beginning. He had persuaded the publishers of the *Atlantic*, for example, to offer Bret Harte the unprecedented sum of $10,000 for twelve contributions to the magazine. The investment had turned sour because Harte's work failed to live up to its earlier promise, but now Howells was backing another writer from California: Mark Twain. He had given favorable notices to *The Innocents Abroad* and *Roughing It* (and had been shocked as well as amused by Mark Twain's remark that when he saw the review of *Roughing It* he was "as uplifted and reassured by it as a mother who has given birth to a white baby when she was awfully afraid it was going to be a mulatto"). He had solicited contributions from Mark Twain for the *Atlantic*, and while he had rejected some inferior offerings, by the end of 1875 he had published eight or ten pieces, including "A True Story" and the seven installments of "Old Times on the Mississippi." He was putting Mark Twain up for election to the Academy at some risk to his own standing among New England intellectuals.

Because the *Atlantic* represented the apex of civilization and refinement, whereas the Far West stood for "barbarism," Mark Twain's relation to the magazine was to say the least problematical, both for him and for Howells. A hostile critic remarked icily in 1877 that Mark Twain's appearance in the *Atlantic* "was in the beginning considered an innovation." In 1874, when Mark Twain submitted the first installment of "Old Times on the Mississippi," Howells had welcomed it and asked for more, but he thought he detected "a sort of hurried and anxious air" in the prose as if the writer were under some constraint. "Don't write *at* any supposed Atlantic audience," he advised, "but yarn it off as if into my sympathetic ear." Although Mark Twain's reply may not have been entirely accurate, it underscored the special character both he and Howells ascribed to the readers of the magazine: "It isn't the Atlantic audience that distresses me; for *it* is *the* only audience that I sit down before in perfect serenity (for the simple reason that it don't require a 'humorist' to paint himself stripèd & stand on his head every fifteen minutes)."

This amounts to saying that as a contributor to the *Atlantic* he might hope to escape the label of humorist and be taken simply as a writer. But the assertion was oversanguine. A widely publicized incident involving his relation to the magazine three years later shows both Howells and Mark Twain taking his role of humorist for granted, with unhappy consequences. The furor arose over a speech delivered by Mark Twain at a dinner given by the publishers of the *Atlantic* to commemorate Whittier's seventieth birthday. The speech itself and the widespread discussion of it in the press provide an opportunity to examine in some detail Mark Twain's relation to the dominant culture a decade after he had achieved a national reputation.

The *Atlantic* dinner was held at seven o'clock on the evening of December 17, 1877, at the Brunswick Hotel in Boston. Fifty-eight men—contributors to the magazine and members of its staff—sat down to a feast on the heroic scale of our ancestors. At a quarter past ten o'clock the doors were opened, additional guests (including ladies) who had been waiting in the halls were admitted, and the speeches began. Henry O. Houghton, publisher of the magazine, made a short address of welcome and introduced Whittier as

guest of honor. Whittier excused himself from speaking and asked
Longfellow to read a sonnet composed by Whittier for the occa-
sion. Houghton then introduced Howells as toastmaster, and
Howells introduced Emerson, who "with much feeling" recited
Whittier's "Ichabod." After Howells had made a short speech,
Holmes read a new poem of his own and Charles Eliot Norton
responded gracefully to a toast to Lowell, who was absent as
Minister to Spain. Howells read several letters from guests unable
to be present. He then introduced Mark Twain in a fashion which
he later thought peculiarly ironic because it praised the speaker for
qualities conspicuously absent from the sketch he was about to
deliver:

> And now, gentlemen, I will not ask the good friend of us all, to
> whom I am about to turn, to help us to forget these absent fellow-con-
> tributors, but I think I may properly appeal for oblivion from our vain
> regrets at their absence to the humorist, whose name is known wherever
> our tongue is spoken, and who has, perhaps, done more kindness to
> our race, lifted from it more crushing care, rescued it from more
> gloom, and banished from it more wretchedness than all the profes-
> sional philanthropists that have live[d]; a humorist who never makes
> you blush to have enjoyed his joke; whose generous wit has no mean-
> ness in it, whose fun is never at the cost of anything honestly high or
> good, but comes from the soundest of hearts and the clearest of heads.
> Mr. Clemens, gentlemen, whom we all know as Mark Twain, will
> address you.

The uncharacteristically involved syntax of this introduction
suggests that Howells felt uneasy. It is true that he was by nature
shy and dreaded any kind of public appearance. But the uneasiness
here goes beyond his chronic dislike of making speeches. Perhaps
without fully realizing it, he was worried about what his protégé
might do, and was uttering a kind of secular prayer. Mark Twain
was being put under instruction not to shock the august company
by making fun of cherished ideals. Since the occasion was intended
to honor Whittier and, through him, the vocation of literature as
represented by the contributors to the *Atlantic,* Howells' admoni-
tion had an obvious reference to the role of the man of letters in
New England and therefore in American culture.

Mark Twain had recognized that the topic was inevitable. His carefully prepared speech, which Howells had not seen, was a little extravaganza exploiting the contrast between the literary life represented by Whittier and the other venerable figures at the head table, and that represented by Mark Twain in his role of the Wild Humorist of the Pacific Slope. We recall that this is the man who had confessed to Mrs. Fairbanks, "There is a fascination about meddling with forbidden things."

Mark Twain said in his speech that some years earlier, when he had just begun to acquire a local reputation as a writer on the Pacific Coast, he "started on an inspection-tramp through the Southern mines of California." Being "callow & conceited," he "resolved to try the virtue of [his] nom de plume."

I knocked at a miner's lonely log cabin in the foot-hills of the Sierras just at nightfall . . . A jaded, melancholy man of fifty, barefooted, opened to me. When he heard my nom de plume, he looked more dejected than before.

Nevertheless, the miner admitted his guest, and after a time explained his somber mood:

"You're the fourth—I'm a-going to move." "The fourth what?" said I. "The fourth littery man that's been here in twenty-four hours—I'm a-going to move." "You don't tell me!" said I; "who were the others?" "Mr. Longfellow, Mr. Emerson, & Mr. Oliver Wendell Holmes—dad fetch the lot!"

Further conversation reveals that "Mr. Emerson was a seedy little bit of a chap—red-headed. Mr. Holmes was fat as a balloon—he weighed as much as three hundred, & had double chins all the way down to his stomach. Mr. Longfellow was built like a prize fighter . . . They had been drinking—I could see that." The visitors are prolific in quotations, or misquotations, from the famous authors mentioned. "Holmes" inspects the cabin with disapproval, and exclaims: "Build thee more stately mansions,/O my Soul!" "Longfellow" begins to recite lines from *Hiawatha:*

> Honor be to Mudjekeewis!
> You shall hear how Pau-Puk-Kee-wis—

but the host breaks in with, "Begging your pardon, Mr. Longfellow, if you'll be so kind as to hold your yawp for about five
minutes, & let me get this grub ready, you'll do me proud." After
supper the intruders begin a game of euchre, with remarks adapted
from well-known poems. When "Emerson" does not like the hand
dealt him, for example, he says:

> They reckon ill who leave me out;
> They know not well the subtle ways
> I keep. I pass, & deal *again!*

Later he points at the host and says,

> Is yonder squalid peasant all
> That this proud nursery could breed?

And next morning when "Longfellow" leaves he steals the host's
boots, remarking:

> Lives of great men all remind us
> We can make our lives sublime;
> And departing, leave behind us
> Footprints on the sands of Time.

Mark Twain, in his capacity of straight character, hastens to
explain the deception to the miner: "Why my dear sir, *these* were
not the gracious singers to whom we & the world pay loving
reverence & homage: these were impostors." But as so often
happens in Mark Twain's anecdotes, the miner, the vernacular
character, turns the tables on his interlocutor: "Ah—impostors,
were they? are *you?*"

The basic impulse here is similar to that which would lead Mark
Twain two years later to link General Grant with the image of a
baby trying to put its toe in its mouth. He is reducing exalted
personages to a low status and is incidentally concocting a literary
burlesque of their work. He was almost certainly unaware of any
hostile feeling toward "the gracious singers" whom he joined the
world in honoring, but the speech goes far beyond the hint of
disrespect, quickly effaced, in the joke about Grant. It is clearly an
act of aggression against the three poets as representatives of the

sacerdotal cult of the man of letters. Mark Twain is quite sincere in his implied confession that he himself feels like an impostor in the role of a contributor to the *Atlantic* (just as he felt "like a barkeeper entering the Kingdom of Heaven" whenever he read Jane Austen). His very candor lends devastating force to the implication that the literary giants of New England may also somehow be fraudulent.

II

Mark Twain's unconscious antagonism toward the literary Titans caused him to feel uneasy while he was delivering his speech and alerted him to the faintest signs of disapproval from the audience. In reminiscences dictated many years later he said that the expression on his hearers' faces "turned to a sort of black frost. I wondered what the trouble was. I didn't know. I went on, but with difficulty . . . always hoping—but with a gradually perishing hope—that somebody would laugh, or that somebody would at least smile, but nobody did." Before he had finished, he recalled, the audience "seemed turned to stone with horror" at the affront to the revered poets who were seated at the head table. His recollection was that the next speaker was unable to utter more than a few sentences before he "slumped down in a limp and mushy pile," and the program "ended there. Nobody rose. The next man hadn't strength enough to get up, and everybody looked so dazed, so stupefied, paralyzed, it was impossible for anybody to do anything, or even try." Howells (in this version) could only lead away Mark Twain and his successor on the program, the young Wisconsin novelist W. S. Bishop, to suffer in the privacy of a hotel room.

Howells likewise recalled later that Mark Twain's speech was greeted with a "silence, weighing many tons to the square inch," which "deepened from moment to moment, and was broken only by the hysterical and blood-curdling laughter of a single guest, whose name shall not be handed down to infamy." Even after Mark Twain's death, Howells considered the speech to have been a "bewildering blunder," a "cruel catastrophe." He continued:

After the scope of the burlesque made itself clear, there was no one there, including the burlesquer himself, who was not smitten with a desolating dismay . . . Nobody knew whether to look at the speaker or down at his plate. I chose my plate as the least affliction, and so I do not know how Clemens looked, except when I stole a glance at him, and saw him standing solitary amid his appalled and appalling listeners, with his joke dead on his hands. From a first glance at the great three whom his jest had made its theme, I was aware of Longfellow sitting upright, and regarding the humorist with an air of pensive puzzle, of Holmes busily writing on his menu, with a well-feigned effect of pre-occupation, and of Emerson, holding his elbows, and listening with a sort of Jovian oblivion of this nether world in that lapse of memory which saved him in those later years from so much bother. Clemens must have dragged his joke to the climax and left it there, but I cannot say this from any sense of the fact. Of what happened afterward at the table . . . I have no longer the least remembrance. I next remember being in a room of the hotel, where Clemens was not to sleep, but to toss in despair, and Charles Dudley Warner's saying, in the gloom, "Well, Mark, *you're* a funny fellow."

Accounts published in Boston newspapers next day show that Mark Twain and Howells had simply invented the notion of a public scandal. Many in the audience laughed at the speech, although some doubtless did not. Howells was correct in saying that Emerson paid little attention to it. Although Whittier, Long-fellow, and Holmes may have felt uncomfortable, they seemed to observers in the room to be politely amused. The program was not interrupted, but continued under Howell's direction along its prearranged course for an hour or more after Mark Twain's speech. The gloomy retreat and private condolences of Mark Twain, Howells, Bishop, and Warner came only at the end of the program, toward one o'clock, when the party broke up.

It may be conjectured that Mark Twain was upset because delivering his speech in the presence of the three poets who are mentioned in it made him aware, for a moment, of his latent hostility toward these representatives of literature as a New England institution. Howells, not protected by Mark Twain's psychic censor, no doubt perceived the aggression even more clearly. And one cannot resist the idea that in some degree he shared it.

Despite the fact that Boston sophistication had put a good face on the incident, and at least one qualified reader of the speech in the papers (Francis J. Child) had found it delightful, Mark Twain and Howells knew that some buried force in the humorist had broken from control. He wrote Howells afterward that he must have been insane when he wrote the speech "& saw no harm in it, no disrespect toward those men whom I reverenced so much." Howells, apologizing for him to Charles Eliot Norton, wrote: "before he had fairly touched his point, he felt the awfulness of what he was doing, but was fatally helpless to stop. He was completely crushed by it, and though it killed the joy of the time for me, I pitied him; for he *has* a good and reverent nature for good things, and his performance was like an effect of demoniacal possession." The abject letter of apology Mark Twain wrote to his three victims ten days later, when Howells had given permission, emphasizes the divorce between conscious and unconscious motives. He interprets his behavior in highly moralistic terms, calling himself a savage by nature with imperfect control over his base impulses, yet innocent of intent to do wrong:

Hartford, Thursday, 27th [December 1877]

To Mr. Emerson, Mr. Longfellow, & Dr. Holmes:
Gentlemen: I come before you, now, with the mien & posture of the guilty—not to excuse, gloss, or extenuate, but only to offer my repentance. If a man with a fine nature had done that thing which I did, it would have been a crime—because all his senses would have warned him against it beforehand; but I did it innocently & unwarned. I did it as innocently as I ever did anything. You will think it is incredible; but it is true, & Mr. Howells will confirm my words. He does not know how it *can* be true, & neither does any one who is incapable of trespassing as I did; yet he knows it *is* true. But when I perceived what it was that I had done, I felt as real a sorrow & suffered as sharp a mortification as if I had done it with a guilty intent. This continues. That the impulse was innocent, brings no abatement. As to my wife's distress, it is not to be measured; for she is of finer stuff than I; & yours were sacred names to her. We do not talk about this misfortune—it *scorches;* so we only think—and think.
I will end, now. I *had* to write you, for the easement of it, even

though the doing it might maybe be a further offense. But I do not ask you to forgive what I did that night, for it is not forgivable; I simply had it at heart to ask you to believe that I am only heedlessly a savage, not premeditatedly; & that I am under as severe punishment as even you could adjudge to me if you were required to appoint my penalty. I do not ask you to say one word in answer to this; it is not needful, & would of course be distasteful & difficult. I beg you to consider that in letting me unbosom myself you will do me an act of grace that will be sufficient in itself. I wanted to write such a letter as this, that next morning in Boston, but one of wiser judgment advised against it, & said Wait.

　　With great & sincere respect

I am

Truly Yours

Sam^L L. Clemens

　　There is no reason to doubt the candor of this painful letter. Mark Twain had indeed been a victim of demonic possession. His unconscious had uttered a truth under the guise of burlesque that was much more frightening to him than to the targets of his derision, for he was obscurely aware of his own guilt, whereas they were protected by their self-confidence and by the public image of them against having to recognize the truth of what the impudent demon proclaimed. Mark Twain was not consciously prepared to repudiate the conception of literature represented by Emerson and Longfellow and Holmes; but he had a half-suppressed awareness that the role assigned to them by the official culture was false and sterile. It was the violent conflict between conscious and unconscious allegiances that made him—and also Howells—suffer so much over what Howells called the "hideous mistake" of his friend.

III

Emerson, Longfellow, and Holmes were too old and too secure to be very much concerned that American culture had shifted out from under them. But the newspaper-reading public was intensely interested in the crisis of values that the Whittier birthday dinner revealed. Mark Twain's speech was published in full (along with other speeches delivered at the dinner) not only in Boston but in

Chicago and probably elsewhere. Within a day or two hostile criticism began to appear in the press—mainly, it should be noted, outside Boston: the geographical distribution of attacks on Mark Twain suggests that conventional assumptions had a stronger hold on what would now be called middlebrow readers in the hinterland than on Boston highbrows. The Worcester *Gazette* made up its mind at once. On December 18 this paper said in an editorial that has already been quoted in part:

Mark Twain made a speech at the Atlantic dinner, last night, which was in bad taste. We refer to it, because Mark's sense of propriety needs development, and it is not his first offence. He told a story in which Messrs. Longfellow, Emerson and Holmes were represented as crowding their society upon a California miner, guzzling his whiskey and cheating him at cards. It was, of course, meant to be a piece of incongruous absurdity, and although the idea was not at all original, it might have seemed funny in some circles, when told with Mark's drawl, but men who have attained the years and fame of Longfellow and Emerson are entitled to some degree of respect amongst a company of their friends. The offence is easier to feel than describe, but it is one which if repeated would cost Mark Twain his place among the contributors to the Atlantic Monthly, where indeed his appearance was in the beginning considered an innovation.

On the same day the Boston *Transcript* said that although there might be a difference of opinion concerning the good taste of the speech, "There was no mistaking the hearty fun elicited by the droll attitude in which these literary lights were represented. They appreciated the joke, as will the public who read, and laugh while they read." But by December 19 this paper had had second thoughts about the occasion, and reported: "The general verdict seems to be that Mark Twain's speech, though witty and well worked-up, was in bad taste and entirely out of place. As one critic puts it, 'if the three gentlemen named in his remarks had been entertained in New York, and a speaker had said what Twain did, Boston would have felt insulted.'"

Nevertheless, the Boston papers were not inclined to participate in the continuing criticism of the speech which some papers in other cities kept alive for a couple of weeks. The Boston *Post* on

December 20 carried a benign pun: "It would have been hard to make a Whittier speech than that of Mark Twain's," and the *Globe* of December 26 reported with some detachment: "the Western papers have just begun to write up the Whittier dinner, and abuse Mark Twain with great unanimity. The Nevada journals have not yet spoken on the subject, but something racy may be looked for in that quarter." "Western" here clearly means Middle Western, and the *Globe* seems to look forward with pleasure to a Far Western counterattack. Unfortunately, the Nevada and California papers did not rise to the occasion. But the Middle West, like inland Massachusetts, did indeed take a stern view of Mark Twain's offense. The *Globe* reprinted by way of documentation a homily from the Cincinnati *Commercial:*

MARK TWAIN'S OFFENCE AGAINST GOOD TASTE

If amazement did not sit on each brow in that assemblage as Mr. Twain went on with his extraordinary narrative, it was because courtesy restrained its expression. It would have read queer enough as a humorous sketch, but delivered, as it was, in the august presence of the men in whose lives there is nothing to suggest such an adventure in the remotest manner, it must have excited far other than humorous emotions . . . Mr. Twain may have . . . thought that by bringing these poets and philosophers, whose lives have been passed amid books, in college cloisters, and in refined society, into intimate relations with whisky, cards, bowie-knives and larceny, he was doing an irresistibly funny thing, that would set the table into a roar and wrinkle a continent with laughter. It was a mistake, however. On the contrary, Mr. Twain has been scored for his exceedingly bad taste, and there is a disposition to deal anything but tenderly with him. It is assumed that he ought to have known better; that even with his innocent desire to enliven the proceedings with something humorously quaint, and mix it with quotations from the respective writings of the poets, the instincts of a gentleman would have forbidden its presentation in a character-sketch so coarse and absurd in every incident. It will require a good deal of ingenuity on the part of the humorist to extricate himself gracefully from the predicament in which he is involved, and soften away the painful sensations that followed his unique performance.

A correspondent of the Chicago *Tribune* wrote from Boston a few days after the speech that although it was "funny in its way," he was appalled at the thought of "making Mr. Emerson, even in travesty, stand for such a vulgar little scamp, and Holmes and Longfellow in such a guise." He could not believe they had enjoyed it even though "Of course they had to laugh." The speech, he admitted, was "very Mark-Twainish; but how he ever made up his face, as the children say, to stand up there and poke his fun at those beautiful, austere old men, is a mystery." On December 26 the *Tribune* implied its support of the hostile critics by reprinting on the editorial page a brief but supercilious article from an unidentified exchange. The reminder that Mark Twain was after all only a jester, and should know his place, must have been especially galling to the unfortunate speaker.

MARK TWAIN has been considered very clever at a *post-prandial* speech, and we recall one or two that were worthy of his reputation as a humorist. If it was his intention on this occasion to say something that would not really be humorous, but sensational, he succeeded, possibly beyond his own anticipation. The effect is not probably what he intended it should be. Boston does not take it kindly, and is as cold as its sharpest winter's day, because of the irreverence of the mad wag. Even a King's jester should know when it will do to shake his cap and bells in the royal presence.

The most rancorous criticism of the speech, however, came from the Springfield (Massachusetts) *Republican.* In a full report of the dinner, on December 19 the *Republican,* after mentioning the remarks of Whittier and Longfellow, said: "Of the other speeches, Mark Twain's was the longest—too long if it had been good; and it was not good, it was vulgar." The *Republican* was displeased by other aspects of the program—it objected for example to Emerson's choice of "Ichabod," which as the "dirge of a great fame" might have led the audience to speculate concerning putative moral lapses of Whittier—but it returned relentlessly to the nuisance committed by Mark Twain:

What would we not have given to watch the Boston and Cambridge men, as they drank in the high-flavored Nevada delirium tremens of

Mark Twain! How exquisitely adapted to the company was this fable of Longfellow and Emerson and Holmes, repeating their own and others' verses, with an accompaniment of hot whisky in a tipsy miner's cabin! It must have been very much as if the Nevada beverage itself had been slyly substituted in their glasses for the delicate wines that should have been there, and they had quaffed it unaware of the change.

On December 24 the paper was still insisting on the heinousness of the speech, which

has doubtless excited more attention than any other feature of the feast. People feel about it as they do about a fly in amber,—

> "The thing, we know, is neither rich nor rare,
> But wonder how the devil it got there."

And on December 27 the *Republican* delivered a long and explicit lecture to Mark Twain in an unsigned letter to the editor. The document throws so much light on the canons of taste and morals Mark Twain was felt to have violated that it warrants full quotation:

MARK TWAIN'S MISTAKE AT THE WHITTIER DINNER

To the Editor of The Republican:—

No one caring in the least for the "fitness of things" can read without a sense of pain the words of "Mark Twain" at the late Atlantic-Whittier dinner. Imagine the scene, the really brilliant company, bright in the best sense of that suggestive word—"shedding much light, opposed to dark," as Webster has it—gathered to celebrate with sober joy and good cheer the 70th anniversary of a man of the most singular delicacy and refinement, combined with a strength, simplicity and sturdiness not always found with so much gentleness! Fit combination of events, the celebration of the progress of a life, which has had for its object the making of to-morrow better than today; and the speeding of an enterprise, which having passed its teens, looks forward to an earnest, ever broadening life. Gathered about the charming board with the gentle poet and the friend whose skill and enterprise enable them to sing to the whole round world, we see him who thinks that "life is not an empty dream," but that it holds high and holy, bright and gladsome things, of which he who has clean hands and a pure heart may taste. Beside him sits the philosopher who has dug deep and brought to light much that makes us think and hope, even if the mines *have* encroached on what are sometimes considered pre-empted claims. Then, also, if wit and fun were wanted, and keen thrusts at sham and pretense, accompanied with a sincere reverence for the beautiful and true, he who sits at the left is able and willing, and there are two others, who, were quiet, delicately delicious humor cared for, could bring it forth. Into this China shop bursts a wild Californian bull. True gentlemen bear insult in silence, and let such things dash on to their own destruction. But there is food for reflection in the incident. The songs, the literature, the wit and humor of a land tell tales, and when a bright, clever man, who does possess genuine humor, and has really discovered a new and curious vein, instead of fitting it to something that will amuse and relax the mind, without polluting it, finds his greatest glory in embellishing with his gift the low, poor, weak parts of our nature, and dressing in the garb of bar-room habitues the men who stand at the other end of life,—is it not well to inquire whether the popularity of this man ought not to have already reached a climax? Literary men in America, where so much is tolerated, ought to aim higher than the gutter, no matter what they have of talent, or even genius. American social life, upon which, by God's aid, must be built the mighty fabric of the future state, is in the formative period, and, jealous as we might have been of our political honor, a thousand times more jealous must we be of that most precious possession—reverence for that which is truly high. According to England's laureate, the good things of time are ours:—

"To shape and use; arise and fly
The reeling Faun, the sensual feast!
Move upward, working out the beast,
And let the ape and tiger die!"

Springfield, December 19, 1877.

IV

This effusion contains a number of ideas—or more properly speaking, prejudices and stock responses—that deserve notice, for they belong to the system of values that had been dominant in American society for a half-century and more. The focus of the letter is the moralistic-didactic conception of literature fittingly indicated by allusions to "A Psalm of Life" and *In Memoriam*. Mark Twain has polluted the minds of his readers by "embellish-

ing with his gift the low, poor, weak parts of our nature"—that is,
the animal impulses in conflict with ideality. The specific offense
seems to consist in linking revered men of letters with the coarse
manners and customs of a Western mining camp. This shows that
the humorist is deficient in "reverence for that which is truly high."
Since the poets were guardians of the ideal, to belittle them was to
weaken the only force that could subdue the beast in man.

Thus we are brought back to the necessity for reverence. As the
reviews of *The Innocents Abroad* had demonstrated, conservative
spokesmen considered this the central issue. Josiah G. Holland,
for example, had written in 1861:

> Nothing is more apparent in American character and American life
> than a growing lack of reverence . . . The parent may be loved, but he
> is much less revered than in the olden time . . . In politics, it is the
> habit to speak in light and disrespectful terms of those whose experi-
> ence gives them the right to counsel and command . . . We nickname
> our Presidents; and "old Buck" and "old Abe" are spoken of as
> familiarly as if they were a pair of old oxen we were in the habit of
> driving . . . What we call "Young America" is made up of about
> equal parts of irreverence, conceit, and that popular moral quality
> familiarly known as "brass."

Holland's contribution to the Whittier dinner had dwelt on the
same theme. Unable to come up from New York, where he was
now editor of *Scribner's Monthly,* Holland sent a letter that
Howells read aloud shortly before he introduced Mark Twain:

> I wonder if these old poets of ours—Mr. Dana, Mr. Bryant, Mr.
> Emerson, Mr. Longfellow and Mr. Whittier—appreciate the benefit
> they confer upon their fellow citizens by simply consenting to live
> among them as old men? Do they know how they help to save the
> American nation from the total wreck and destruction of the sentiment
> of reverence? Why, if they will only live and move and have their being
> among us from seventy years of age to 100, and consent to be loved
> and venerated, and worshipped and petted, they will be the most use-
> ful men we have in the development of the better elements in the
> American character . . . The influence which these beloved and ven-
> erated poets exercise upon the public mind and character, simply by
> being lovely and venerable, is, in the highest and sweetest degree, salu-

tary and salvatory. May heaven bless them and spare them all to us these many, many years.

Holland was saying substantially the same thing he had been saying sixteen years earlier; and Mark Twain's critics in general had not really changed their tune since the publication of *The Innocents Abroad*. Then they had been made uneasy by his treatment of historical monuments, especially those with Biblical associations; now they were defending the ideal of the man of letters. The weakening of the underpinnings of religious orthodoxy had led defenders of tradition to exalt poets to the status of surrogate priests, commanding (in Howells' phrase) a "species of religious veneration," and to assign to literature the function of holding institutions in place.

As Howells had implied in his introduction of Mark Twain at the Whittier dinner, reverence was ordinarily taken to be incompatible with humor. Most people who prided themselves on having a cultivated taste considered vernacular humor to be vulgar, if indeed not actually immoral. James Russell Lowell, in the introduction to the second series of *Biglow Papers* (1867), was careful to explain that he had written in a comic dialect only for the sake of reaching a wider audience with antislavery and Union sentiments:

> If I put on the cap and bells and made myself one of the court-fools of King Demos, it was less to make his majesty laugh than to win a passage to his royal ears for certain serious things which I had deeply at heart. I say this because there is no imputation that could be more galling to any man's self-respect than that of being a mere jester.

Edmund Clarence Stedman, writing to Bayard Taylor in 1873, blamed the *"horrible* degeneracy in public taste" in the United States on such humorists as John Hay (in his *Pike County Ballads*), Bret Harte, Josh Billings, and "the Danbury *News* Man." The tendency to look down on humorists was if anything even more pronounced in the South. A biographer of Johnson J. Hooper (creator of Simon Suggs) wrote in 1872:

> His ambition had been . . . to enjoy the respect of men; but he had unfortunately obtained a reputation [that is, that of being a humorist]

which cut off all such hopes. It was an evil day to his fortunes and to his happiness when he embarked in that class of literature, or otherwise became a *chronic* story-teller for his companions.

In 1888, when Matthew Arnold cited "the addiction to 'the funny man' " as one of the principal forces making against "distinction" in the United States, and a prime illustration of the American lack of "the discipline of awe and respect," he was merely repeating what had been a conventional opinion in this country for decades.

V

By the 1870's the system of values implied in the cult of ideality was rapidly losing the authority it had exercised in the decades before the Civil War. The changes brought about by the rise of previously submerged segments of the population to political and economic power during the nineteenth century seemed to men like Holland and Stedman sheer barbarism. Looking back from the vantage point of the present, we can see that the disintegration of the traditional culture was part of a transition that would lead to the formation of a new system of values and a new literary mode in the twentieth century. Cultural history is a procession of such transitions, but only in retrospect do the outlines become clear. The articulate spokesmen for American culture, the writers and editors in control of the leading magazines and publishing houses, were unable to comprehend what was happening because they were committed to the preservation of a complex institutional structure and the body of assumptions supporting it. They thought of themselves as the garrison of a beleaguered citadel and, being on the defensive, tended to find all kinds of novelty threatening.

One can sympathize with their attitude because so much of the emergent popular culture was merely a vulgarization of the high culture of the past. The germs of a new system of values and a new literature were buried in the debris. It is difficult even now to discriminate between the vital crudity of fresh insights and the sterile crudity of traditional attitudes degraded into clichés and stereotypes. Nevertheless, Mark Twain's place in American cultural history cannot be properly understood unless we are prepared to make distinctions that could not be made by either his critics or his defenders in his own lifetime. Both the best and the worst of his work derived from the popular culture—the tastes and assumptions of the "average practical American public" which Howells said must be his final court of appeal. In an often-quoted letter to Andrew Lang protesting against British attacks on *A Connecticut Yankee in King Arthur's Court* Mark Twain claimed that he had never addressed himself to "the cultivated classes," "the thin top crust of humanity," but only to "the mighty mass of the uncultivated who are underneath." He deliberately placed his work among the kinds of art dear to the mass audience: "cheap terra cotta groups" like those of the sculptor John Rogers, gaudy chromolithographs, "the hurdy-gurdy and the villagers' singing-society," the poems of Riley and Kipling.

In the domain of prose—although Mark Twain interestingly enough mentions no examples of work he considers comparable to his own—such a list would include two quite different types of writing: on the one hand, native humor; on the other, theatrical melodramas and the "sensation fiction" purveyed by the weekly story papers that during the 1850's and 1860's attained the first mass circulations in American publishing history. To mention these genres is to demonstrate that the popular culture embraced violent contrasts. Sensation novels were a hybrid of sentimental and Gothic conventions. So far from challenging the cult of ideality, they carried refinement to the point of unconscious caricature. They were emptily grandiose imitations of the silver-fork manner of Disraeli and Bulwer-Lytton or the medieval glamour of Scott. As we have seen, Mark Twain enjoyed burlesquing this kind of thing. Representative examples are the Legend of Count Luigi in *The Innocents Abroad* and the chapter on *The Weekly Occidental* in *Roughing It,* which contains thumbnail burlesques of half a dozen types of the sensation novel. Yet at the same time he could use characters and situations from popular fiction and drama with perfect seriousness, and his experience in writing literary burlesques provided him with structural patterns for *Tom Sawyer, The Prince and the Pauper,* and later books, including *Huckleberry Finn.*

The mass audience itself had an ambiguous attitude toward boiler-plate drama and fiction. When Fred G. Maeder's play *Buffalo Bill, the King of Bordermen* (based on a serial by Ned Buntline in the *New York Weekly*) began its successful run at the Bowery Theater in New York in 1872, a burlesque was rushed into production as a matter of course at Hooley's Opera House in Brooklyn under the title *Bill Buffalo, with His Great Buffalo Bull*. The two plays were presumably aimed at an identical clientele. Straight melodrama and burlesque could appear side by side in the same work, as in James J. McCloskey's *Across the Continent* (1870), which held the boards for ten seasons. At the other end of the spectrum the taste for sensation fiction was not confined to the semiliterate. The story papers had at least a few cultivated readers. In the 1860's Edward Everett found members of his own social circle reading the *New York Ledger,* chief of the story papers; and Spencer Baird, the paleontologist of the Smithsonian Institution, declared that *"Ledger* day" was "an epoch in his family." He added that although he received "over a hundred periodicals a week, the *Ledger* is the only one that would be really missed." For years during the 1860's Henry Ward Beecher conducted a regular column in the *Ledger;* and his novel *Norwood,* combining didactic conversations with a sensational plot, was serialized in the paper in 1867. (He received for it the enormous sum of $30,000.)

The significance of American humor was difficult for the critics to grasp because it seemed to appeal to exactly the same audience as sensation fiction and melodrama. During the 1860's and 1870's most of the story papers, following the lead of the *Ledger,* began to publish the work of humorists such as Josh Billings, and some carried a regular section devoted to humor. The bizarre consequences of this practice are illustrated by the fact that Mark Twain's anecdote about Mother Utterback was reprinted in the same issue of the San Francisco *Golden Era* that carried the first installment of a preposterously genteel novel by Mary Braddon, editor of the London magazine *Belgravia*.

A mass audience that responded to both Miss Braddon and Mark Twain must have been confused in its tastes. Its aspiration to rise in the social scale was apparently gratified by the exaggerated ideality of characters, settings, and style in sensation fiction. Yet it did not have a traditional commitment to the cult of gentility; most members of it had received only a few years of schooling and were still close to their nonliterate rural origins. They could therefore respond with pleasure, if a little guiltily, to the coarse but fresh and vigorous work of the humorists—which they took to be entirely distinct from literature. If this interpretation is correct, the growing taste for native humor can be seen as an intrusion of attitudes originating in remote rural areas into the prim middlebrow world of the story papers, which ostensibly derived its standards from the upper-class traditional culture.

In the absence of reliable historical knowledge about levels of literary taste in the United States, we must make inferences from fragmentary data. These indicate that a few writers and critics at the top of the scale of sophistication, such as Francis J. Child and Thomas Sergeant Perry, appreciated the vitality of native humor. Even Emerson, according to his daughter, had often asked to have read to him "certain passages of *The Innocents Abroad*," and Holmes, although he himself mildly deprecated the "broad farce" of the Whittier dinner speech, reported that two of his friends, "gentlemen of education and the highest social standing, were infinitely amused" by it and "stoutly defended it against the charge of impropriety." Although Howells was distressed over the personal affront offered to honored guests by this particular speech, he had from the beginning praised the "delicious impudence" of his friend's "colloquial drolling." But the bulk of Mark Twain's vast audience was in the conventional sense uncultivated. His primary appeal was to the tens and hundreds of thousands of readers who delighted in Artemus Ward and Petroleum V. Nasby and Bill Nye—readers of whom Lincoln is the best known representative. Somewhere between Lincoln and Child along this dimension of tastes must be placed the middlebrow readers and critics represented by Holland, Mrs. Fairbanks, and Mrs. Severance. Olivia Langdon belonged to this group when Mark Twain met her, and she never entirely graduated from it. The geographical pattern of newspaper attacks on the supposed irreverence of the Whittier

dinner speech permits certain further inferences. Boston, more
secure in its sophistication than the rest of the country, was freer
from the rigidity of taste imposed by the cult of gentility. As the
strength of the traditional culture declined, it was finding its last
stronghold in the middlebrow provinces, the upcountry of New
England and the Middle West.

VI

The confusion of tastes and attitudes in nineteenth-century American culture made it impossible for Mark Twain to arrive at a
workable idea of his vocation. If he hoped to be accepted as a
serious writer, he was apparently obliged to conform to the priestly
role of the man of letters. If he devoted himself to humor he must
be content with the humble function of providing comic relief from
higher concerns. The program of the Whittier dinner was virtually
a pageant translating his problem into quasi-dramatic terms. He
was invited to enact as if on a stage the role of harmless jester
offered him by the dominant culture. But he had also been invited
to write his own lines, and the assignment had stirred his imagination to an act of expression more revealing than either he or
Howells, the director of the pageant, intended. Despite Howells'
contention that his friend was free of the crudities of other
humorists, Mark Twain's humor was basically irreverent. When he
went beyond a perfunctory gesture of politeness his speech was
bound to be shocking to his sponsor.

Lacking a satisfactory rationale of his position, Mark Twain
suffered a succession of pendulum swings of emotion. Howells
remembered that "not so very long" after the dinner Mark Twain
had reacted from his depression, declaring "with all his fierceness,
'But I don't admit that [the speech] *was* a mistake.'" Within two
or three weeks he was able to write with self-possession to Mrs.
Fairbanks, who had called to his attention an item about his
apology in the New York *Sun:*

I am pretty dull in some things, & very likely the Atlantic speech
was in ill taste; but that is the worst that can be said of it. I am sin-

cerely sorry if it in any wise hurt those great poets' feelings—I never wanted to do that. But nobody has ever convinced me that that speech was not a good one—for me; above my average, considerably.

He went on to draw a dubious analogy ignoring the charge of personal affront to men who were present when the speech was delivered:

I could as easily have substituted the names of Shakespeare, Beaumont & Ben Jonson, (since the absurd *situation* was where the humor . . . lay,) & all these critics would have discovered the merit of it, then. But my purpose was clean, my conscience clear, & I saw no need of it.

His final argument is more cogent, for the insecurity of the defenders of ideality had made them unable to bear any suggestion of varied perspectives regarding questions of value:

Why anybody should think three poets insulted because three fantastic tramps choose to personate them & use their language, passes my comprehension. Nast says it is very much the best speech & the most humorous situation I have contrived.

Mark Twain's difficulty in discovering a role and an identity for himself condemned him to further changes of mind about the speech. In March of 1882, writing to Howells, he said that the news of Longfellow's death "had a peculiar effect upon me; for it brought back that infernal breakfast and made me feel like an unforgiven criminal." (He had by that time confused the Whittier dinner with a ceremonial breakfast honoring Holmes two years later in the same hotel.) Almost thirty years after the speech was delivered, a woman wrote him from New York to ask where she might find the text; she remembered enjoying it from a newspaper report in 1877. He caused the files of the Boston *Transcript* to be searched and the speech copied out for him. In his autobiographical musings, he talks of the Whittier dinner at length. Upon first rereading the speech in 1906 he found it admirable:

I have read it twice, and unless I am an idiot, it hasn't a single defect in it from the first word to the last. It is just as good as good can be. It is smart; it is saturated with humor. There isn't a suggestion of coarseness or vulgarity in it anywhere.

He could only conclude that on the fateful evening his technique
had been uncertain because he had lost courage when he saw
"those great men up there whom I was going to describe in such a
strange fashion." With an impulse to secure vindication, he
thought of delivering the speech before the Twentieth Century
Club of Boston, or at a banquet of newspapermen in Washington
to which he had been invited. But a few days later he told Twichell:

I have examined that speech a couple of times since, and have
changed my notion about it—changed it entirely. I find it gross, coarse
—well, I needn't go on with particulars. I didn't like any part of it,
from the beginning to the end. I found it always offensive and detest-
able. How do I account for this change of view? I don't know. I can't
account for it . . . I expect this latest verdict to remain.

Nevertheless, there was to be yet one more swing of the pendulum.
On the typescript of this passage in the Autobiographical Dictation
is a footnote in Mark Twain's hand:

May 25th. [1906.] It did remain—until day before yesterday; then I
gave it a final and vigorous reading—*aloud*—and dropped straight back
to my former admiration of it. M.T.

JAMES M. COX

✪

The Muse of Samuel Clemens

If a wife's influence upon her husband's literary work is measured by the importance his imagination accords her presence, Olivia Langdon Clemens is one of the most influential wives in the nineteenth century—which amounts to saying that she is one of the most influential wives in any century. For it was in the nineteenth century that the wife came into her own in the study as well as in the parlor. Not, to be sure, the dominant figure in that bearded century, she nevertheless hovered by the threshold of the imagination almost as much as by the hearthside in the manner of an attendant spirit approving rather than brooding over the creative process. The eighteenth-century writer had had his mistress, the Romantic artist his sister, the Victorian author his wife.

Yet even in such a period—which produced an Elizabeth Barrett, an Emily Selwood, a Virginia Clemm, a Sophia Hawthorne—Olivia Langdon was the object of extreme adoration. From the moment when, as Mark Twain remembered it, he saw the ivory miniature of her in her brother's stateroom in the *Quaker City* she was, he confidently asserted, never out of his mind. And throughout his thirty-four years of married life he did all in his power to make a legend of their happiness together. Sustained by his seemingly boundless devotion, she rose out of the semi-invalidism of her adolescence to become the mother of four children. Though

Reprinted from *The Massachusetts Review,* Vol. V, No. 1 (Autumn 1963), pp. 127–141, © 1963, The Massachusetts Review, Inc.

never strong, she clearly enjoyed a degree of health and energy she had never known before her marriage. And though misfortune, disaster, and finally something akin to despair overtook Mark Twain, causing him to doubt the fabric of his own experience, there is never a hint that he ceased to believe absolutely in Olivia Langdon. To see the arc of his career is to recognize that she was the one thing he did believe in and that all else—even himself—he came to doubt.

Yet for all his proclaimed adoration, the literary immortality he bestowed upon her was hardly flattering, for he insistently presented her as his censor, not as his muse. Much of his talk about her censorship was of course part of the humorous game he played with his intimate friends, particularly with William Dean Howells. Nevertheless the consequence of his humorous accusations and his feigned stupidity in matters of literary taste was a shifting of the responsibility for his shortcomings and failures upon the shoulders of others, chief among them his wife. This does not mean that he intentionally made her the scapegoat for his self-advertised failure; but he made possible, no matter how unwittingly, the attacks which were to be made upon her. It was no mere accident that she came to be seen as the figure representing all the social and artistic values antithetical to Mark Twain's native genius. Even the unctuous praises which Mark Twain, and Albert Bigelow Paine, lavished upon her were interpreted by Van Wyck Brooks and others as shameless demonstrations of his acquiescence to an impotent gentility.

It is fair to say that the chief reason she came to be singled out for attention and attack was her apparent activity in curtailing Mark Twain's "free" expression. For Mark Twain succeeded in conveying to posterity an image of himself as a writer repressed by the society. Interestingly enough, his chief efforts in creating such an image were made after Olivia's death in 1904. Long before her death Mark Twain had complained of the innumerable shackles which enslaved him and frustrated his creative instincts, but after 1904 he made a concerted effort to prove that at last he was going to write and speak his true mind. This final phase of his creative life is largely given over to books which were in one sense or another "repressed." There were of course many works published

during his last years, but the projects which were to be memorable
—the projects in which Samuel Clemens heavily invested—per-
petuated the last of the Mark Twain myths, the myth of the
repressed artist. At one pole of the myth lay *What Is Man?;* at the
other, the *Autobiography.*

What Is Man?, a philosophical account of man's fundamental
helplessness, was published anonymously—simply one more way
of dramatizing the difficulty of "free" expression—in 1906 in an
extremely limited edition and copyrighted under the name of J. W.
Bothwell, a clerk working in the law offices that handled Mark
Twain's accounts. The preface to the volume is worth quoting in
full:

Feb. 1905. The studies for these papers were begun twenty-five or
twenty-seven years ago. The papers were written seven years ago. I
have examined them once or twice per year since and found them satisfactory. I have just examined them again, and am still satisfied that they
speak the truth.

Every thought in them has been thought (and accepted as unassail-
able truth) by millions upon millions of men—and concealed, kept
private. Why did they not speak out? Because they dreaded (*and could
not bear*) the disapproval of the people around them. Why have I not
published? The same reason has restrained me I think. I can find no
other.

Here in succinct terms is a definition of the repressed artist. He
appears at last with a truth which he has kept secret for half his
creative life because he could not face the disapproval of those
around him. It is not simply his truth but the truth of all men that
he undertakes to publish.

If in *What Is Man?* Samuel Clemens anonymously revealed
his—and all men's—secret thought, in the *Autobiography* he set
about to disclose his secret self. Here he was not simply publishing
work which had hitherto been repressed; he was actually writing—
or, to be more precise, *speaking*—freely and frankly for the first
time in his life. He had begun dictating the *Autobiography* in
earnest in Florence shortly before Olivia's death, and during the
remaining years of his life he devoted more of his creative energies
to his autobiographical dictations than to any other production. He
did not keep his labors secret but kept reminding the world that his

autobiography was to be the greatest self-revelation ever written.
The secret self he was to unveil would be so intimate, he argued,
that the complete *Autobiography* could not be published for a
hundred years. "It has seemed to me," he announced at the end of
his preface, "that I could be as frank and free and unembarrassed as
a love letter if I knew that what I was writing would be exposed to
no eyes until I was dead and unaware and indifferent." For that
reason he spoke to the reader "as from the grave."

His determination to disclose his secret self was by no means an
innocent urge. Never one to forget the financial possibilities in-
herent in any of his creative instincts, Mark Twain did not fail to
attempt a double capitalization on his repressions; he published
extended portions of his *Autobiography* in *The North American
Review* before he died, thus realizing an immediate return upon his
recollections at the same time he was advertising the great revelation being withheld for posterity.

In view of Samuel Clemens' concerted effort at the end of his
career to present himself as a victim of repression it is hardly
surprising that Van Wyck Brooks could develop a fairly substantial thesis that Samuel Clemens was a repressed artist. And given
the myth of repression—few authors have tried harder to create
the illusion that their unpublished work held The Great Secret—it
was inevitable that Olivia Langdon Clemens would in time become
implicated in the drama. For Samuel Clemens had himself invented her in the role of censor. The invention dated all the way
back to the autumn of 1868 when he began the written phase of
his courtship with her. Even at that early time he was prepared to
assign her a more important part in his creative life than any
subsequent critic has been willing to grant her. She was, by virtue
of the power he himself invested in her, both his muse and censor,
or, to put it more precisely, his muse *as* censor. The manner in
which he invented her role during their courtship will go far
toward defining the significance of her presence to his art.

II

The first and possibly the last fact to remember about Samuel
Clemens' courtship of Olivia Langdon is that he fell in love with

her image—or so he maintained—before he saw her in the flesh. And that image, which he said was never out of his mind, is really all that remains of Olivia. Considered apart from her husband, she seems no more than a portrait having no personality, no essential individuality. Like Virginia Clemm, she lacks personality because her identity has been relocated in her husband's image of her. That is why both Virginia and Olivia seem more ideal than individual. It is why Olivia is seen—and cannot really be seen otherwise—as a kind of apotheosis of respectability.

Olivia was by nature no doubt more representative than individual. Certainly her taste, wherever it declares itself before her marriage to Samuel Clemens, seems the very epitome of respectability, as if conventionality were rooted in the core of her imagination. Her commonplace book, which she kept as a young girl—and which is now in the Mark Twain Papers in Berkeley, California— is so commonplace that it seems more like a transcript of standard passages chosen by the head matron of a female seminary than a private individual's favorite literary selections. In her neat and absolutely regular schoolgirlish hand are copied the most familiar and edifying passages from the approved writers. Portia's speech from *The Merchant of Venice* is there, along with innumerable platitudes culled from such worthies as Holmes, Ruskin, Horace Greeley, Theodore Parker, Thackeray (*The English Humorists!*), and her own Elmira pastor, Thomas K. Beecher. Beecher's more famous brother, Henry Ward, is amply represented by allegorical profundities such as "The past belongs to Gratitude and Regret; the present to Contentment and Work; the future to Hope and Trust." As a matter of fact, the prose of Henry Ward Beecher seems to have represented to Olivia a pattern of moral and literary excellence quite as satisfactory as one could wish. When Samuel Clemens began the extensive correspondence with her which culminated in engagement and marriage, she sent him regularly as a kind of spiritual tonic the weekly sermons issuing from Beecher's Plymouth pulpit.

The commonplace book provides an index of how completely she embodied conventional, respectable taste, and the point remains that, according to the myth he made, he "recognized" Olivia from her image and wanted her before he saw her. He clearly did not submit to her wiles, but aggressively spent his energies in winning her. He was thirty-two when he met her, thirty-four when he married her, and for all his mock innocence he was experienced in range and depth beyond any man she could have known. He was experienced enough to discover in the pose of innocence a power which no American before him, with the single exception of Franklin, had begun to realize. He was also experienced enough to know that he wanted her more than anything else he had ever wanted. Even so, he approached cautiously, not recklessly. He saw her in person for the first time in New York on December 27, 1867, six weeks after the *Quaker City* voyage had ended; and again during the week which followed, on one occasion going so far as to accompany her to a reading by Charles Dickens. After that first week, however, there is only his word that she was never out of his mind. Obeying the conventions of nineteenth-century courtship, he so discreetly kept his distance that during the entire eight months he spent in revising his *Quaker City* travel letters into *The Innocents Abroad* he did not write to her or indicate his love to anyone.

His correspondent during that period was Mary Mason Fairbanks of Cleveland, Ohio. Mrs. Fairbanks had been a reporter for the Cleveland *Herald*—her husband was one of the owners of the paper—and had accompanied the *Quaker City* party. During the excursion Mark Twain had formed a friendly attachment with her, calling her "Mother," and for the remainder of his twenty-year correspondence with her he continued to use the affectionate epithet. How much of a mother she actually was during the voyage is difficult to say because the relation is projected almost entirely through the magnifying lens of his imagination. His letters cast her in the role of the kind, straight-laced but indulgent mother whose desire was to reform her Prodigal Son. In the little drama he composed for them, she had cured him of bad habits, kept his clothes clean, sewed on his buttons, fed him jam when he behaved, and lectured him when he had not. As her character emerges in the course of his letters, it is possible to discern the outlines of Aunt Polly.

Yet she was not simply the "mother" for the bad boy; she was the "editor" for her "cub." She was, as he insisted, his "mentor" and copyreader who corrected his travel letters to the San Francisco *Alta California*. Mrs. Fairbanks' duties as mother and mentor were more than merely compatible tasks; they were mutually reinforcing aspects of the character which Samuel Clemens was inventing for her. His letters to her are the record of a surprisingly fertile little game which both players played with energy and imagination. As invented by her "son," Mrs. Fairbanks is a kind, shrewd, fairly intelligent keeper of the conventions, who scolds her cub for his use of slang, takes upon herself the education of his taste, and instructs him in the proprieties of authorship. He in turn is her eager disciple, assuring her that her good work of the recent voyage has not been in vain, that her reforms are still in force, and that her literary tutelage has carried beyond the schoolroom of the *Quaker City* to become a permanent influence for good in all the work that he will do. Informing her that the early letters he had written to the *Alta California* had little to recommend them, he adds that he looks forward with hope to the later ones which she had edited. "I may think better of those you weeded of slang," he remarks in one letter, and goes on to say, "There will not be any slang in this book except it should occur in a mild form in dialogues."

More than providing a framework for playing with the conventions, his correspondence with Mrs. Fairbanks formed a preparation for the invasion of Elmira. For in addition to securing the advantage of a valuable ally—a "mother" whom he could consult and in whom he could confide—Samuel Clemens was refining and polishing his skills as a letter writer. Though he did not write to Olivia and though he did not mention her to Mrs. Fairbanks until late in the summer of 1868, the concentration he devoted to the assault which began in September, 1868, makes it difficult for a skeptic to deny his contention that from the time he saw her image she was never out of his mind.

Upon finishing the manuscript of *The Innocents Abroad* and turning it over to his publisher, Elisha Bliss, in Hartford, he secured an invitation to visit the Langdons, and accordingly made his pilgrimage to Elmira. Bringing matters directly to a point, he

apparently proposed—or at least made a reckless declaration—
and was as immediately repulsed by his frail lady and her parents.
He was not completely banished, however, being allowed to
address her in letters as his "honored sister." From this initial
defeat he literally wrote his way back into her favor. First he
regained a position where he no longer had to call her "sister";
from there he moved close enough to declare his love; then to the
point where he persuaded her to declare her own; on to engagement; and finally—on February 2, 1870, eighteen months after his
early setback—to marriage. During the most crucial period of his
courtship he was on a vast lecture tour, writing her from such
towns as Lockport, New York; Titusville, Pennsylvania; Ravenna,
Ohio; Tecumseh, Michigan; and Galena, Illinois. Despite the
exhaustion of traveling, lecturing, and the inescapable social en-
gagements which attended his performances, he wrote her as much
as a hundred pages a week. This correspondence in the year and a
half of their courtship and engagement—less than twenty per cent
of which is in Wecter's edition of the *Love Letters*—makes up a
manuscript as long as that of *The Innocents Abroad*.

But it is a remarkably different manuscript. For if Mark Twain's
journey to the Holy Land is rooted in irreverence and skepticism,
Samuel Clemens' "manuscript" to Olivia which grew during the
months *The Innocents Abroad* was being prepared for publication,
chronicled the pilgrimage of a reverent lover toward the object of
his worship and belief. She was, he playfully contended, his
Human Angel, and he drew upon all the chivalric, royal, and
religious associations at his command to encompass her elevation.
Thus he spoke of her at one time as the "matchless little princess"
whom he wished to enthrone,[1] and at another as "a little martyr"
(Feb. 28, 1869, MTP). The attitude throughout is one of complete reverence sustained by a continual offering of every style at
the lover's command to the service and devotion of his love in an

---

[1] Unpublished letter of December 9, 1868, in the Mark Twain Papers.
Letters and dates will hereafter be cited parenthetically in the text. This and
other quotations from Mark Twain's unpublished letters are used by permission of the Trustees of the Mark Twain Estate. © Copyright 1961 by
the Mark Twain Company.

I were to lose you it seems to me that to lose memory and reason at the same time would be a blessing to me" (May 8, 1869, MTP).[6] The image of Olivia did, as I shall try to show, make both memory and reason possible for him. She was the single object of faith which allowed Samuel Clemens to "believe" in the tall tale of "Mark Twain" and possessing her at the center of his imagination he came into a particular possession of a past which he had never really owned before he won her.

The authoritative definition of her role in his imaginative undertaking is to be found in a letter—unquestionably one of the most interesting and important letters Samuel Clemens ever wrote. It was written on February 6, 1870—four days after his marriage—to Will Bowen, a boyhood friend. He had written to Bowen two years earlier, "I have been thinking of schooldays at Dawson's, & trying to recall the old faces of that ancient time—but I cannot place them very well—they have faded out from my treacherous memory."[7] All that he could remember was a single incident involving a louse which Will had purchased from one Arch Fuqua. Two years later, however, he could reply that Bowen's recent, and evidently nostalgic, letter had stirred him "to the bottom." "The fountains of my great deep are broken up" he sonorously began, "& I have rained reminiscences for four & twenty hours." Continuing in this vein of nostalgic oratory, he eloquently proclaimed:

The old life has swept before me like a panorama; the old days have trooped by in their old glory again; the old faces have looked out of the mists of the past; old footsteps have sounded in my listening ears; old hands have clasped mine; old voices have greeted me, & the songs I loved ages & ages ago have come wailing down the centuries! Heavens what eternities have swung their hoary cycles about us since those days were new!—

Then, as easily as he had assumed the grand manner, he cast it aside in order to detail a particular past:

[6] © Copyright 1961 by the Mark Twain Company.
[7] Theodore Hornberger, ed., *Mark Twain's Letters to Will Bowen* (Austin, 1941), p. 17.

—Since we tore down Dick Hardy's stable; since you had the measles
& I went to your house purposely to catch them; since Henry Beebe
kept that envied slaughter-house, & Joe Craig sold him cats to kill in
it; since old General Gaines used to say "Whoop! bow your neck &
spread!"; since Jimmy Finn was town drunkard & we stole his dinner
while he slept in the vat & fed it to the hogs in order to keep them still
till we could mount them & have a ride; since Clint Levering was
drowned; since we taught that one-legged nigger, Higgins, to offend Bill
League's dignity by hailing him in public with his exasperating "Hello,
League!"—since we used to undress & play Robin Hood in our shirt-
tails, with lath swords, in the woods on Halliday's Hill on those long
summer days; since we used to go in swimming above the still-house
branch—& at mighty intervals wandered on vagrant fishing excursions
clear up to "the Bay," & wondered what was curtained away in the
great world beyond that remote point; since I jumped overboard from
the ferry boat in the middle of the river that stormy day to get my hat,
& swam two or three miles after it (& got it,) while all the town collected on the wharf & for an hour or so looked out across the angry
waste of "white-caps" toward where people said Sam. Clemens was
last seen before he went down; since we got up a rebellion against Miss
Newcomb, under Ed Stevens' leadership, (to force her to let us all go
over to Miss Torry's side of the schoolroom,) & gallantly "sassed"
Laura Hawkins when she came out the third time to call us in, &
then afterward marched in in threatening & bloodthirsty array,—&
meekly yielded, & took each his little thrashing, & resumed his old seat
entirely "reconstructed"; since we used to indulge in that very peculiar
performance on that old bench outside the school-house to drive good
old Bill Brown crazy while he was eating his dinner; since we used to
remain at school at noon & go hungry, in order to persecute Bill Brown
in all possible ways—poor old Bill, who could be driven to such extremity of vindictiveness as to call us "You *infernal* fools!" & chase
us round & round the school-house—yet who never had the heart to
hurt us when he caught us, & who always loved us & always took our
part when the big boys wanted to thrash us; since we used to lay in wait
for Bill Pitts at the pump & whale him; (I saw him two or three years
ago, & was awful polite to his six feet two, & mentioned no reminiscences); since we used to be in Dave Garth's class in Sunday school
& on week-days stole his leaf tobacco to run our miniature tobacco
presses with; since Owsley shot Smar; since Ben Hawkins shot off his
finger; since we accidentally burned up that poor fellow in the cala-

effort to claim for her a state of earthly perfection. Thus, while all traditional styles in *The Innocents Abroad* had been subverted by the irreverent Mark Twain who impersonated them, styles in the love letters are the offerings which Samuel Clemens brings to the worship of his earthly goddess.

His courtship involved a game similar to the one he had played with Mrs. Fairbanks. Again he offered himself as the repentant Prodigal begging to be reformed and asking to be schooled in the tender refinements which only Olivia could teach. And again he asked for criticism, appointing her his "darling little Mentor" (Dec. 27, 1868, MTP) and telling her that she must read each thing he wrote, keep a scrapbook of the clippings he sent her, collect his fugitive newspaper articles, advise him in matters of style, censor him when he was incorrigibly "bad," and edit his works after his death. Such were the duties of his new editor and mentor. He assured her as he had assured Mrs. Fairbanks that her presence was having the most salutary effect upon his spiritual and imaginative life. He dropped the use of alcoholic beverages and went so far as to offer to give up cigars if she demanded such a sacrifice.

Yet Olivia's role was considerably more complex and elevated than the one Mrs. Fairbanks had played. Whereas Mrs. Fairbanks had been invented as the Mother, Olivia was cast as the Human Angel. Thoroughly playful, the term indicated precisely the areas of the imagination which were at stake. Mrs. Fairbanks had been operative in matters of convention and taste; Olivia, in addition to handling these concerns, was delegated authority over regions of sex and faith. The game of love with her included not merely the task of reforming Samuel Clemens; she was to take up the burden of saving him from physical ruin and mental doubt. Constantly holding her up as the one object he could believe in and adore, he reminded her that the responsibility for his salvation lay inexorably in her hands. When she deprecated the crown he insistently offered her, contending that it was unchristian to be so worshiped, he blandly replied that perhaps his idolatry might lead him toward her God. He told her of the grave doubts which seized him despite his earnest efforts to believe, "confessing" to her upon occasion that there were hopeless periods when "religion seemed well-nigh unattainable, & when one feels grimly like jesting with holy things, & giving up in despair" (Dec. 30, 1868, MTP).[2] And at times he was filled with self-abasement and a sense of unworthiness in the face of her spiritual perfection. Apologizing for having caused her pain, he wrote, "I do despise myself to think that all your precious love & all your patient gentleness & your beautiful nature were not puissant enough to curb my little peevish spirit & bridle my irreverent tongue. I was not fit to stand in such a presence in such a mood" (Aug. 8, 1869, MTP).[3] In addition to succeeding Mother Fairbanks as his mentor, she was to be his partner in a relationship at once physically passionate but "pure." Thus he closed an early letter with the following fragmentary outburst: "If I could take you in my arms *now,* & imprint upon your forehead the kiss of reverent Honor, & upon your lips the Kiss of Love, imperishable & undefiled!" (Dec. 4, 1868, MTP).[4]

Through all the reverence of his style Olivia was quick to sense the heresy of his courtly love. She perceived it much more clearly than Mark Twain apologists who explain away his reverence as an unfortunate sentimentality which occasionally threatened his rough frontier masculinity; and more clearly than the critics who point to his chivalry as proof of just how conventional Mark Twain finally was. The heresy was plain enough to see. Early in the game he put the matter abruptly: "I have a faith in you—a faith which is as simple and unquestioning as the faith of a devotee in the idol he worships" (Wecter, *Love Letters,* p. 25). Even a parishioner in the liberated Congregationalism of Elmira could see that such a profession was hardly Christian. Though he assured her that her love might redeem him, she rather helplessly encouraged him to believe in God rather than in her and sent him Beecher's sermons in an effort to give him spiritual instructions. He replied—not without a touch of savagery—that he was learning to "devour" religious literature. Olivia betrayed increasingly weakening resistance to his worship, for against the tide of reverence which flooded toward her from the pen of Samuel Clemens the easy religion of Henry Ward Beecher afforded little protection indeed. Her early fears proved prophetic. Less than two years after they were married, when he was on another great lecture tour, she wrote half wistfully and half playfully that she had fallen away from God, adding that if she could only feel toward God what she felt toward her husband she would feel no anxiety whatever about religion.

The whole course of the courtship raises the inevitable question of how "serious" Samuel Clemens was in his efforts to be "saved." Did he really wish to be converted, or was he simply acting a part? Like all questions concerning Mark Twain, this one comes down to style. The reason the question is asked in the first place is that an uncertainty exists concerning the "sincerity" of the style—an uncertainty which runs the length and breadth of his work. The reverent style is finally difficult to distinguish from the irreverent. Here is a sample of Mark Twain's reverence; it could easily be duplicated a hundred times in the love letters. Responding to Olivia's troubled reactions to Anna Dickinson's radical expressions on women's rights, he exhorted her to accept her fate:

Therefore be content. Do that which God has given you to do, & do not seek to improve upon His judgment. You cannot do Anna Dickinson's work, & I can freely stake my life upon it, she cannot do yours. —Livy you might as well reproach yourself for not being able to win bloody victories in battle like Joan of Arc. In your sphere you are as great, & as noble, & as efficient as any Joan of Arc that ever lived. Be content with the strength God has given you, & the station that He has given into your charge—& don't be discouraged & unsettled by Anna Dickinson's incendiary words [Jan. 22, 1869, MTP].[5]

The entire passage has about it the air of being borrowed instead of created; thus the manner in which the language echoes the conventional rhetoric of piety takes precedence over the argument of the passage. Instead of creating a new style, Mark Twain is impersonating an old style. As his own Tom Sawyer would later love to do, he is "putting on" style as if it were a garment. That is why the whole structure of his rhetoric seems more ready-made

[5] © Copyright 1961 by the Mark Twain Company.

than hand-woven. His "seriousness" is questioned in proportion to the sense of play manifesting itself in his use of a particular style.

His very willingness to employ and play with styles was mirrored in the play world the letters were creating for himself and Olivia. For it was a play world, and it would be a somber person who failed to see the play from which Mark Twain could never save himself. The list of diminutives he used to describe her is an index to the perspective he was inventing. He constantly referred to her as his little mentor, his little angel, his little martyr, his little princess, his little darling. But it would be a blind person, who seeing the dimension of play, dismissed the activity of impersonation as not "serious." The seriousness lies precisely in the imaginative engagement in the process by which Mark Twain was converting the conventional Olivia Langdon into a mock-solemn companion of his art. She was, to use his own favorite term for her, his "dear little gravity"—a kind of straight woman who was to collaborate in the creation of his humor.

Thus, her censorship and tutelage did not constitute an alien authority impinging upon Mark Twain's imagination; rather, as Bernard DeVoto shrewdly recognized, Olivia was his self-appointed censor, and her censorship was really his own. It was, like his image of her, part of his imagination. In being his editor she played a part for him in a comic dialectic of his own arrangement. The fact that, beginning with *The Innocents Abroad,* she was his literary advisor until her death serves to emphasize how inextricably she was involved in his whole creative enterprise. Her role of editor and censor was in fact merely a concrete manifestation of the power he invested in his image of her as Human Angel.

For as his Angel, she was nothing less than his self-created muse. She was the good angel whose presence was not merely a protection against demonic forces but an assurance of sanity itself—as necessary to his imagination as the past which lay behind him waiting to be reconstructed. Writing to her from Hartford shortly before *The Innocents Abroad* was published, he assured her with all the conviction the reverent style would carry: "Livy, you are so interwoven with the very fibre of my being that if

I were to lose you it seems to me that to lose memory and reason at the same time would be a blessing to me" (May 8, 1869, MTP).[6] The image of Olivia did, as I shall try to show, make both memory and reason possible for him. She was the single object of faith which allowed Samuel Clemens to "believe" in the tall tale of "Mark Twain" and possessing her at the center of his imagination he came into a particular possession of a past which he had never really owned before he won her.

The authoritative definition of her role in his imaginative undertaking is to be found in a letter—unquestionably one of the most interesting and important letters Samuel Clemens ever wrote. It was written on February 6, 1870—four days after his marriage—to Will Bowen, a boyhood friend. He had written to Bowen two years earlier, "I have been thinking of schooldays at Dawson's, & trying to recall the old faces of that ancient time—but I cannot place them very well—they have faded out from my treacherous memory."[7] All that he could remember was a single incident involving a louse which Will had purchased from one Arch Fuqua. Two years later, however, he could reply that Bowen's recent, and evidently nostalgic, letter had stirred him "to the bottom." "The fountains of my great deep are broken up" he sonorously began, "& I have rained reminiscences for four & twenty hours." Continuing in this vein of nostalgic oratory, he eloquently proclaimed:

The old life has swept before me like a panorama; the old days have trooped by in their old glory again; the old faces have looked out of the mists of the past; old footsteps have sounded in my listening ears; old hands have clasped mine; old voices have greeted me, & the songs I loved ages & ages ago have come wailing down the centuries! Heavens what eternities have swung their hoary cycles about us since those days were new!—

Then, as easily as he had assumed the grand manner, he cast it aside in order to detail a particular past:

[6] © Copyright 1961 by the Mark Twain Company.
[7] Theodore Hornberger, ed., *Mark Twain's Letters to Will Bowen* (Austin, 1941), p. 17.

—Since we tore down Dick Hardy's stable; since you had the measles & I went to your house purposely to catch them; since Henry Beebe kept that envied slaughter-house, & Joe Craig sold him cats to kill in it; since old General Gaines used to say "Whoop! bow your neck & spread!"; since Jimmy Finn was town drunkard & we stole his dinner while he slept in the vat & fed it to the hogs in order to keep them still till we could mount them & have a ride; since Clint Levering was drowned; since we taught that one-legged nigger, Higgins, to offend Bill League's dignity by hailing him in public with his exasperating "Hello, League!"—since we used to undress & play Robin Hood in our shirt-tails, with lath swords, in the woods on Halliday's Hill on those long summer days; since we used to go in swimming above the still-house branch—& at mighty intervals wandered on vagrant fishing excursions clear up to "the Bay," & wondered what was curtained away in the great world beyond that remote point; since I jumped overboard from the ferry boat in the middle of the river that stormy day to get my hat, & swam two or three miles after it (& got it,) while all the town collected on the wharf & for an hour or so looked out across the angry waste of "white-caps" toward where people said Sam. Clemens was last seen before he went down; since we got up a rebellion against Miss Newcomb, under Ed Stevens' leadership, (to force her to let us all go over to Miss Torry's side of the schoolroom,) & gallantly "sassed" Laura Hawkins when she came out the third time to call us in, & then afterward marched in in threatening & bloodthirsty array,—& meekly yielded, & took each his little thrashing, & resumed his old seat entirely "reconstructed"; since we used to indulge in that very peculiar performance on that old bench outside the school-house to drive good old Bill Brown crazy while he was eating his dinner; since we used to remain at school at noon & go hungry, in order to persecute Bill Brown in all possible ways—poor old Bill, who could be driven to such extremity of vindictiveness as to call us "You *infernal* fools!" & chase us round & round the school-house—yet who never had the heart to hurt us when he caught us, & who always loved us & always took our part when the big boys wanted to thrash us; since we used to lay in wait for Bill Pitts at the pump & whale him; (I saw him two or three years ago, & was awful polite to his six feet two, & mentioned no reminiscences); since we used to be in Dave Garth's class in Sunday school & on week-days stole his leaf tobacco to run our miniature tobacco presses with; since Owsley shot Smar; since Ben Hawkins shot off his finger; since we accidentally burned up that poor fellow in the calaboose; since we used to shoot spool cannons, & cannons made of keys, while that envied & hated Henry Beebe drowned out our poor little popguns with his booming brazen little artillery on wheels; since Laura Hawkins was my sweetheart—

The mention of Laura Hawkins served to recall Samuel Clemens from this series of memories covering the whole spectrum of experience which was later to constitute the adventures of Tom Sawyer and Huckleberry Finn.

Hold: *That* rouses me out of my dream, & brings me violently back into this day & this generation. For behold I have at this moment the only sweetheart I ever *loved,* & bless her old heart she is lying asleep upstairs in a bed that I sleep in every night, & for four whole days she has been *Mrs.* Samuel L. Clemens! . . . & she is the *best* girl, & the sweetest, & the gentlest, & the daintiest, & the most modest & unpretentious, & the wisest in all things she should be wise in & the most ignorant in all matters it would not grace her to know, & she is sensible & quick & loving & faithful, forgiving, full of charity—& her beautiful life is ordered by a religion that is all kindliness & unselfishness. Before the gentle majesty of her purity all evil things & evil ways & evil deeds stand abashed—then surrender. Wherefore without effort, or struggle, or spoken exorcism, all the old vices & shameful habits that have possessed me these many years, are falling away, one by one, & departing into the darkness.[8]

This letter to Bowen forms a fitting end to any account of Samuel Clemens' courtship. The reverent description is in effect a summary and distillation of all that he had said again and again in his love letters.

But the letter also marks the recovery of a past. For what is new four days after the marriage is the presence and particularity of a vast memory of boyhood. Moreover, the letter makes clear how the presence of the princess upstairs is related to the stream of memories being recorded. It is not simply that the memory of Laura Hawkins reminds Samuel Clemens of Olivia; rather, under the protection of the reverent spirit of Olivia the old vices and shameful habits of the intervening years are falling away, leaving

[8] *Ibid.,* pp. 18–20.

the past free from evil and available to the memory. The remarkable feature of this "purification" is that it occurs without effort on his part. Olivia is thus more than a protector; she represents the presence of a grace which blesses the memory, opening a window upon the territory of boyhood.

Finally the very structure of the letter reveals as no document can—for the letter is in its way a work of art—how Olivia was a censor, not merely in the role of being a copyreader but in the deepest psychic meaning of the term. Even the "innocent" memories in the letter were being written to his boyhood friend while she slept. The letter is, in the last analysis, a dramatic summary of Mark Twain's act of writing. His "dream" of the past is made possible not only by her grace but by her sleep. And it is not an exaggeration to say that all of his "dream" of the past which lay before him was to be made possible by her presence and her sleep. When he had completed his dream and she had awakened, he dutifully submitted his manuscript for her "approval." This last gesture in his invented drama marked the ritual which exposed her function and assured them both that nothing was amiss.

Thus, in making Olivia his editor he was explicitly and "humorously" defining the much deeper role her image played in his creative memory. She was, by virtue of his imagination, part of his identity as a man and as a writer. His headlong determination to have her had been in its way an expression of himself. After their marriage he insisted not without reason that theirs was a true marriage in that each shared the other's identity, she being his other self. And when she was stricken with her last illness, Mark Twain measured her necessity to his genius in a letter to Frederick Duneka of Harpers. "My wife being ill," he wrote, "I have been— in literary matters—helpless all these weeks. I have no editor—no censor."[9]

In the death which he saw approaching her, he could hardly help feeling a grave threat to himself as a writer. For with the exception of a single volume of early sketches, distinguished only

---

[9] Unpublished letter in the Berg Collection, New York Public Library. Typescript in the Mark Twain collection in University of California Library, Berkeley, California. © Copyright 1961 by the Mark Twain Company.

by the Jumping Frog yarn, his entire literary work had been sub-
jected to her benign censorship. His comic genius required such a
resistance in order to achieve expression in the same way that Tom
Sawyer required Aunt Polly's indulgent repression in order to
create the dream of freedom. Mark Twain's "humor" was itself a
conversion of real tyranny and slavery into play and adventure;
and Olivia, his straight woman, had been at once his muse and
censor whom he had "converted" to serve himself instead of
Beecher's God. By winning this figure who both embodied and
represented the forms of reverence and respectability, Samuel
Clemens had possessed the style which Mark Twain would endlessly impersonate and parody.

With her death, he pursued the last illusion left him—the
illusion that after years of evasion and subterfuge he was at last
going to speak the truth which he had so long kept secret. Yet for
all his brave attempts to re-create himself one last time in *What Is
Man?* and the *Autobiography,* the reader of those works discovers
that there was nothing left to tell. All that remained of worth were
characters like Captain Stormfield and Satan whom he had invented in her lifetime and whom he turned back upon during the
long twilight of his career. He was at last tricked into believing—
or was it his last hopeless wish to believe?—that there was a
substantive truth about himself and about the universe which he
had been afraid to tell. Actually, of course, Mark Twain was at
last the fool of his illusion, for the truth lay behind him in all the
tall tales he had told. It had been no accident that the greatest
truth he had told had been spoken by the finest liar he could
invent, for Mark Twain, who was at once the signature and
personality of Samuel Clemens' genius, was himself a tall tale. The
only truth he could tell in a world of lies was the lie which did not
pretend to be the truth. Such a lie was the tall tale as Mark Twain
told it. Instead of creating the illusion that the fiction was the
truth, the tall tale in Mark Twain's hands exposed itself as a lie.
Mark Twain distrusted and despised fiction because fiction as
traditionally practiced appealed to the reader to believe in its
ultimate reality. The tall tale on the other hand frankly invited the
listener to question its reality. The one is essentially transcendental

in its assumptions; the other radically skeptical. The one tells the lie as the truth; the other tells the truth as a lie. Thus Mark Twain, who exposed rather than concealed Samuel Clemens, was the liar whose compulsion to exaggerate was his "humor." The truth of his tall tale lay always in the telling. That is why Mark Twain's chief concern in literary criticism lay in how to *tell* a story; it is also why he maintained throughout his life the twin identity of writer and talker and no doubt why when he came to reveal the "truth" in his autobiography he instinctively hit upon the happy plan of dictating his reflections.

Finally this necessity of his art was why—if one believes even remotely in the fatality of genius—that there could be no substantive truth for Samuel Clemens at the end of his career. His much lamented doubt and "despair" to which so much speculation has been devoted—he is often scolded for the failure which he begged posterity to explain—is in its way the inexorable expression of the radical skepticism at the heart of his humorous form. And yet it was equally inevitable that Mark Twain should have come to believe in his repression. The whole comic strategy of telling the truth as a lie had necessitated the illusion that the *truth could not be told*. But here again the illusion was a further irony to which the genius of Samuel Clemens exposed him. For the illusion of repression was what he had invented throughout his career as both a motive and a means of *expression*. That was why, unlike the traditional muse which enabled the artist to escape the earthly shackles binding his divine imagination, the muse of Samuel Clemens was his editor and censor.

The Yankee and the Machine:
Mark Twain's Perfectible World

In 1886, Mark Twain, fifty years old, was at the pinnacle of his multiplex career. Eight books, including, most recently, *Huckleberry Finn,* had established him as a major American writer who had a popular following as well as an international reputation. He was enormously successful as lecturer, public performer, and the publisher of General Ulysses Grant's *Personal Memoirs.* He was rich and famous and lived in a great mansion in Hartford with a wife and three daughters whom he adored. He had, it seemed, everything a man would want. Even so, possessed by the same restlessness and faith in limitless possibility that characterized his country in his century, he embarked on two new ventures. They were apparently unrelated, but they came out of the same central core of aspiration and belief, and they both contained elements of self-destruction.

Mark Twain had just begun serious work on *A Connecticut Yankee in King Arthur's Court,* his tale of a Hartford master mechanic and superintendent at the Colt Arms Factory who is hit on the head with a crowbar in the course of an argument and begins to imagine himself bringing nineteenth-century enlightenment, technology, and venture capitalism to sixth-century England. And only a week before this apparent return to full-time writing after a year of publishing involvements Mark Twain organized a company to perfect, manufacture, and market all over the world a typesetting machine invented by a man named James W. Paige. Paige's machine was a "mechanical marvel," Clemens declared, which makes "all the other wonderful inventions of the human brain . . . sink nearly into commonplace." In comparison, he said, the telephone, telegraph, locomotive, cotton gin, and sewing machine were "mere toys, simplicities."

The Connecticut Yankee and the Machine were twinned in Clemens' mind. Both were tests of a perfectible world in which, contrary to all his experience and expectations, friction and mechanical difficulties were to be the precise equivalents of ignorance and superstition. Both were expression of a covert secular religion which, as an unexamined article of faith, believed in perpetual motion instead of eternal life. "Wait thirty years and *then* look out over the earth," Clemens wrote in 1889, as a birthday greeting to Walt Whitman: "You shall see marvels upon marvels, added to those whose nativity you have witnessed; and conspicuous above them you shall see their formidable Result—Man at almost his full stature at last!—and still growing, visibly growing, while you look." Mark Twain was capable of two modes of belief at the same time. The opposite of this paean to progress is the conclusion of *A Connecticut Yankee*. The ambivalences, disillusions, destructive furies, and, finally, homicidal tantrums of this novel were fire drills in his imagination for the actual failure of the typesetting machine, machine values, and his dream of a capitalist democracy in which he expected to be a tycoon among tycoons.

Mark Twain the writer saw the omens of disaster long before Mark Twain the promoter, who all his life believed that he was lucky and also, like inventors and prophets in general, maintained a mulish faith that despite constant delays, breakdowns, and disappointments, the machine would turn up trumps eventually. Acknowledging a magical kinship between a writer writing words and a machine setting them in type, he planned to finish his novel the day the machine was finished. Four years before he formally conceded that the machine had defeated him, he wrote of it in terms that make it clear that what was at stake for him was not simply a business venture bigger and more promising than most, but an entire framework of aspiration, for himself and for his century. "I watched over one dear project of mine five years," he said in 1890, "spent a fortune on it, and failed to make it go—and the history of that would make a large book in which a million men would see themselves as in a mirror; and they would testify and say, Verily this is not imagination, this fellow has been there—and after would they cast dust upon their heads, cursing and blaspheming."

With one operator seated at its keyboard Paige's machine set entire words at a time; it fed itself from a galley of type that had already been used, and later distributed—sorted out by letter—its own type. An assistant removed the sticks of type from the machine and did the handwork of justifying the lines, that is, inserting space so that they aligned at the right. In Paige's final machine the assistant had been replaced by a built-in mechanical justifier. Even at an early stage of its development the machine was doing the work of four men. It set six-point type at the rate of about 3,000 ems an hour, which was four times the best speed Sam Clemens ever achieved when he was an itinerant practical printer, and it would eventually be capable of setting 5,000 ems and then 8,000 and more an hour.

Until he saw it in action Clemens had not believed such a miraculous machine could exist. Soon after he saw it and fell under the spell of its inventor, he began to believe that it was about the only machine of its kind that did exist. Actually, a similar machine designed by Henry Bessemer, the inventor of the iron converter, had set type commercially as early as 1842, a number of other machines had seen limited practical service, and the basement of the London *Times* was said to be filled with typesetting machines that had been tried and discarded. All of them, and especially the one Mark Twain backed, represented successively intricate elaborations, unworkably delicate and temperamental, of the same principle. These machines were designed to imitate the work of a *man* setting, justifying, and distributing single types *by hand*. Type distribution, half the function of Paige's early machine, was, in fact, no longer even necessary. The London *Times* was using a rotary typecaster, patented in 1881, which worked so fast—it turned out 60,000 characters an hour from its 100 molds—that instead of distributing type at the end of the day the printers simply melted it down and started all over again with fresh type. This significant bypass of the human analogy was the basic principle of the modern Linotype machine which went into service in 1886: it cast its own type from its own matrices in single slugs of a line's length, which were afterward thrown back into the melting pot.

A mechanical typesetter would have to *think* in order to work, Clemens persisted in believing, and the machine Paige demonstrated for him in the workshop appeared to be able to think. The inventor of such a machine must therefore be a divine magician, Clemens also believed, and the machine itself a living, intelligent organism which, as Paige improved it and articulated it, began to parallel human ontogeny: it became, in Clemens' phrases, "an inspired bugger," "a cunning devil," and after passing through a "sick child" stage, a "magnificent creature" ranking second only to man. (We shall be returning to this last comparison.) What Clemens was expressing in personifications like these was not only his veneration for the machine but also his basic layman's ignorance, his credulity in the face of what seemed to him a divine mystery only because he knew hardly anything about mechanics.

"He is a poet," Clemens wrote of Paige even in 1890 (when he had the phantasy that he would like to lock the inventor in a steel trap and watch him die), "a most great and genuine poet, whose sublime creations are written in steel. He is the Shakespeare of mechanical invention." Mark Twain, a passionately believing child of the Great Century, defined his writer's role as that of teacher, entertainer, and moralist of the masses. He deferred to another order of "poet" altogether, for the inventor, as the Connecticut Yankee says, is "after God" the creator of this world. Paige bestrode the two sacred temples of nineteenth-century progress, the patent office and the printing office. The Yankee's first official act in Arthur's England was to start a patent office: "A country without a patent office was just a crab," he says, "and couldn't travel any way but sideways or backwards." And he goes on to hammer away at sixth-century mind shackles by starting a newspaper. For Mark Twain and Walt Whitman the rotary press and its great whirling cylinders symbolized dynamic democracy, for it both whetted and fed the word hunger of a new mass audience.

Paige's final machine had 18,000 separate parts, including 800 shaft bearings. The patent application, which contained 275 sheets of drawings and 123 pages of specifications, was pending for eight years, during which time two patent examiners died, one of them insane, and the patent attorney also died insane. But the machine was no hoax. It was probably the most ambitious and complex device of its sort, and when it worked it worked like a miracle. But it was impossibly delicate and highstrung, broke down frequently and expensively, and even by 1889 it had become altogether too much like a mechanical human being, exciting for a laboratory demonstration but not as sturdy and practical as the real thing. And it was scarcely likely that the machine would ever be finished, for Clemens, even while he was figuring up the potential profits in the millions, shared Paige's fatal reluctance to release it from its machine shop shrine into the world of commerce, and it became, to return to the inevitable analogy, a pampered and overprotected child, precocious but accident-prone. "It did seem to me to be the last word in its way," said William Dean Howells, but he felt that that last word "had been spoken too exquisitely, too fastidiously." He recognized that both Clemens and Paige were trying to bring the machine "to a perfection so expensive that it was practically impracticable." Clemens' psyche as well as his fortune came to be disastrously overinvested in the machine's gears and levers, and when the machine died, more than money died with it.

Hartford's most prominent literary man was to be seen in New York at the Union League Club or on Wall Street singing the virtues of the machine to skeptical tycoons who agreed with him that the purse was big but were not so sure he had picked just the right horse to win it. Some of them, as he discovered when it was too late, had been betting all along on Ottmar Mergenthaler's

Linotype machines, twelve of which went into service at the New York *Tribune* in July, 1886; soon after came *The Tribune Book of Open Air Sports,* the first book printed from machine-set type. The typesetting machine, an invention as important as the rotary press, had finally proved workable. But Clemens, putting down the first bitter intimations of his own impending failure, was sure that Mergenthaler's victorious machine was "just a racehorse" and consequently "can't run no competition with a railroad." His own machine was rarely together in one piece for more than a week at a time, but he planned all sorts of public demonstrations and contests, to be witnessed by assorted financiers, newspaper proprietors, and the government printer.

Despite his confidence Clemens had the growing feeling that the mire was sucking at his boots. Even when he wanted to write, he found that the machine had eaten up all his energies. During most of 1886 and 1887 the combined expense of Paige's salary and the bills at Pratt and Whitney averaged about $2,000 a month; then the monthly drain went up to $3,000. By the end of 1887 the typesetter had cost Clemens about $50,000, and before he finished with it in 1895 it had bankrupted him and his publishing house and cost him nearly $190,000 altogether. "We go on and on, but the type-setter goes on forever," he complained. And the predictions also went on and on—finished by April, finished by May, finished by August, finished in eighty-five days, and with all these distractions he managed to force himself to work on *A Connecticut Yankee.* He was determined as ever that the machine and the book had to be finished at the same time.

"Machine O.K.," Paige telegraphed to him in New York on January 2, 1889, "Come and see it work." Three days later, a date Clemens noted for history—"Saturday, January 5, 1889, 12:20 P.M."—he scrawled in his notebook the block letters of EUREKA! He wrote: "I have seen a line of movable type, *spaced and justified by machinery!* This is the first time in the history of the world that this amazing thing has ever been done," and he signed his statement. A few hours later, writing to his brother Orion, he went on to describe "the immense historical birth" at which every one of the six men present seemed "dizzy, stupefied, stunned," drunk, even though there had been nothing to drink. The machine even made a perverse demonstration of its powers, for just when it seemed that the marvel was misbehaving again and might have to be taken apart, Paige discovered the trouble. "We are fools," he said, "the machine isn't." Its superfine intelligence— which went along with its unviably fastidious nature—had simply been making allowances for an invisible speck of dirt on one of the types. But even in this demonstration the future of the delicate machine was foretold. While Clemens was writing his jubilant account—and two weeks later, when a newspaper as far away as London announced that Mark Twain's "patient toil" has at last been "crowned with success"—Paige was taking it apart once more, his purpose, as he told his backer, to work the stiffness out of its joints and make it smooth and supple as a human muscle. The same story was beginning all over again. Mark Twain was cramped for money, he expected to be for some time. Never mind, he told himself wearily: "All good things arrive unto them that wait—and don't die in the meantime."

Clemens managed to finish *A Connecticut Yankee* that summer, three and a half years after having a dream about being a knight errant, itching inside his armor, and looking for pockets. But over the years, this comic idea, his response to a reading of Malory's *Morte d'Arthur,* changed its course, headed away from burlesque and toward an apocalyptic conclusion at which chivalric England and the Yankee's American technology destroy each other. Writing this book Mark Twain was in effect acting out his own disintegration, measuring the failure of that precarious equilibrium by which he had functioned for ten good years and more. In response not to a traumatic reversal but to an erosion of belief speeded by the machine, his center ceased to hold. For the rest of his life his imaginative energies were to be baffled and scattered.

By the early part of 1886, when he was writing the first three chapters, the comic idea had already taken on grim overtones. At the same time that he planned for the Yankee to do battle armed with a hayfork instead of a lance, Mark Twain also planned a conflict with the supreme medieval authority. "Country placed under an interdict," he noted, anticipating his account of a desolate and muted England punished by the Church for accepting the Yankee's ideas. And from the very start, the dream about knight errantry was joined in his mind by the idea of a great battle, at first between Crusaders and a modern expeditionary force fitted out with ironclad warships, torpedoes, 100-ton cannon, and Gatling guns. In other early notes for the book the Yankee, like Mark Twain yearning for Hannibal as it had been in his boyhood, yearns for an Arcadian past which "exists" only in his dream: a pre-Boss Camelot, drowsing and idyllic, "sleeping in a valley by a winding river." Caught between dream and reality, past and present, the Yankee approaches the impossible position of needing to return to a place which never had a real existence—or no longer exists, because he destroyed it himself.

Visiting Hannibal just when he was under the spell of Malory, Clemens felt himself swept under by "infinite great deeps of pathos," by waves of regret and longing for a lost Eden and his boyhood there. His mother, too, he found increasingly dislocated from the present: she asked for news about people who had been dead for fifty or sixty years, she even was not quite sure at times what relation he was to her. Like her, the Yankee has lost the power and desire to shake off his dream. "He mourns his lost land," Clemens said in a note for the book, "has come to England and revisited it, but it is all so changed and become old, so old— and it was so fresh and new, so virgin before." And then he went on to outline the only possible ending: "He has lost all interest in life—is found dead next morning—suicide."

But the nihilistic implications were too unpleasant to face, and neither Clemens—at first—nor those on whom he tried out the idea acknowledged that it might lead to something other than a splendidly funny book. "That notion of yours about the Hartford man waking up in King Arthur's time is capital," William Dean Howells said, after the story had been talked to him (and even in 1908 Howells still believed that it was the "most humane, sweetest fancy that ever was"). When Clemens read the first three chapters and outlined the rest to a public audience at the end of 1886 it seemed simply and harmlessly hilarious. The final battle had reached the tadpole stage: Under contract from King Arthur the Yankee kills off fifteen kings and acres of hostile knights—squadron after squadron they charge, while from behind an electrified barbed-wire fence he slaughters them with Gatling guns. Having done this, driven the ogres out of business, and abolished courtly love and armor, he puts the kingdom on a strictly business basis: Arthur's knights set themselves up as a stock exchange, and seats at the round table go for $30,000.

To allay the fears of a bluestocking friend of his that he was committing a crime of cultural lese majesty against King Arthur, and the entire body of Arthurian legend hallowed by time, Thomas Malory, and Tennyson, Clemens wrote what now seems an extraordinary letter, because it shows how tangled and mutually exclusive his aims were, and how obscure they were to him. "The story isn't a satire peculiarly," he wrote to her, "it is more especially a *contrast*" of daily life in Arthur's time and now. He had no intention of smirching or belittling any of Malory's "great and beautiful *characters*," and he went on to explain—in a literary-lofty-sentimental vocabulary that he often favored when writing to women—that Galahad ("the divinest spectre") will still gallop through the "mists and twilights of Dreamland" and Arthur will still keep his "sweetness and purity." He was determined, he said, that the disruption of the Round Table and the final battle—"the Battle of the Broken Hearts, it might be called"—should lose none of their "pathos and tears" through his handling. Writing a book which, if it preaches anything, preaches irreverence, the guillotine, a reign of terror, and a kind of generalized despair, its author believed he was writing a blameless, instructive tale for women and children.

Some months later Clemens was invited to give a talk to a meeting of Union veterans in Baltimore. He chose as his subject his own service as a Confederate irregular in 1861: after two weeks of retreating and hiding from the Yankees, Second Lieutenant Clemens and his soldiers simply deserted. The deciding event, as he was fond of telling and had told publicly before, was the moonlight shooting of an unarmed, unidentified man whom Clemens and his terrified band of warriors thought was a Union

scout. As he told the story in Baltimore, however, the killing of
this solitary "poor fellow" is no longer a small tragedy of war but
just a hyperbolic joke: "So began and ended the only battle in the
history of the world where the opposing force was *utterly extermi-
nated,* swept from the face of the earth—to the last man." Having
demonstrated that, like the Connecticut Yankee, he is invincible in
battle, Lieutenant Clemens, professing fear of his own powers,
decides to withdraw to civilian life, let the Confederacy collapse,
and give the Union a chance to survive—a wise decision, he now
realizes, because the United States in 1887 is, he says, the "one
sole country nameable in history or tradition where a man *is* a man
and manhood the only royalty."

To a great extent the Connecticut Yankee *is* Mark Twain: Both
love showmanship and gaudy effects; their hearts melt before the
vanished past; both combine idealism, shrewd practicality, and a
devotion to profit; their revolutionary, humanitarian zeal is tem-
pered and at times defeated by their despairing view of human
nature. Now, by an ironic reversal, the Rebel soldier's battle with
the Yankee scout has the symbolic content of the Connecticut
Yankee's battle with the enemies of his "republic." Having made
the connection in terms of his own experience Mark Twain was
able to go on and explore in his book certain implicit parallels
between Arthur's England and the American South: slavery; a
chivalric code which, as Clemens was fond of arguing, came to the
South filtered through Sir Walter Scott and kept the South mawk-
ish, adolescent, verbose, and addicted to leatherheaded anachro-
nisms like duels and tournaments. In the course of writing the
book Mark Twain compelled his original matrix of a "contrast"
rather than a "satire" to accept and contain such a remarkable
range of conflict and anger that finally it burst. He ended up
cursing both terms of the contrast.

The sixteen chapters he wrote during what began as a "perfect"
summer in 1887 trace a pattern of mounting anxiety, bitterness,
and invective. All his experience, his business involvements, his
worries about the machine and his impatience, and even his
reading of history pointed to a single conclusion and a single
mood. Early in July he was too occupied with the typesetter to get

started. Later, writing seven hours a day, he was tense and anxious, unable to sleep at night. He sat up late smoking and thinking—"not pleasantly." "I want relief of mind," he complained to his nephew after one of these bad nights. "The fun, which was abounding in the Yankee at Arthur's Court up to three days ago, has slumped into funereal sadness, and this will not do. . . . The very title of the book requires fun, and it must be furnished. But it can't be done, I see, while this cloud hangs over the workshop." Two weeks later, his mood, characteristically, had turned all the way around. Now he was proudly writing "an uncommonly bully book" which would sell twice as many copies as *Huckleberry Finn,* and for a while he deluded himself into believing that he could put the machine, with all its delays and postponements, out of his mind altogether, and only work on the book. But soon the machine and his publishing house were in the saddle again and riding him hard. Mired deeper and deeper in business he was not able to finish the Yankee, as we saw, until five months after his triumphant cry of Eureka!

During all this time the abounding "fun" never really returned. The book contains episodes as richly comic and satiric as anything Mark Twain ever wrote, but they are more and more frequently, finally compulsively, presented in terms of havoc. It was apparent to Mark Twain himself that he had passed through some crisis of ebbing faith in the Great Century, a negative conversion which was in part symbolized by the machine and which he could hardly help but dramatize in the final chapter of his book. "The change," he wrote to William Dean Howells in the summer of 1887, "is in *me*—in my vision of the evidences." He had been rereading Carlyle's *The French Revolution,* and he was full of hatred for all the ancient forms of authority: monarchy, aristocracy, the Catholic Church. None of these, it is significant, posed much of a threat to him or to America in the late 1880's. Like Arthur's England their very remoteness made them permissible scapegoats for an anger whose real objects were much closer to home. True, modern Europe offered him few "evidences" that it was any better than it had been centuries earlier. He loathed the French for what he considered their traditional incapacity for independent thought and

their depraved sexual mores. Matthew Arnold's celebrated stric-
tures on American civilization enraged him when they were published in 1888 because they seemed merely to demonstrate that the
English were as servile, conformist, and brutalized as they had
been in the darkest ages, their national character combining the
primary traits of the dog and the lion. From the lecturer and
traveler George Kennan, Clemens, and the American people in
general, were learning of the horrors of life under the Czar.
Kennan's accounts of Siberian slave labor shed in the contrast a
wanly charitable light on slavery as it had been in England and the
United States. "If such a government cannot be overthrown except
by dynamite," Clemens exclaimed after hearing Kennan lecture in
Boston, "then thank God for dynamite!"

Yet what the Yankee dynamites is not only the old chivalric and
autocratic order—Europe, symbolically—but all the apparatus of
that "new deal" he tried to impose on what he now bitterly
acknowledges to be "human muck." "All our noble civilization
factories went up in the air and disappeared," he says: "We could
not afford to let the enemy turn our own weapons against us."
And it becomes clear that this apparatus of progress and enlightenment is in some way a "weapon" which destroys its
beneficiaries as well as its "enemies." The busy factories hidden all
over England, the Yankee says, are like a "serene volcano, standing innocent with its motionless summit in the blue sky, and giving
no sign of the rising hell in its bowels." Throughout the book there
are similar metaphors which suggest that Clemens, for all his
expressed enthusiasm for what he called "machine culture,"
nursed the covert belief that the machine was a destructive force.
For Clemens and his contemporaries the most familiar epitome of
the two-facedness of the machine was the steam locomotive tearing
and shrieking its way through the heart of the American Eden.
Clemens' concurrent experience with Paige's typesetter confirmed
his worst fears. The very names the Yankee gives to his institutions—"civilization factories" and, a dehumanizing pun, "man
factories"—evoke not the fervent brotherhood of Whitman's
democratic utopia but instead a bleak, industrial collectivism, the
nightmare society of a monolithic state ruled by the Boss.

Working through a crisis of belief in fictional terms, Clemens found himself unable, either ideologically or emotionally, to cope with the historical extremes that lay on either side of his pastoral, drowsing Hannibal. He chose the way of the anarch. The final combat—more a massacre along the lines of Custer at Little Bighorn than a "Battle of the Broken Hearts"—is a gruesome practical joke. Virtuoso of dynamite, electricity, hydraulics, and the inevitable Gatling gun, the Yankee slaughters the chivalry of England, twenty-five thousand men. He surveys the bodies lying on the field—for reasons of taste Clemens at the last moment suppressed a reference to four million pounds of human meat—and with a tragic overconfidence he declares that "We fifty four were masters of England!" But he is trapped within three walls of dead men, he is the victim of his own victory. Wounded, the Boss is carried into the cave by his band of boys—in effect, young Sam Clemens has come back to Hannibal for good. Having rejected all the values and both the "contrasts" of the book he makes one further withdrawal, as Clemens himself was shortly to do, into the world of the dream.

By an ironic accident Mrs. Clemens, her husband's vigilant editor, had a severe case of pinkeye when the proofs of *A Connecticut Yankee* were ready, and she was forbidden by her doctor to read or write. She insisted that Clemens ask William Dean Howells to read the proofs. "She is afraid I have left coarsenesses which ought to be rooted out," Clemens explained to his friend, "and blasts of opinion which are so strongly worded as to repel instead of persuade." For once, despite their remarkable rapport, the two might have been talking to each other across the Grand Canyon. "Last night I started on your book, and it sank naturally into my dreams," Howells wrote from Cambridge: "It's charming, original, wonderful—good in fancy, and sound to the core in morals." And from Hartford three days later answered a man who knew that in the course of writing the *Yankee* his demons had been loosed and could never be kennelled again. "Well, my book is written—let it go. But if it were only to write over again there wouldn't be so many things left out. They burn in me; and they keep multiplying; but now they can't ever be said. And besides, they would require a library—and a pen warmed up in hell."

Despite his deep anxieties about the machine, Clemens, in

optimistic moments, believed that it was about to make him rich, gargantuanly rich, and he expected never to have to write or lecture for money again. But his own resources were nearly exhausted, he acknowledged that he was in a desperately tight corner, and it was in the hope of finding a financial backer that he planned a demonstration of the machine for the millionaire Senator from Nevada, John Percival Jones.

In actuality, there was rarely anything for even the most eager investor to see. For all their calculations of wealth Clemens and Paige were also reluctant to expose their model of perfectibility to the scrutiny and corruptive touch of the market place. The machine was so pampered, obsessively tinkered with and "improved" that it was rarely in working order. It stayed in pieces for about six months after its Eureka demonstration. Then despite Clemens' insistence that the experiments stop, Paige began to install a new device to keep the keys from jamming. By the time it was put together again in September, 1889, one potential investor, who might have been convinced by a demonstration, had left for a year abroad. Throughout its life span the typesetter again and again showed the same character defects—grimly traceable to its two parents—of a foolish virgin and an overprotected child. In November, even though it was already "as perfect as a watch," it was taken down again, this time with Clemens' entire approval. This was to be the final polishing, he and Paige believed, which would eliminate "even the triflingest defect" and make the prodigy "perfecter than a watch," "letter-perfect"—such rapt phrases were about to become the epitaphs for the enterprise.

By the end of February, 1890, when the machine was in a brief and rare state of readiness to be demonstrated, Senator Jones was delayed on other business. Two months later he arrived in Hartford on a week's notice with some other capitalists in tow. Clemens met them at the station and drove them home to a sumptuous dinner, plied them with punch, champagne, brandy, cigars, and his best stories, and then loaded them once again into the family carriage. At the Pratt and Whitney factory they found that Paige, again with Clemens' approval, had got so engrossed in putting in an air-blast to blow motes off the types that he had not had time to reassemble the machine properly. What was on display was not the mechanical marvel Clemens had talked about over the canvasback ducks and fillet of beef, but a crazy tangle of gears, keys, wheels, cams, springs, cogs, levers, and other hardware. The Senator and his consortium marched out in disgust and headed for the first train back to New York. After this disaster—a psychologically predetermined "accident" in which his own conflicts figured quite as much as Paige's—Clemens began to sink into what his wife recognized as a serious depression. "I don't believe you ought to feel quite as desperate as you do," she wrote to him in New York, where he was once again trying to raise money. By some chain of miracles, however, Clemens managed to lure Jones back to Hartford, the machine actually performed, and Jones agreed to take on the job of financing the machine. He expected to raise the money by February, 1891, and he said he anticipated no difficulty provided Paige and the machine, both of whom had to be supported through the winter by Clemens, did their part.

The conditions were now ripe for that entrepreneurial tragedy of aspiration and credulity in which, as he said, "a million men would see themselves as in a mirror." In the Yankee's image, the volcano was about to pour out its hellfire.

"Dear Mr. Clemens," Paige wrote on January 2, 1891: "The cast iron lever which owing to the poor quality of the iron broke the other day, and the cast iron part accidentally broken by Mr. Parker, have both been replaced by new, substantial, and durable *steel parts,* and the machine has run since that time without bruising, breaking, or damaging a type of any sort and gives promise of working continuously without delays of any kind. This is the best New Year's greeting that I can send you." And it was now time, Paige was soon saying almost daily, for Jones and Clemens to exercise their option before it ran out.

In Washington Clemens waited in his hotel room for two days before Jones consented to talk to him, gave him a grudging few minutes, told him he was too busy with Senate affairs, and rushed him out. Suddenly sick with worry, Clemens went back to Hartford and began bombarding Jones with letters that grew more and more shrill and desperate in their claims: the machine will pay about

$55 million a year to begin with, Clemens now said; it was a more important invention than the telephone or the telegraph; the Mergenthaler Linotype was no competition at all. And while Jones maintained his silence, from Paige came harsher reminders that the option expired "absolutely" on February 13. On February 11 Jones finally telegraphed: It was impossible for him to do anything, he said, a letter would explain. But when it arrived on the thirteenth his letter added to this flat refusal only a transparent contradiction. He and other prudent men of substance felt that conditions in the money market were not at the moment favorable for such a venture; moreover, a number of these same men of substance already had large investments in Mergenthaler's Linotype. "For a whole year you have breathed the word of promise to my ear to break it to my hope at last," Clemens started to write, sitting alone in the Hartford house which he could no longer afford to live in: "It is stupefying, it is unbelievable."

A week or so later he was able to return to a more nearly normal idiom. Jones, he said, was nothing but a fraud, a "penny-worshipping humbug and shuffler," "really a very good sage-brush imitation of the Deity." On February 20 he noted that it had been two weeks since he had last seen Paige and his machine and that during that time he had been hard at work on a new novel. Five days later he gave his brother further news—horribly premature, as it turned out—of his apparent recovery from a deep addiction. "I've shook the machine and never wish to see it or hear it mentioned again. It is superb, it is perfect, it can do ten men's work. It is worth billions; and when the pig-headed lunatic, its inventor, dies, it will instantly be capitalized and make the Clemens children rich." For the first time in twenty years he was compelled to be a full-time writer and a lecturer too, the only sure ways he knew to rebuild his wasted fortunes.

The vital signs seemed to be reappearing. Still, it soon became clear that he and the machine had not really let go of each other and that, in fact, he had not even begun to grasp the full and disastrous extent of his involvement with it. To finance the machine he had spent his wife's fortune as well as his own. His publishing house was not only seriously undercapitalized but fatally committed to desperate projects beyond its capabilities. In April, 1894, the firm went bankrupt and carried him into bankruptcy with it. At the age of nearly sixty Clemens had to commit himself to earning about $100,000 to pay off his creditors, and more than that to restore his family to some measure of security. But he was not at all despairing at first, for by some electro-convulsive movement the machine appeared to be alive all over again and promising its usual millions.

During the dark winter that followed the Panic of 1893 the machine had gone into production in Chicago and was to be given its first really practical test at the Chicago *Times-Herald.* "Our ship is safe in port," Clemens cabled to his wife, and when he held in his hands examples of the newspaper work the machine had actually done, he felt like Columbus sighting land. But soon the machine began to break down, the stoppages became longer and longer; it was simply too delicate to be practical. The newspaper proprietors ended the test. The machine was a proven failure. The news hit Clemens like a "thunderclap," and he wandered through the streets of Paris in a daze; at the end of the afternoon he found himself at a steamship office on the Rue Scribe, about to buy a ticket on the 6:52 boat train to Le Havre. This time the machine was truly dead, and with it had gone his certainty that his luck would never run out. "All my life I have stumbled upon lucky chances of large size, and whenever they were wasted it was because of my own stupidity and carelessness." The machine had disappointed him lots of times, he said, "but I couldn't shake off the confidence of a lifetime in my luck."

Only then did he begin to comprehend his bankruptcy as not only a financial reverse but also a loss of faith and a kind of symbolic failure of manhood. The machine—or, rather, his faith in the machine—had ruined him, and when, in 1896, his favorite daughter died suddenly of meningitis he felt that he had suffered the last conceivable affront to his sense of plenitude and possibility. For both Mark Twain and his America the frontier was closed.

And all the while, during the slow and painful death of the machine, some corrosive process of change, prefigured and rehearsed in *A Connecticut Yankee,* had taken place in his vision and morale as a writer. He began to make notes for a novel which he never wrote: Tom and Huck, both 60, come back from wandering the world, talk about old times, mourn all the good things that are now dead, and agree that life for each of them has been a failure—"They die together." After his daughter died, Mark Twain, very close to madness, began to live in a self-induced dream state in which, over and over and over again, in any number of unfinished manuscripts, he tried to find out where he had gone wrong and why he felt so guilty. For a while, like the Yankee, he became the captive of his dream, unable and unwilling to distinguish between dreams and reality. What saved him from madness was undoubtedly work, and he succeeded not in understanding but in rationalizing his guilt, but it left him with an insatiable appetite for approval and adulation which he spent a good part of the last ten years of his life trying to feed. He had decided that life lacked dignity and meaning, that each and every member of what he called "the damned human race" was driven only by self-interest, the need to conform, the need, above all others, to win the approval of his neighbors. And the Paige typesetter, that mechanical marvel which had seemed capable of thinking and second only to man became, by a reversal which sums up the entire bitter story, the model for man himself. In the despair of his old age Mark Twain said: "Man's proudest possession—his mind—is a mere machine; an automatic machine."

A Selected Bibliography

BOOKS BY MARK TWAIN:

The Celebrated Jumping Frog of Calaveras County, and other Sketches (1867); The Innocents Abroad (1869); Roughing It (1872); The Gilded Age (with Charles Dudley Warner; 1873); Sketches: New and Old (1875); The Adventures of Tom Sawyer (1876); A Tramp Abroad (1880); The Prince and the Pauper (1882); Life on the Mississippi (1883); The Adventures of Huckleberry Finn (1885); A Connecticut Yankee in King Arthur's Court (1889); The Tragedy of Pudd'nhead Wilson (1894); Personal Recollections of Joan of Arc (1896); Following the Equator (1897); How to Tell a Story and Other Essays (1897); The Man That Corrupted Hadleyburg (1900); What Is Man? (1906); The $30,000 Bequest and Other Stories (1906); Christian Science (1907); Is Shakespeare Dead? (1909); Mark Twain's Speeches (1910); The Mysterious Stranger (1916); Europe and Elsewhere (1923); Mark Twain's Autobiography (1924); Mark Twain in Eruption (1940); The Autobiography of Mark Twain (1959); Letters from the Earth (1962).

LETTERS, NOTEBOOKS, AND PAPERS:

Letters (1917); Notebook (1935); Love Letters (1949); Mark Twain to Mrs. Fairbanks (1949); Mark Twain–Howells Letters (1960). Fourteen or so volumes of Mark Twain's Papers are being planned for publication by the University of California Press. The first three volumes in this series appeared in 1967: Letters to His Publishers; Satires and Burlesques; and Which Was the Dream?

BIOGRAPHICAL AND CRITICAL WRITING ABOUT MARK TWAIN:

Albert Bigelow Paine's authorized, often uncritical but thoroughly indispensable *Mark Twain: A Biography* was published in 1912, two years after another book based on intimate acquaintance, William Dean Howells' affectionate portrait, *My Mark Twain* (1910). Among many biographical studies which have since appeared are: Van Wyck Brooks, *The Ordeal of Mark Twain* (1920; revised in 1933); Bernard DeVoto, *Mark Twain's America* (1932) and *Mark Twain at Work* (1942); Samuel C. Webster, *Mark Twain: Business Man* (1946); Kenneth R. Andrews, *Nook Farm: Mark Twain's Hartford Circle* (1950); Dixon Wecter, *Sam Clemens of Hannibal* (1952); and Justin Kaplan, *Mr. Clemens and Mark Twain* (1966).

Some major, recent critical studies are: Kenneth S. Lynn, *Mark Twain and Southwestern Humor* (1959); Walter Blair, *Mark Twain & Huck Finn* (1960); Henry Nash Smith, *Mark Twain: The Development of a Writer* (1962); and James M. Cox, *Mark Twain: The Fate of Humor* (1966).

General bibliographies can be found in: Robert E. Spiller et al., *Literary History of the United States* (1948; supplement 1959); Floyd Stovall (ed.), *Eight American Authors: A Review of Research and Criticism* (1956); and E. Hudson Long, *Mark Twain Handbook* (1957). Issues of the quarterly *American Literature* (1929–   ) contain running bibliographies of the periodical literature.

Among useful collections are: Arthur Scott (ed.), *Mark Twain: Selected Criticism* (1955); Lewis Leary (ed.), *A Casebook on Mark Twain's Wound* (1962), which documents the reaction to Brooks's *The Ordeal of Mark Twain;* and Henry Nash Smith (ed.), *Mark Twain: A Collection of Critical Essays* (1963).

Contributors

VAN WYCK BROOKS (1886–1963), critic and literary historian, was the author of the Pulitzer Prize winning history *The Flowering of New England* (1936), and of *New England: Indian Summer* (1940), *The World of Washington Irving* (1944), *The Times of Melville and Whitman* (1947), and *The Confident Years* (1952).

JAMES M. COX, born in 1925, is Professor of English at Dartmouth. He is the author of *Mark Twain: The Fate of Humor* (1966) and is the editor of *Twentieth-Century Views: Robert Frost* (1962).

BERNARD DEVOTO (1897–1955), historian, novelist, and teacher, succeeded Albert Bigelow Paine as Literary Editor of the Mark Twain Estate. He wrote a three-volume history of "the American Continental experience": *The Year of Decision* (1943), *Across the Wide Missouri* (1947), which was awarded a Pulitzer Prize, and *The Course of Empire* (1952).

PAUL FATOUT, born in 1897, is Professor of English at Purdue University. He is the author of *Mark Twain on the Lecture Circuit* (1961) and *Mark Twain in Virginia City* (1964).

LESLIE FIEDLER, born in 1917, critic and novelist, has written *An End to Innocence* (1955) and *Love and Death in the American Novel* (1960). He is Professor of English at the State University of New York at Buffalo.

WILLIAM DEAN HOWELLS (1837–1920), novelist, critic, and editor, was Mark Twain's intimate friend and adviser for forty years. Their relationship is chronicled in Howells' memoir, *My Mark Twain,* and in the cycle of correspondence, *Mark Twain–Howells Letters* (1960).

KENNETH S. LYNN, born in 1923, is Professor of English at Harvard and author of *The Dream of Success* (1955) and *Mark Twain and Southwestern Humor* (1959).

DWIGHT MACDONALD, born in 1906, has been staff writer for *Fortune* and *The New Yorker,* an editor of *Partisan Review,* and founder and editor of *Politics.* He has written *Memoirs of a Revolutionist* (1957) and edited the anthology *Parodies* (1960).

WINFIELD TOWNLEY SCOTT, born in 1910, for ten years Literary Editor of the Providence *Journal,* is a poet and critic. Among his books are *Exiles and Fabrications* (1961), *Collected Poems: 1937–1962* (1962), and *New and Selected Poems* (1967).

HENRY NASH SMITH, born in 1906, former Literary Editor of the Mark Twain Estate, teaches at the University of California, Berkeley. He has written *Virgin Land: The American West as Symbol and Myth* (1950), which received the John H. Dunning prize and a Bancroft Award, and *Mark Twain: The Development of a Writer* (1962).

DIXON WECTER (1906–1950) was Professor of English at the University of California, Berkeley, and Literary Editor of the Mark Twain Estate. He wrote *The Saga of American Society* (1937), *The Hero in America* (1941), and the biography *Sam Clemens of Hannibal* (1952).

JUSTIN KAPLAN was born in New York City in 1925, attended the Horace Mann School, and did his undergraduate and graduate work at Harvard. He returned to New York in 1947 and for several years wrote and edited in the fields of literature, art history and criticism, and medicine. The Washington Square Press published his selected editions of Aristotle and the Dialogues of Plato. In 1955 he became a senior editor at Simon and Schuster but he gave up his editing four years later to begin work on *Mr. Clemens and Mark Twain,* his celebrated biography, which in 1967 won the Pulitzer Prize for Biography and the National Book Award for Arts and Letters. Mr. Kaplan, who now lives in Cambridge, Massachusetts, is married to novelist Anne Bernays and has three daughters.

✪

AÏDA DiPACE DONALD, General Editor of the American Profiles series, holds degrees from Barnard and Columbia, where she taught American history, and a doctorate from the University of Rochester. Mrs. Donald has been awarded A.A.U.W. and Fulbright fellowships and has edited *John F. Kennedy and the New Frontier.* She is also co-editor of the *Charles Francis Adams Diary.*

regarded this incident reveals the massiveness of the genteel tradition in New England and the probationary status upon which Mark was kept for so many years.

Between the publication of the *Innocents* and this indiscretion, Clemens had taken a wife whose remolding influence has been the subject of much debate. The story of their courtship is familiar: his first sight of her delicate face in a miniature carried by her brother on the *Quaker City* cruise; Twain's meeting with the original, Olivia Langdon, ten years his junior, a semi-invalid who had turned to faith healing; their two years' betrothal while her father, the richest businessman in Elmira, and her kin were slowly won over; and their wedding early in 1870, with Clemens the bridegroom trying unsuccessfully to establish himself as a solid newspaper editor in Buffalo, but moving to Hartford in 1871 to resume a free-lance life. His veneration of women and their purity was almost fanatical. "I wouldn't have a girl that *I* was worthy of," he wrote "Mother" Fairbanks before his engagement. *"She* wouldn't do."

About the sexual make-up of Mark Twain speculation has been indulged since the Freudian era. In that famous sophomoric sketch *1601,* written in mid-career to amuse his clerical friend Joe Twichell, he had Sir Walter Raleigh describe "a people in ye uttermost parts of America, y^t copulate not until they be five-&-thirty yeeres of age." This, it happens, was the age when Clemens married a semi-invalid wife, as if some inadequacy in himself, some low sexual vitality, made such a woman his fitting mate. And yet respecting their physical love for each other and the fruitfulness of their union, with its four children, no doubt can be raised. What illicit experience might have come to a boy growing up in the accessible world of slavery, and passing his green manhood upon riverboats and in bonanza towns, can only be guessed at. In later years, respecting the idealized Hannibal of his boyhood, he went so far as to deny the existence of sexual irregularities; and by confining his two great novels about Hannibal to adolescence he was able in a manner to carry his point. Obviously certain taboos about sex, personal as well as conventional, appear in his writings from beginning to end. Unlike his friend Howells, he attempted no probings of desire, no analysis of the chemical affinity between man and woman beyond the calf love of Tom and Becky and the implausible treatment of Laura the siren of *The Gilded Age*. Only under the protective shield of miscegenation, in the person of the warm-blooded Negress Roxana in *Pudd'nhead Wilson*, does he venture even to approach passion which overleaps the bounds of society. Joan of Arc, a virgin of exquisite purity, plainly is the heroine after his inmost heart. A certain fear of sex, like the shrinking of primitive races and some adolescents from carnality as if it meant degradation of the body, seems to lie at the root of Mark Twain's nature. The exceptions of his occasional bawdry— in *1601* and a few unprinted works like his speech before the Stomach Club in Paris and his manuscript "Letters from the Earth"—but prove the rule, in ridiculing the body and its ways sufficiently to suit the most fanatic Puritan.

Yet Twain was in no sense a misogynist. He loved the company of women, of the refined women whose tastes and restraints fitted his own presuppositions about them. His understanding of the feminine mind has left no more delightful evidence than "Eve's Diary," written in 1905 shortly after Olivia's death, so that Adam's final bereavement becomes the epitaph of his own loss: "Wherever she was, *there* was Eden." In summary, Mark Twain's personal make-up and the conventions of gentility surrounding the kind of success he aspired to, joined to suppress the recognition of sex as a key motive in human actions—leaving woman not an object of desire but of reverential chivalry.

The effect of his wife upon Twain the artist has provoked latter-day discussion. One school of thought holds that Clemens was forced, first by his mother and then by his wife, to "make good," i.e., to make money and be respectable. Moreover, thanks to the censorship of his wife, they say, he became not the New World Rabelais but a frustrated genius incapable of calling his soul or vocabulary his own. It is clear, however, that proof of Livy's "humiliating" dominion rests largely upon Twain's letters to Howells: that pair of devoted husbands married to invalids who made a gallant little joke over being henpecked. The notion that women exercised a gentle tyranny over their menfolk, for the latter's good, always appealed to Mark Twain, schooled in Western theories that man was coarser clay and woman a rare and special being (as among the Washoe miners in *Roughing It,* who chipped in $2,500 in gold as a gift at the miraculous sight of a live woman). All his life he encouraged women to reform him, improve his taste and manners. His three little daughters who shared in the family rite known as "dusting off Papa," and the "angelfish" of adolescent girls in his Bermudian Indian summer, were among the youngest of the sex whose devoted slave he rejoiced to be. It was a kind of game in the feudal tradition, which he adored. But to assume therefore that Twain the genius was henpecked, baffled, unmanned by women in general and Livy in particular is to convert a jest into a cry of anguish. About the converse influence of husband upon wife something deserves to be said. For Twain's vitality rescued her from abysses of timorous living, his banter relaxed her serious disposition, and his religious skepticism destroyed her Christian faith.

As for the specific question of censorship, we know that Twain liked to read aloud *en famille* the results of his daily composition, usually n.. ating the approval he craved, sometimes encountering a chill disfavor to which he was equally sensitive. He was a poor self-critic and knew it. He plunged into writing without much plan or foresight. Livy's judgment in matters of simple good taste and in pruning wordiness and irrelevance was clearly superior to his own in the heat of incubation. A careful examination of his manuscripts shows that Mrs. Clemens, like that other long-standing adviser William Dean Howells, objected to certain vivid words and phrases—"wallow," "bowels," "spit," "rotten," and realistic allusions to stenches and putrefaction which always tempted Mark Twain, so that he grumbled about her "steadily weakening the English tongue"—but that in mild profanities (like Huck Finn's "comb me all to hell") and in rare inclinations toward the risqué (such as the farce of "The Royal Nonesuch") the author on second thought was his own most attentive censor. He was not above playing an occasional hazard with his critics to see how far he could skate on thin ice; then doubled on his own track back to safety. Just as he dreamed of the unabashed nakedness of a boy's freedom on a raft floating down the Mississippi, now and again he yearned for the lusty old ways of medieval speech, "full of unconscious coarsenesses and innocent indecencies," "good old questionable stories," as the Connecticut Yankee says. But quickly he reminded himself, as he observes in *A Tramp Abroad,* that the license of the printed word had been "sharply curtailed within the past eighty or ninety years." To this curb in the main he gave unstinting consent.

IV

Up to the time of his anchorage in Hartford in 1871, the most important facts about Mark Twain are the things that happened to him, shaping his development as an artist and filling the granaries of memory. After that date the chief milestones are the books he wrote out of that accumulation. His maturity and self-assurance can be gauged, growing from book to book through the next two decades, as he lectured at home and abroad, met the captains of literature and politics and finance, read widely if desultorily, and perfected his early journalistic manner until it became one of the great styles of American letters—easy, incisive, sensitive to nuances of dialect, rich in the resources of comedy, satire, irony, and corrosive anger.

One group, of secondary importance, consists of his travel books. Between *The Innocents Abroad* (1869) and *Roughing It* (1872) he learned, under emancipation from newspaper reporting, to take greater liberties with fact for art's sake. Both books owe such structure as they have to a rough chronology. Upon this thread Mark Twain the raconteur strings one story after another. The latter volume offers us almost all the classic types which Americans in general, frontiersmen in particular, had long since favored: the tall tale, the melodramatic shocker, the yarn of pointless garrulity, malapropian humor, the canard of impossible coincidence, the chain of free association that wanders farther and farther from its announced subject; the comedy of man in his cups, the animal fable, and the delusions of a lunatic. Paradox, surprise, and understatement often heighten his effects. Anecdote continues